International Perspectives on Bilingual Education: Policy, Practice, and Controversy

A volume in
International Perspectives on Educational Policy, Research, and Practice
Kathryn M. Borman, *Series Editor*

International Perspectives on Educational Policy, Research, and Practice

SERIES EDITORS

Kathryn M. Borman
University of South Florida

This series is an extension of the internationally known journal of similar title, the International Journal of Educational Policy, Research and Practice. This book series seeks to extend the research on internationally important issues within education, while providing a platform for deliberation among practitioners, policy-makers and researchers. The scope of topics to be published ranges from technology-based instruction and diverse methodologies to educational practices in developing nations and issues of contemporary concern. A leading forum for informed discussion, this series draws upon projects from institutions around the globe.

International Perspectives on Bilingual Education: Policy, Practice, and Controversy

edited by

John E. Petrovic
The University of Alabama

INFORMATION AGE PUBLISHING, INC.
Charlotte, NC • www.infoagepub.com

Library of Congress Cataloging-in-Publication Data

International perspectives on bilingual education : policy, practice, and controversy / edited by John E. Petrovic.
    p. cm.
Includes bibliographical references.
 ISBN 978-1-60752-329-1 (pbk.) — ISBN 978-1-60752-330-7 (hardcover) — ISBN 978-1-60752-331-4 (e-book)
1. Education, Bilingual. 2. Language and education. 3. Education and state. I. Petrovic, John E.
LC3715.I47 2010
370.117'5–dc22

2009042509

Printed in the United States of America

CONTENTS

SECTION I

POLICY

SECTION II

PRACTICE

SECTION III

CONTROVERSY

FOREWORD

Terrence G. Wiley
Arizona State University

This collection is offered largely as a defense of linguistic pluralism, in an attempt to "provide scholars an international comparative understanding of language policy, its relation to educational policy and practice, and current debates within the field" (Petrovic, herein). Explicitly or implicitly, most of the contributions deal with language policies, ideologies, needs, practices, and discourses. Language policies may be *official*, result from *implicit institutional practices*, or be derived from the *agency of language strategists* who have been able to influence the linguistic market through mass sales of dictionaries, primers, and/or literature that provide models for "common" language usage (Weinstein, 1983).

An important contribution of this collection is its emphasis on the role of understanding the varied contexts in which policies are prescribed and its chapters that cast a critical eye on accepted theories of bilingual education (e.g., MacSwan & Rolstad). Many of the chapters help to demonstrate the importance of language policy as an instrument of *social control,* in facilitating or limiting access to the political arena, education, and social and economic benefits (Leibowitz, 1969, 1974, 1976).

During the past five centuries, in those parts of the world dominated by eurocentric nationalism and colonialism, language policies have been in the domain of educators, missionaries, and colonial functionaries. In Africa, Asia, and Latin America, educational policies often went hand in hand with the colonial project (Willinsky, 2000) and grand narratives that constructed hierarchical language and racial statuses (Blaut, 1993; Mignolo, 2003; Wiley, 2006). Educational language policies have often been framed in terms of acquisition planning. Acquisition planning has focused on national languages and colonial languages, as well as languages of literacy and mass communication, in postcolonial contexts.

The chapters in this volume may be indexed to many of the themes regarding language policy that have developed over the past several decades. These include discussions regarding language policy and planning that have moved from technocratic prescriptions for linguistic standardization and how they relate to various modernist and nationcentric ends regarding linguistic assimilation, unification, mass literacy, and universal education. This has been followed by focus on the value of mother tongue(s) in promoting educational access and equity while fostering positive identity and concerns regarding policies that result in rapid language shift and negative social and psychological consequences associated with language loss, the loss of language as societal resources, concerns over the relationship between linguistic genocide as a form of cultural genocide, and comparisons of linguistic diversity as being analogous to the loss of biodiversity, followed by efforts to reverse language shift. Along with these concerns, there has been a struggle to promote minority language rights as linguistic human rights. Recently, the field has entertained internal debates among scholars regarding the role that applied linguists and educators should play in shaping language policies, and there has been concern that scholars can become complicit, wittingly or unwittingly, in formulating or implementing policies that undermine language as a resource or that result in linguistic discrimination. More recently, there has been critical reflection among scholars who support language maintenance, choice, and linguistic human rights concerning the role of language policies in promoting educational, political, social, and economic access and equality, as well as introspection regarding the very discourse and metaphors that are used in defense of these goals. For some, long-used constructs such as *native speaker* and even *language* have become suspect.

No single collection could address all of these issues, but *International Perspectives on Bilingual Education: Policy, Practice, and Controversy* makes an important contribution to many of the important issues and debates within the field. The division of this text into three major sections—national policies, applied considerations, and debates within the field—is a reasonable way to organize the various topics presented, but we can also note the intersection of many themes across these boundaries. One motif that is largely implicit in the various chapters is the role that language ideologies play in privileging one language over another, which has relevance in Part I (Petrovic, Ricento & Cervatiuc, and Balcazar) in terms of national language policies. Ideologies also have bearing in Part II in considering educational language policies that have been designed to promote monolingualism and monoliteracy or bilingualism and biliteracy (Escamilla & Hopewell; Rao, Shanbal, & Khurana; and Vila i Moreno) and multilingualism and multiliteracy, or that privilege-school-taught varieties of language and academic discourse practices (MacSwan & Rolstad, in Part III).

Petrovic notes that monolingualist policies favoring English-only (Chapter 1) or castellanización, for example, in Guatemala (see Balcazar, herein) have been dominant in many modern nation-states, regardless of whether they have positive immigration, as in the case of the United States, or negative immigration, as in the case of Guatemala. In modern nation-states, statuses have often been ascribed to speakers of various languages. The U.S. case is often framed only in terms of immigration, but it involves also historical modes of incorporation of others, including so-called involuntary immigrants who were enslaved and transported against their will or forced to be assimilated (as in the case of indigenous peoples, initially conceived as *dependent domestic nations*). Thus, seemingly similar language policies favoring English have had differential impacts on language minorities depending on their legal status during the initial mode of incorporation and their subsequent treatment after incorporation (Wiley, 2000).

Monolingualist ideologies as a basis for modern conceptions of language policy have been influential tools for "unifying" nation-states. Schools have been major instruments in this process through imposing normative language practices. Five centuries ago, the scholar Antonio de Nebrija was among the first to advocate for overt instruction in a standardized language as a means of advancing the interests of the Castilian state (Illich, 1979). We can trace the origins of modernist prescriptivism, which privileges literate discourse, to the promotion of Nebrija's Castilian grammar and consider how notions of alphabetic literacy were used to position indigenous peoples in the ideological schemas and grand narratives of colonialism (Blaut, 1993; Mignolo, 2003). Similarly, the promotion of standard languages has been seen as the tool for national hegemony and strength in modern France since the time of François I of France (Christ, 1997) and as a model for the emerging Meiji Japan and its efforts to promote modernization through mass education (Carroll, 2001; Weinberg, 1997). Educational expansion was tied to reforms in the writing system and the unification of spoken and written language, as well as the incorporation of new concepts into the Japanese language from abroad (Coulmas, 1990). The hegemony of such ideologies has provided the rationale for linguistic assimilation around reified notions of language as well as deficit views that have positioned bilingualism, multilingualism, and codeswitching as aberrant. As Stroud notes in the final chapter, "language has been socially and politically construed in ways that serve to regiment and order peoples into administrative constituencies, in constructing moral images of speakers, and in the semiotic framing of discourses of tradition and modernity, agency, and citizenship."

Vernaculars, patois, dialects, idioms, pidgins, and mixed codes all became suspect forms of speech, marked as "nonstandard," "substandard," or even so-called "semilingual" indicators of an alleged cultural, technological, and intellectual *great divide* between schooled "literates" and "polyglot hordes." Some vernaculars were redeemed as national or regional languages once they became standardized based on classical models of grammar and then promoted as national languages. With the rise of common public schooling during the mid to late nineteenth century, in a number of western European countries, as well as in the United States, ideologies and discourses of monolingualism and standard language have been implicitly at the core of teacher education when teacher education itself has been available (Wiley, 2008).

Language diversity is often presented as being a "problem" in the popular media. Within applied linguistics, however, it has generally been defended as a human right or societal and individual "resource." Ruiz (1984), in a frequently cited article, argued for the merits of the language-as-resource (LAR) orientation. Although the resource orientation has been widely endorsed, some scholars (see Ricento, 2005, and Petrovic, 2005) have critiqued the position for its instrumentalist stance, which can be appropriated in the service of the neoliberal state. Certainly, the resource metaphor has been co-opted in recent years in the United States by those interested in promoting foreign language study for purposes of national security (Wiley, 2007a, 2007b), but appeals to this orientation have long been prevalent and independently constructed outside of the field of applied linguistics (see Simon, 1988). Ruiz's reflection on the LAR orientation in Chapter 7 thus provides a thoughtful, measured clarification and response.

Stroud's final chapter provides a fitting conclusion for the book as he provides a useful critique of discourses related to linguistic human rights and notions of citizenship. As he notes, historically the notion of "rights" has been understood either positively (involving access to resources) or negatively (requiring from the state) (see Stroud, herein). Calls for policies that promote "linguistic justice" (cf. Ricento and Cervatiuc, this volume) can be interpreted as a call for positive rights. Appeals for promoting language rights have resource implications (as Ruiz also notes). Appeals for linguistic justice require an equitable allocation of resources for the maintenance or promotion of community languages, which implies some form of distributive justice that requires a formula for a more equitable allocation of resources within the neoliberal state.

As Stroud notes, linguistic rights discourses "tend to channel discourses on diversity into specific predetermined cultural and linguistic identities." They also raise the question of where the locus of agency for language promotion and preservation should be—that is, *from the state* on behalf of the group (positive rights), or *from groups* based on their own resources without interference from the state (negative rights). Whichever the case, Stroud notes that "LHR, as currently conceived, also privileges the official and group values and perceptions of what might constitute the language in question" without considering "alternative-language practices as part of the language." These result in new "hierarchies of difference and disadvantage . . . rather than consensus and accommodation." Stroud encourages us to think beyond linking languages and notions of citizenship to "national borders" and to reconceptualize them as "meeting places" where speakers of different languages and dialects nevertheless communicate. Drawing from notions of *deliberative democracy* and *cosmopolitan citizenship,* he sees languages as political resources that are both a "prime means (rather than a problem) for the material realization of democracy."

This collection offers a number of perspectives in defense of linguistic pluralism within a variety of contexts. The final section helps to elucidate some of the schisms that persist in the field. Beyond its critique of linguistic human rights discourses, Stroud's concluding chapter offers a fresh perspective that locates language diversity within the discourses of citizenship as "the very medium whereby citizenship is enacted and performed." This ideal certainly relates to and informs the positive language policies and educational practices endorsed in Parts I and II of this volume, respectively, just as the other two chapters in the final section have implications for policy and practice.

REFERENCES

Blaut, J. M. (1993). *The colonizer's model of the world: Geographical diffusionism and Eurocentric history.* New York: Guildford Press.

Carroll, T. (2001). *Language planning and language change in Japan.* Richmond, VA: Curzon.

Christ, H. (1997). Language policy in teacher education. In D. Corson (Ed.), *Encyclopedia of language and education, Vol. 1* (pp. 219–227). Dordrecht: Kluwer.

Coulmas, F. (1990). Language in Meji Japan. In B. Weinstien (Ed.), *Language policy and political development* (pp. 69–86). Norwood, NJ: Ablex.

Illich, I. (1979). Vernacular values and education. *Teacher's College Record, 81*(1), 31–75.

Leibowitz, A. H. (1969). English literacy: Legal sanction for discrimination. *Notre Dame Lawyer, 25*(1), 7–66.

Leibowitz, A. H. (1974, August). Language as a means of social control. Paper presented at the VIII World Congress of Sociology, University of Toronto, Toronto, Canada.

Leibowitz, A. H. (1976). Language and the law: The exercise of political power through the official designation of language. In O'Barr & O'Barr (Eds.), *Language and politics* (pp. 449–466). The Hague: Mouton.

Mignolo, W. D. (2003). *The darker side of the renaissance: Literacy, territoriality, and colonization* (2nd ed.). Ann Arbor: University of Michigan Press.

Petrovic, J. E. (2005). The conservative restoration and neoliberal defenses of bilingual education. *Language Policy, 4,* 395–416.

Ricento, T. (2005). Problems with the "language as resource" discourse in the promotion of heritage languages in the USA. *Journal of Sociolinguistics, 9*(3), 348–368.

Ruiz, R. (1984). Orientations in language planning. *NABE Journal, 8*(2), 15–34.

Simon, P. (1988). *The tongue-tied American: Confronting the foreign language crisis* (2nd ed.). New York: Continuum.

Weinberg, M. (1997). *Asian-American education.* Mahwah, NJ: Lawrence Erlbaum.

Weinstein, B. (1983). *The civic tongue: Political consequences of language choices.* New York: Longman.

Wiley, T. G. (2000). Continuity and change in the function of language ideologies in the United States. In T. Ricento (Ed.), *Ideology, politics, and language policies: Focus on English* (pp. 67–86). Amsterdam: John Benjamins.

Wiley, T. G. (2006). The lessons of historical investigation: Implications for the study of language policy and planning. In T. Ricento (Ed.). *Language policy: Essential readings* (pp. 136–152). London: Blackwell.

Wiley, T. G. (2007a). The foreign language "crisis" in the U.S.: Are heritage and community languages the remedy? *Critical Inquiry in Language Studies, 4*(2–3), 179–205.

Wiley, T. G. (2007b). Beyond the foreign language crisis: Toward alternatives to xenophobia and national security as bases for U.S. language policies. *Modern Language Journal, 91*(2), 252–255.

Wiley, T. G. (2008). Language policy and teacher education. In S. May & N. Hornberger (Eds.), *Language policy and political issues in education* (pp. 229–242), vol. 1. In N. Hornberger (Gen. Ed.), *Encyclopedia of language and education,* (2nd ed.). New York: Springer.

Willinsky, J. (2000). *Learning to divide the world: Education at empire's end.* Minneapolis: University of Minnesota.

INTRODUCTION

The unifying theme of this book is a defense of linguistic pluralism generally and of language policies and practices in education that sustain that ideal. While I hope that the phrase "bilingual education" captures the general purpose of the book, the title is, in fact, misleading. In the United States, for example, bilingual education has historically referred to the idea of using a child's native language as a language of instruction in addition to the second language, English. In Canada, however, one might consider French immersion programs for English speakers as bilingual education since the goal is bilingualism. In Cataluña, students might attend a school wherein both Castillian and Catalán are languages of instruction even as the student's first language is something different.

Educational meanings and models are influenced by different populations and different social and historical contexts. Thus, it is important to look at these issues internationally as social contexts change the meanings of, and needs around, linguistic pluralism. Therefore, the purpose of the book is to provide scholars an international comparative understanding of language policy, its relation to educational policy and practice, and current debates within the field. The aim is to develop, in some small way, a greater sense of the commonalities and differences in perspectives, issues, and approaches across the globe. The book is divided into three sections dealing with the general topical areas of policy, practice, and controversy.

In the first section of the book, the authors consider national level language policies and their relation to educational policy. Specifically, these first three chapters present the historical development and impact of language policy in the United States, Canada, and Guatemala.

In Chapter 1, I provide a brief definition of language policy and present a historical overview of the development of language policy as it has impacted education in the United States. I argue that language policy in the United States has frequently been driven by "reactionary attempts to maintain an imagined national community," and that these reactions "have given rise to negative language policy." I divide this history into distinct periods, analyzing each in terms of the primary language policy goal that distinguished them: to maintain, to reform, or to transform extant patterns of access in U.S. society.

In Chapter 2, Thomas Ricento and Andreea Cervatiuc trace the roots of the current official bilingualism paradigm in Canada that frames educational policymaking for the teaching of foreign, second, and heritage languages. They review the "mixed results" of enactments, such as the Official Languages in Education Program, that have come from this paradigm. In addition to the bilingual paradigm, Ricento and Cervatiuc argue that Canada has "a distinctive multicultural paradigm" which is "unique in the world." This has raised a great deal of debate and demanded a great deal of compromise. In the end, they argue, multiculturalism must promote linguistic justice "in which all ethnic groups . . . have the right and financial support to preserve both their languages and cultures."

In Chapter 3, Ivonne Heinze Balcazar discusses the history and contemporary status of language policy in Guatemala. In a contrast to the first two chapters, the focus of this chapter is solely upon the effects of language policy on the educational experiences of indigenous peoples. Unlike the United States and Canada, Guatemala has a negative net migration rate. Thus, linguistic diversity owes almost completely to the various indigenous communities. Therefore, Heinze Balcazar's primary language policy concern is about language shift, the shift toward the use of the majority language, Spanish, by indigenous peoples at the expense of their own language. She notes that grassroots movements have "successfully channeled the focus of the Ministry of Education to issues of . . . educational quality and . . . cultural relevance" and that bilingual education is a key component of these educational efforts.

On the one hand, the histories and policies discussed in these chapters have many similarities. For example, restrictive language policies, such English-only or *castellanización,* have had negative consequences on language minority and indigenous groups. Such consequences have included, in each of the cases, language shift and loss, denial of equal educational opportunity, and the squandering of linguistic resources and cultural enrichment. The authors of each chapter argue that commitment to an ideology of "one nation, one language" is fatally misguided.

On the other hand, it is important to understand that the historical and sociopolitical contexts do differ greatly. Therefore, while we can learn much through international comparisons, we must resist the temptation to generalize approaches to addressing issues of language diversity outside of their particular contexts. As Ricento and Cervatiuc point out in the concluding section of their chapter, policymakers "in the United States who seek to avoid what they consider to be a fragile accommodation achieved between French- and English-speaking Canadians by declaring English the only official language of the United States fail to understand" the different realities of the situations. For example, the language demographics (the number of speakers of various languages and their geographic concentration), language shift (the stability of these various languages over generations), and language prestige (the correlation between language spoken and economic wellbeing) are in no way comparable between Canada and the United States and Belgium and the United States (Canada and Belgium being oft-cited cases in which linguistic instability leads to political strife) (cf. Petrovic, 1997/1999).

In its own manner, each of the chapters in the first section highlights the ways in which language has served as a proxy for what are in fact other historical sources of ongoing political strife (e.g., oppression). These histories must be taken into account in the current development of relevant and just language policy.

In the second section of the book, the authors address more practical considerations of language policy, one aspect of which is acquisition planning. Acquisition planning considers the processes by which the goals stated in given language policies will be achieved. Schools are, of course, among the primary institutions upon which the achievement of given language policies rests. Thus, this section addresses the program models and practices needed to serve children of multilingual backgrounds in order to promote linguistic pluralism.

Cooper (1989) presents three overt goals of acquisition planning: acquisition of a language as a second or foreign language, reacquisition of a language by populations for whom it was once a vernacular or language of specialized function, and language maintenance. One of the overarching values of each of these chapters is the lens through which bilingualism is viewed. While each of these authors embraces the ideal of becoming bi- or multilingual (as in Cooper's first overt goal), they argue, each in his or her own way, that effective, positive language policy cannot proceed from this singular position. In each of the contexts described in these chapters, the default position is being (as opposed to becoming) bilingual, and that bilingualism is a natural state of affairs. The bilingual person is not simply someone who can translate from one language to another. Policy must derive from a much more robust theory of bilingualism—a theory that sees the bilingual person as someone engaging in language in much more complex ways, using language in different situations for different purposes, and acquiring, processing, and making sense of information in ways unique from a monolingual person or from someone acquiring a second or foreign language.

In this vein, Kathy Escamilla and Susan Hopewell, distinguish in Chapter 4 between simultaneous bilinguals and sequential bilinguals. They report the results of their empirical study of a literacy intervention program designed specifically for simultaneous (Spanish–English) bilingual children. The question of whether literacy should be introduced in a child's first language, second language, or both has nagged bilingual educators for many years. August and Hakuta (1997) summarize this research as follows:

> The evidence that better academic outcomes characterize immigrant children who have had 2 to 3 years of initial schooling (and presumably literacy instruction) in their native countries is consistent with the claim that children should first learn to read in a language they already speak. However, it is clear that many children first learn to read in a second language without serious negative consequences. (p. 60)

Escamilla and Hopewell's research sheds important light on this question. In the end, I suspect they would quarrel with any policy and practices that might emerge from August and Hakuta's summary of the research to the extent that it proceeds from a theory of sequential bilingualism.

The idea of simultaneous bilingualism is put into starker relief, and thus becomes even more important, in the case of India where, as is not the case in the United States, bilingualism is the norm rather than the exception. In Chapter 5, Prema K. S. Rao, Jayashree C. Shanbal, and Sarika Khurana provide an overview of the immense linguistic diversity in India and the implications for educational policy and practice. Most important, as concerns the purpose of this section of the book, the authors review their own and other studies in the Indian context that examine certain factors such as linguistic and orthographic structures that influence acquisition of multiliteracy. The subtle differences in the processing of languages and scripts, particularly between those of Indian languages and English, are examined from the perspective of deriving the best possible policy and practice for the bilingual/multilingual children in India.

In Chapter 6, F. Xavier Vila i Moreno presents the case of Catalan. The story of Catalan takes us through each of the goals of acquisition planning presented by Cooper. For example, during the dictatorship of Franco, (negative) language policy was designed to force language shift among the Catalan people, encouraging the acquisition of a second language (many Catalans would argue a *foreign* language), Spanish. Subsequent to this, Catalan had to be reacquired by many people of Catalan heritage, and current policy seeks to maintain Catalan as a national language in the region. In this chapter, Vila i Moreno explores the extent to which, and ways in which, Catalan is being promoted and maintained in schools in Catalan-language areas spread through Spain, France, Andorra, and Italy.

As I reviewed the chapters in this section, especially the ones on India and Catalonia, I was reminded of the ignorance of policymakers in the United States, and of a comment made by former Speaker of the House

Newt Gingrich. In the midst of debate on English-only legislation, Gingrich quipped, "I think that anyone who thinks we should have more than one national language doesn't understand how human societies operate." In fact, human societies operate bilingually/multilingually. Progressive language policy demands that this condition be reflected in school practices. What such practices might be is the concern of these chapters.

As will be outlined in the first section of the book, the purpose of language policy, very generally, is to manage, encourage, and/or discourage the use of particular languages. On the one hand, multilingualism is simply a fact in human societies. On the other hand, promoting it is certainly not uncontroversial. For the most part, what controversy exists is driven by ideological presumptions of one nation–one language in the age of the modern nation-state—recall the Gingrich comment above. Such presumptions dictate negative language policy nationally, locally, and educationally.[1] In education, debates swirl mainly around the issue of providing literacy and content area instruction in more than one language. Empirical debate has resolved overwhelmingly in favor of providing bilingual/multilingual instruction, yet political debate continues. The minister of education in the Northern Territory of Australia, for example, continues to support severe restrictions on bilingual education. She maintains her position in spite of two recent reports from her own department—corroborated by research conducted by the Australian Council for Educational Research—concluding that indigenous children taught through their own language ultimately achieve better English literacy skills (Northern Territory News, 2008).

The first two sections of the book proceed unapologetically from a belief (no less ideologically) in language pluralism and bilingual education. The third and final section of the book continues in this vein. But the controversies covered here are not between language pluralists and assimilationists, as might be anticipated. This section instead considers current debates and disagreements among language pluralists who are nevertheless in general agreement about bilingual/multilingual education. Such disagreements "among friends" (as Richard Ruiz puts it in his chapter) are healthy and an important component of our continuing efforts to promote positive language policy.

---

[1] To provide some examples from the U.S. context, we can consider at the national level the movement to make English the official language. While the movement has been so far unsuccessful at the national level, it has enjoyed broad success at the state level. Locally, in 1987, the City Board of Monterrey Park, California, dissolved the library board after the latter accepted a large gift of Chinese-language books from the Lions Club International of Taiwan (see Betancourt, 1992, for details). Similarly, after passage of Proposition 227, a ballot initiative that severely restricted bilingual education in California, a Californian principal removed all Spanish library books from his school's library (see Cline and Necochea, 2001).

Richard Ruiz's original "orientations" to language planning (language-as-problem, language-as-right, and language-as-resource) have been generative for many years. In these increasingly conservative times, Ruiz's original defense of language-as-resource has raised concerns over its seeming embeddedness in neoliberal, instrumentalist discourse. In Chapter 7, Ruiz "reorients" language-as-resource, addressing these concerns, as he puts it in the chapter, "not so much as a defense of an entrenched position but as a way to understand how intellectual colleagues can frame arguments that will have positive influences on policies we can support."

In Chapter 8, Jeff MacSwan and Kellie Rolstad argue that prescriptivism and the related construct of semilingualism wield powerful, political force and lead to wrongheaded ideas about children's language and subsequent explanations of academic underperformance. For these authors, neither the practices of prescriptivism nor the construct of semilingualism is supported by linguistic evidence. In this project, MacSwan and Rolstad provide an important critique of some of the theoretical constructs employed by Jim Cummins. Although Cummins's work is widely cited—and, I believe, has certainly advanced the field—MacSwan and Rolstad (among others they cite) argue that it supports a deficit model, showing how it is related to the almost universally dismissed construct of semilingualism.

In Chapter 9, Christopher Stroud provides a critique of "linguistic human rights." Linguistic human rights presents a particular way of viewing the relationship between language(s) and society and is thus a political philosophy of language, making normative claims about the demands that language communities can make of the state and vice versa. The construct simultaneously operates discursively, calling into being certain views of language itself. This, in turn, defines minority language speakers in particular ways, especially as *citizens*. Drawing on specific examples from South Africa, Stroud argues that this particular discourse is inadequate "for understanding the semiotic practice of citizenship in contemporary late modern society." His alternative is to frame multilingualism within a postliberal (linguistic human rights being liberal) ideal of citizenship. Stroud highlights some of the implications for language policy and practice in education that come from his new frame.

REFERENCES

August, D. & Hakuta, K. (1997). *Improving schooling for language minority children: A research agenda.* Washington, D.C.: National Academy Press.

Betancourt, I. (1992). "The Babel myth": The English-only movement and its implications for libraries. *Wilson Library Bulletin, 66*(6), 38–41.

Cline, Z. & Necochea, J. (2001). ¡Basta ya! Latino parents fighting entrenched racism. *Bilingual Research Journal, 25*(1–2), 89–114.

Cooper, R. L. (1989). *Language planning and social change.* New York: Cambridge University Press.

Petrovic, J. E. (1997/1999). Balkanization, bilingualism, and comparisons of language situations at home and abroad. *Bilingual Research Journal, 21*(2–3), 233–254.

Northern Territory News (2008, November 22). Department's reports undermine minister. Retrieved from http://www.ntnews.com.au/article/2008/11/22/17631 _ntnews.html.

SECTION I

POLICY

CHAPTER 1

LANGUAGE MINORITY EDUCATION IN THE UNITED STATES: POWER AND POLICY

John E. Petrovic
The University of Alabama, USA

INTRODUCTION

Language policy and planning involve a body of ideas, laws, regulations, rules, and practices enacted to promote systematic linguistic change in a community of speakers. Language policies might be enacted through legislation, court decisions, executive action, or other means. A traditional definition is that language policy is simply language planning by governments. Language planning, then, refers to the efforts and activities necessary to implementing given policy. Or, as Herriman and Burnaby (1996) describe, it is the actual realization of language policy. In this process, officials determine the linguistic needs, wants, and desires of a community and then seek to establish policies that will fulfill those goals. Such goals might include cultivating language skills needed to meet national priorities; establishing the rights of individuals or groups to learn, use, and maintain languages; promoting the growth of a national lingua franca; or promoting or discouraging multilingualism (Petrovic, 2007). Although this fairly conventional

International Perspectives on Bilingual Education: Policy, Practice, and Controversy, pages 3–20
Copyright © 2010 by Information Age Publishing

understanding of language policy and planning has been criticized (cf. Tollefson, 1991) and there are certainly more nuanced distinctions between policy and planning, this general understanding serves the purposes of this chapter.

Unfortunately, language policy in the United States has developed absent a consistent language ideology, or an ideal of the language goals that we, as a nation, should seek to fulfill. Instead, it has evolved through a number of important court cases and some ad hoc legislation. Arguably, there has been no language policy, per se, in the United States. But, as Herriman and Burnaby (1996) observe, when there is no language policy, the linguistic status quo becomes de facto policy.

Language policy in the United States, instead of following a smooth path toward some particular language goal, has been laid out in fits, starts, and stops shaped by various political, social, and economic forces. As regards language diversity (as follows from Herriman and Burnaby), this path has been formed against an assimilationist backdrop: one that discourages multilingualism. However, the *specific* ebb and flow of language policy in the United States is somewhat more complex. Historically, we can trace roughly three distinct periods: a period of benign neglect in which language diversity was tolerated, a period of severe restriction with an emphasis on assimilation, and a period of opportunism that saw a revived importance placed on language learning and maintenance (Ovando, 2003). As will be described, recent policy enactments indicate a return to restrictionism.

This chapter provides an historical overview of the development of language policy in the United States, especially as relates to language in education policy. Despite Heinz Kloss's (1977) classic presentation and defense of an "American Bilingual Tradition," reactionary attempts to maintain an imagined national community have given rise to negative language policy. Such policy rose in the wake of World War I, was beaten partially back during the civil rights movement, and has had a resurgence most recently.

LANGUAGE POLICY AND REFORM

In seeking to define language policy, Brian Weinstein (1990) provides a straightforward way to frame analyses, asking, "Does one wish to maintain the identity and patterns of access in a society, to reform them, or to transform them?" (p. 19). While Weinstein defines these broad goals by example in specific ways, depending on the sociopolitical context and the more specific purposes, each of them can represent positive or negative language planning. As Kaplan and Baldauf (1997) explain, "Certain types of language planning are intended not to increase the number of linguistic options, but rather to restrict severely the number of such options" (p. 230). The purpose of this section is to review examples of language planning in these general ways in order to then analyze the historical development of language policy in the United States.

As an example of maintaining the identity and patterns of access in a society, Weinstein cites the corpus planning of the Commissariat de la Langue Française, whose goal is to purify the French language by removing and punishing the use of non-French (mainly American English) lexicon and to establish a list of approved French terms and expressions for frequently used foreign expressions. The goal of the Commissariat is to maintain the identity of France by way of the maintenance of the linguistic status quo as not only French but more specifically standard prescribed French.

By limiting the linguistic options (in this example by prescribing what variety of French should lead to access in society), this sort of prescriptivist planning is an example of negative language planning. A parallel example in the United States is the debate around Ebonics, or African American Vernacular. Despite its syntactic integrity and its importance in American society (cf. Labov, 1973; Baugh, 1999), Ebonics is usually seen as slang or "bad English" to be overcome. This view helps to maintain the linguistic privilege of those who happen to speak a variety of English that more closely resembles what is merely a socially constructed standard.

As a broader example, federal legislative efforts in the United States to make English the official language exemplify status planning with the goal of maintaining the status quo. Even though the officialization of English would be a change in its current status, it would serve to maintain the status quo since English is already the de facto lingua franca and language of power and access in the United States.

Moving to efforts to reform identity and patterns of access in a society, Weinstein offers the co-officialization of Catalan with Castilian in Cataluña as one example. After many years of linguistic oppression, the Catalonian Linguistic Normalization Law raised the status of the Catalan language in 1983. After a decade of litigation, the law was upheld by the Spanish Supreme Court. An example of reform in the United States that will be discussed in more detail later is the Bilingual Education Act, signed into law by President Lyndon Johnson in 1968. Another significant example of reform is found in one of the 1975 amendments to the Voting Rights Act (1965). As amended, the Act requires states and political subdivisions to conduct elections and provide certain election materials in languages other than English. The Act is invoked whenever more than five percent of the voting-age citizens in a state or other political subdivision are members of a single language minority group. Notice that these reforms represent positive language planning—increasing linguistic options for participation. Furthermore, in these examples of reform, the increase in linguistic options opens access to opportunity both societally and educationally.

Weinstein defines language policy to transform as an effort "to change a state and society in radical ways: changing identities, replacing one elite by another in the state apparatus, and altering patterns of access to reflect the replacement of a dominant class or ethnic group" (p. 14). The goal of changing identities is forcefully illustrated in language policy vis-à-vis Native Americans in the United States. This is especially true of language policy as carried out in Bureau of Indian Affairs schools. These schools were explicitly designed, as infamously observed by Richard Pratt, founder of the Carlisle Indian School, to "kill the Indian . . . and save the man" (Pratt, 1892).

HISTORICAL TRAJECTORY OF LANGUAGE POLICY IN EDUCATION

The focus of this chapter is language policy in education. Therefore, this section provides an overview of the history of bilingual education, including the Bilingual Education Act, as well as of more recent policy developments. In this presentation, I choose to cast "bilingual education" more broadly as a history of primary language instruction, as explained below.

History of Bilingual Education

Some time ago, Linda Chavez (1991) lamented,

> It is a social contract between the person welcomed into the home and the host: when in Rome, do as the Romans do. When Hispanics insist that they do not have to follow the same rules as every group before them, they threaten this contract. (p. 94)

With this, Chavez would have us believe that language minorities in the United States today are making unprecedented demands on U.S. society. Chavez' claim is not unique. Indeed, a common understanding of our history suggests that previous generations of immigrants came to the United States without bilingual education, did not demand bilingual education, learned English, and did quite well, thank you very much. But the historical record is not quite as straightforward or consistent as Chavez and other assimilationists would have us believe. Let me address the historical claims regarding bilingual education specifically.

First, bilingual education has always existed in the United States in a variety forms. Second, the history of education clearly demonstrates the great importance that immigrant groups placed on their own languages and cultures. Immigrant groups rejected coercive assimilation and, contrary to Chavez's claim, often demanded that their children be given the opportunity to maintain their first languages. In other words, the demands that some language minority groups and families today are making for bilingual education are not unique. The United States has a long and constant history of bilingual education (Kloss, 1977).

Andersson and Boyer (1978) observe that "the history of bilingual education in the United States falls into two distinct periods: the first from 1840 to 1920 and the second beginning in 1963" (p. 21). First, I would like to point out that the history of bilingual education, to be thorough, must be more generally a history of "primary language instruction." A common definition of bilingual education in the United States is the use of both students' native language and English as languages of instruction for content area instruction.[1] But if we stick to this definition, we are apt to miss many episodes in our history that demonstrate the strong and continuous language loyalties of the myriad speakers of other languages in the United States. Therefore, for the purposes of refuting the inaccurate claims mentioned, I use the term primary language instruction (PLI) to mean all of the following: (1) bilingual education as defined above, (2) use of the native language of a group of students as the sole language of instruction, and (3) instruction in the native language as a subject in and of itself—but not necessarily as a language of instruction in other core subjects.

Second, Andersson and Boyer imply that 1840 was the beginning of bilingual education in this country. If we use PLI as a measure, 1840 was certainly not the beginning. In fact, given the philosophy of homogeneity inherent to the common school movement around this time, it is arguable that 1840 or so marked the beginning of a general decline in PLI. I do agree with Andersson and Boyer that 1963, roughly, marked the renaissance of PLI, including bilingual education. But the period between 1920 and 1963 is equally important in the history of PLI because of both the efforts to do away with PLI and the struggles against such efforts.

a. PLI from 1700s–1917

The Colonial Period to World War I can be identified as a period of "democratic localism" as regards the control of schools and, per Ovando

---

[1] This definition owes much to the historical record of language use in the United States, given that most immigrants saw, and continue to see, the acquisition of English as a necessity. The definition owes much also to the debates surrounding the Bilingual Education Act. The Act proposed bilingual education primarily as a compensatory program to serve the special needs of language minority students (the focus then was on Spanish-speaking students) and to promote academic achievement as well as English-language acquisition. This is not to say that broader definitions-developing from other sociohistorical conditions—are not accurate. For example, many students in India receive education in two (or more) languages, which may or may not include their first language (cf. Petrovic and Majumdar, in press).

(2003), a "permissive period" toward languages. The colonists, while acknowledging the importance of education, "did not believe the creation of an extensive and well-organized system of education was necessary" (Spring, 2001, p. 32). Schools, in the modern sense, existed only in certain areas, depending on the number of children and parents' desire for a school.

Immigrants tended to settle in the country and to form language pockets. Thus, families were not only isolated geographically by the large tracts of land needed for farming, but they were also isolated culturally. Schools reflected these different populations. In many cases, the immigrant population was monolingual in a language other than English, and all instruction was given in the students' language. This was reinforced by the fact that teachers were hired from the local monolingual population and were thus themselves monolingual (Faust, 1969).

Nonetheless, bilingual schools were also quite common during this period. Missionary schools were set up for the various Indian nations (Keller & Van Hooft, 1982; Castellano, 1983), and French/English schools were not uncommon in the Louisiana Territory and in the Northeast. By 1840, Germans had become the most educationally established language minority group. They were able to provide either all German or bilingual schools for their children through the end of this period—and, in many instances, well into the next period. Kloss (1977) notes that the superintendents of public schools in Pennsylvania again and again recognized the right to a German as well as a bilingual school. The report of the Superintendent of 1836, for example, reads: "Care has been taken during the last year to correct the impression that a German school cannot be a (public) common school" (p. 149).

Support for PLI reached its zenith in 1840. Governor Seward of Ohio exemplified the position when he proclaimed that

> [a]s a result of obstacles which arise from differences of language and religion, children of immigrants are all too often robbed of the advantages of the public educational system . . . . Therefore, I do not hesitate to recommend the establishment of schools in which they are taught by teachers who speak the same language and confess to the same creed as they do. (Kloss, 1977, p. 62)

Although social forces would begin to erode it, support for PLI continued throughout the nineteenth and into the twentieth century. As late as 1875, the superintendent of St. Louis schools, William T. Harris, was defending the use of German in the schools, if only as a separate subject in the curriculum, in the name of eradicating "caste distinctions" and maintaining "national memories and aspirations, family traditions, customs, and habits" (Tyack, 1974, p. 107).

The Germans themselves clung tenaciously to a more robust version of bilingual education. In Colorado, the school law of 1867 required school boards in districts with at least 25 German children to establish a bilingual school; several bilingual schools were established in Maryland in 1874 as well (Kloss, 1977). In some Maryland schools, as well as in cities such as Cincinnati and St. Louis (Tyack, 1974), German was the sole language of instruction in many classes.

It was not until the end of the 1800s that a sharp decline in bilingual schooling became evident. By 1888, for example, the use of German was abolished even in William T. Harris's former school district. German was abolished not only as a language of instruction but also as a subject. This decline was provoked by a number of things, such as the common school movement, the Industrial Revolution, and the assimilation demanded by industrial leaders (Katz, 1987).

Furthermore, increased immigration, mainly from Eastern and Southern Europe, helped give rise to early nativist movements such as the American Protective Association, the National Americanization Committee, and the Know Nothings. Anti-immigrant sentiment was not the sole prerogative of such organizations, but was more widely held. Ellwood P. Cubberley (1919), head of the Department of Education at Stanford University at the time, perhaps exemplified the mood of the nation when he wrote that the Eastern and Southern European immigrants were "of a very different type from the North and West Europeans who preceded them" (p. 338). He went on to describe them as "largely illiterate, docile, lacking in initiative, and almost wholly without the Anglo-Saxon conceptions of righteousness, liberty, law, order, public decency, and government," arguing that "their coming has served to dilute tremendously our national stock and to weaken and corrupt our political life" (p. 338).

As regards immigrants and primary language instruction, the common schools came to reflect this broad sentiment and the specific order of the nativist organizations. For example, for the Superintendent of Public Instruction of Pennsylvania, the purpose of the common school vis-à-vis the children of immigrants[2] was to ensure their Americanization by putting them "under the definite culture of our language and life" so that they will "grow up into an affectionate fellowship with American habits," becoming with us "colingual and congenial" (*Forty-ninth Annual Report*, 1884, p. 267). The intent was a denationalization of immigrant children from their origins. Such denationalization could not occur among their parents whose "habits and forms of thought [were] too deeply ingrained to be removed"

---

[2] This is not to say that adult immigrants were ignored by Americanizers. They were encouraged to attend English classes in both day and night schools and many of their places of work offered classes as well. (cf. Ettinger, 1919; Immigrants and night schools, 1916; National committee of one hundred, 1916).

and who "[clung] to their mother-tongue as a hallowed possession not to be lost" (*Forty-ninth Annual Report*, 1884, p. 267).

Baron (1990) points out that although nativist movements like the Know Nothings had subsided by the end of the Civil War, "attempts to extend the legal sway of English did not" (p. 114), and the sway of English as the sole language of instruction was widely established. Furthermore, these earlier, more radical movements set the stage for "a new and even more pervasive form" (Baron, 1990, p. 133) of nativism: the Americanization movement of the early twentieth century. The "restrictive period" beginning in the late 1800s would reach its nadir with the onset of World War I.

b. PLI from 1917 to 1946

The years just before, between, and after the World Wars were characterized by isolationism and strict quotas on immigration. The increasing patriotism (read: nativism) and xenophobia experienced in the pre–World War I years remained throughout this period. This is exemplified by a statement by the Council of Defense in Victoria County, Texas in 1918:

> As a high evidence of patriotism and love for those tenets of freedom for which our sons are dying we call upon all loyal Americans to abandon the use of the German language, in public and private, as an utmost condemnation of the rule of sword. (cited in McNab, 2003, p. 2)

The extent of this "patriotic" sentiment can be seen in state legislation concerning foreign languages. Before World War I only three states (Connecticut, Maine, and Rhode Island) had any kind of English-only legislation. By the end of 1917, legislation had been passed in 34 states. In 1919, for example, the Siman Act in Nebraska "prohibited instruction in any foreign language in any public, private, or parochial school, except that foreign languages could be taught as languages to students who had passed the eighth grade" (Ross, 1994, p. 94). In that same year, legislation passed in Iowa that was almost identical to Nebraska's. Ohio's law of 1919 was not quite as severe; it only prohibited the instruction of German, a trend which included 21 other states (Baron, 1990).

These types of prohibitions met their end in the landmark *Meyer v. Nebraska*, a case brought by the state against a teacher who was observed using German in his classroom. The Supreme Court ruled in 1923 that states could not prohibit PLI. However, even this ruling could not reverse the damage done. European immigrant groups still felt great pressure to assimilate, while the rest of the public continued to view instruction in a language other than English as unpatriotic. In schools, students who did not speak English were simply expected to sink or swim.

Despite the general anti-immigrant sentiment and negative language policies, it is important to note the will and efforts of minority groups to maintain their languages. This is evidenced by the number of PLI programs maintained. For example, in 1917 in Nebraska alone, there were a total of 262 schools in which it was estimated that 10,000 children received instruction in "foreign" languages. In many of these schools, instruction was given entirely in the "foreign" language—chiefly, German. The situation was similar in other states. For example, in Minnesota, 213 bilingual schools were still operating in 1917. Of these, 195 were German and English schools; 10 were Polish and English; 4 were French and English. The remaining four used Bohemian [sic], Dutch, Norwegian, and Danish, along with English, as languages of instruction (Thompson, 1920). But the extent of these programs caused "Americans" great concern. And the period 1917–1946 ushered in the abandonment of PLI.

c. PLI from 1945 to 1980

The end of World War II marked the beginning of the Cold War, creating concern in the ability of the United States to maintain its "edge" in the world power struggle. On the one hand, many of the effects of maintaining this edge were pernicious in the U.S.: state-sponsored terrorism, the establishment of a corporate welfare system (the military–industrial complex that supported companies like Lockheed Martin, Boeing, IBM, Union Carbide, etc.), and a domestic system of ideological control of the population such that the first two effects were (and still are) rendered invisible. On the other hand, language pluralists must also consider three largely positive government-sponsored initiatives as regards language policy: a return to the instruction of foreign languages, a survey of all living languages, and a survey of language resources.

The first initiative was highlighted by the National Defense Education Act (NDEA) in 1958. With this act the U.S. government promoted and funded the teaching of modern foreign languages in the secondary schools. The Act also encouraged the return to Foreign Languages in Elementary Schools (FLES) programs, abandoned since the 1920s.

The second initiative, the survey of all living languages, was intended to identify all of the languages used in the world. Experts in each language were identified. The operation focused specifically on languages that were not taught in schools at that time. If the United States were to be able to exert its influence throughout the world, it had to be able to communicate.

The third initiative was the survey of language resources of American ethnic groups conducted by Joshua Fishman in 1960. The intent of this survey was to identify the native languages used by the different ethnic groups in the United States. It focused not only on the numbers of different languages used, but also on the numbers of speakers and their proficiency. In his contact with the different groups Fishman observed:

The maintenance and preservation of your mother tongue is important both to you and to the country at large. What steps can be taken to perpetuate the language and culture of your ethnic group in this country, how can difficulties that stand in the way be overcome, how can greater interest in an awareness of this problem be secured? (cited in Kloss, 1977, p. 34)

This view, while it foreshadowed the debate to come in the following years, was not representative of government policy at the time. Government basically wanted to know who and how many spoke what languages. It was not committed to answering the kinds of important questions posed by Fishman. This was evident in the programming, founded on cultural deprivation theory, that developed for language minority students.

Cultural deprivation theory held that these students did worse in school because they lacked American culture. This led to coercive Americanization and English as a Second Language (ESL) pullout programs. There was no room or justification for PLI, which was seen as promoting neither the American culture nor English language learning.

Legislation in the 1950s did nothing directly to affect the status of PLI, at least in its more thorough-going bilingual forms. However, the attitudes toward non-English languages and their speakers in the United States were becoming more positive in the 1950s. Also, advances in second-language teaching, tested and proven in Army language schools, helped to improve ESL instruction. Even though they were mainly in the area of foreign language education and gave short thrift to maintaining and developing the language abilities of students who already spoke a language other than English, the advances in this period arguably set the stage for the rebirth of PLI.

THE REBIRTH OF BILINGUAL EDUCATION (AND REFORM?)

The rebirth of bilingual education owes much to the Cuban revolution and the exiles, mainly to Florida, who wanted their children to both learn English and maintain their own language and culture. Of equal importance to the revival of PLI was the civil rights movement of the 1960s. The civil rights movement included political activism and legal activity in bilingual education, the most significant case being *Lau v. Nichols* (1974). Additionally, Title VII of the Elementary and Secondary Education Act—commonly known as the Bilingual Education Act—was enacted in 1968. The BEA recognized the special educational needs of language minority students and provided financial assistance to local educational agencies to develop innovative programs to meet those needs. The architect of the bill, Senator Ralph Yarborough of Texas, argued that bilingual education would do this best. The Civil Rights Act of 1964 helped set the stage for the inclusion of

Title VII in the ESEA, and the unanimous Supreme Court decision in Lau was explicitly based on it.

Unfortunately, these legislative and court induced reforms, while positive, did not signal any reasoned or systematic approach to language policy in the United States. Thus, we have a history of varying degrees of activism leading to different approaches in different eras. This has direct ramifications for education. If we are to be a monolingual society, what is the best way to educate children? If we respect families' rights to their own language and culture, need we supply the resources to promote them? If we want to respect private bilingualism but promote societal monolingualism, how should we educate language minority children?

Positive language planning seeks ways to reform, as outlined previously. In the educational arena, both the Bilingual Education Act and the Supreme Court case of *Lau v. Nichols* could be argued to represent such reform (but not necessarily planning). Even though the Bilingual Education Act was explicitly compensatory, it left some ambiguity as to whether its goal was merely to speed the transition to English-only instruction or whether it could be interpreted as a way to promote bilingualism (Crawford, 2004). Nevertheless, as August and Hakuta (1997) observe, the primary focus of the Bilingual Education Act, among other legislative and court actions, "has been on providing meaningful and equitable access for English-language learners to the curriculum, rather than serving as an instrument of language policy for the nation through the development of their native languages" (p. 16). Indeed, the first reauthorization of the Act in 1974 explicitly states that the native language was to be utilized only "to the extent necessary to allow a child to progress effectively through the educational system . . ." (Sec. 703[a] [4][A][i]). Allowing schools to use children's first languages as languages of instruction at least part of the time has been a key, but contentious, idea in the struggle for equity in education for language minority students.

In *Lau*, a group of Chinese-speaking students in San Francisco sought relief against unequal educational opportunities created by English-only instruction. While lower courts absolved the school district of any responsibility, the Supreme Court, in a unanimous decision, disagreed. They found instead that the sink-or-swim mentality and practices of the school were a violation of the students' civil rights. Even though the Court declined to offer any specific remedy, the *Lau* decision, by requiring that the special needs of English language learners be attended to, represented a major reform. At the end of its tenure, the Carter administration tried to take this reform a step further by issuing the "*Lau* Remedies." These remedies included the requirement that—at least in the elementary schools—bilingual instruction be provided to limited English proficient students (Crawford, 2004).

While the *Lau* case was brought on behalf of a group of Chinese students, much of the debate around bilingual education has centered on the Hispanic community, seeing that Spanish is, by far, the most widely spoken language in the United States after English. In fact, the Bilingual Education Act and the *Lau* decision were followed by a series of lawsuits brought by Hispanic communities across the country seeking equal educational opportunity for their children (e.g., *Cintron v. Brentwood* [New York, 1978]; *Rios v. Reed* [New York, 1978]; *Castañeda v. Pickard* [Texas, 1981]; *Gomez v. Illinois* [1987]).

These reforms, through legislation (e.g., the BEA) and through court decisions, have driven policy changes. Nevertheless, they also reflect the ad hoc nature of language policy in the United States and bring into stark relief a complete lack of planning. Perhaps the closest the United States has come to even beginning the discussion of the development of language planning was in 1978, with Executive Order 12054. With this order, President Jimmy Carter established the President's Commission on Foreign Language and International Studies. The purpose of the Commission was to make recommendations to the president in accordance with the following research objectives:

> (1) Recommend means for directing public attention to the importance of foreign language and international studies for the improvement of communications and understanding with other nations in an increasingly interdependent world;
>
> (2) Assess the need in the United States for foreign language and area specialists, ways in which foreign language and international studies contribute to meeting these needs, and the job market for individuals with these skills.
>
> (3) Recommend what foreign language area studies programs are appropriate at all academic levels and recommend desirable levels and kinds of support for each that should be provided by the public and private sectors.
>
> (4) Review existing legislative authorities and make recommendations for changes needed to carry out most effectively the Commission's recommendations. (Executive Order 12054, 1978)

The final report of the Commission plaintively concludes, "Americans' incompetence in foreign languages is nothing short of scandalous . . ." (President's Commission on Foreign Language and International Studies, 1980, p. 12). The Commission focused on acquisition planning, making some 65 recommendations that have been largely ignored in the 30 years since the report's release.

RECENT BACKLASH AND PROMISE

A backlash against language minorities, especially Spanish speakers, rose in the wake of these somewhat progressive language policies in education. In 1983, two years after introducing a (failed) constitutional amendment that would make English the official language of the United States, Senator S. I. Hayakawa founded "U.S. English." The organization quickly became, and remains, a tenacious political interest group lobbying for an amendment to make English the official language of the United States. One of its other stated goals is to "reform" (read: eliminate) bilingual education. Similarly, anti-bilingual education policies became a cornerstone of the Department of Education under the leadership of Secretary William Bennett in the 1980s.

Hispanic leaders organized quickly against the English-only backlash. In 1985, the league of United Latin American Citizens (LULAC) and the Spanish American League Against Discrimination (SALAD) joined forces to launch a campaign known as English Plus (Crawford, 2004). Attracting more than 50 other organizations opposed to official English and the English-only movement, the English Plus campaign resulted two years later in the formation of the English Plus Information Clearinghouse (EPIC). Two of the primary purposes of EPIC were to (1) foster the development of second or multiple language skills of everyone and, especially, (2) promote the retention and development of a person's first language.

While the English Plus movement has served a very positive role in the fight against the English-only movement, it certainly has not been the success supporters hoped it would be. If successful, the English Plus movement would represent a significant shift in language planning and policy. It would move current language policy from its stagnation in the reforms of 30 years ago to a new level.

Historically, language planning to transform—changing identities, replacing one elite by another in the state apparatus, and altering patterns of access to reflect the replacement of a dominant class or ethnic group—is most readily seen in policies designed to make languages disappear. Historical examples include France's policies toward Alsace, Spain's policies toward Cataluña, and the United States' policies toward Native Americans. In educational policy, this negative language planning has often meant severe repression of the minority language in schools, including punishment for its use. Language policy actively seeking to promote bilingualism, as proposed by English Plus, would indeed be historic reform.

English Plus represents a policy position that would promote deeper, positive reform than has been witnessed historically by providing second-language instructional programs throughout K–12, especially through effective approaches such as bilingual education for both language minority and language majority students. While the goal would not be to de-emphasize English, the transformation here would be an emphasis on individual bilingualism never before pursued in the United States.

It seems, however, that one of the fears of English-only proponents is that such progressive policies would lead to transformation—the replacement of one elite by another—rather than reformation. This fear was made explicit in the late 1980s by a leader of U.S. English when he asked, "Will the present majority peaceably hand over its political power to a group that is simply more fertile?" (Tanton, 1986). Similarly, commenting on a column in the San Francisco Examiner from the 1980s in which the author condemns the supposed "anti-assimilation movement" as an attempt by the Hispanic elite and liberals "to turn language minorities into permanent power blocs," Sandra del Valle (2003) observes that

> Here, at least, is one almost honest rationale for supporting English-only: it will help keep ethnic minorities from becoming powerful voting blocs. The possibility of the political power of ethnic minorities must be the overriding reason for this kind of restrictionist movement since no other makes sense. . . . (p. 57)

Today the fear of a change in power relations may be couched in less vitriolic language, but it remains a common feature of the restrictionist movement. For example, Mauro Mujica, Chairman of U.S. English, argues that

> The lack of an assimilation policy for immigrants to the United States is rapidly changing the successful integration ways of the past. Gone are the days of the American Dream and the upwardly mobile society for immigrants. In its place are low expectations and government policies that encourage Americans to learn the language of the immigrants, instead of the other way around. (Mujica, 2008, emphasis added)

It is similarly implicit in such shrill headlines as "Keep the US English Speaking,"[3] which presumes the English language to be in danger in the United States.

Unfortunately, recent changes in language policy in education portend a dire future. Policies that have severely curtailed bilingual education in favor of English immersion have passed in California (Proposition 227, 1998), Arizona (Proposition 203, 2000), and Massachusetts (Ballot Question 2, 2002). These initiatives are a return to negative language planning and have limited the educational options available. It should be noted that the people most affected by these initiatives voted overwhelmingly against them. In both California and Arizona, Hispanics voted two to one against the initiatives. In Massachusetts, 92 percent of the Hispanic population voted against the measure. In other words, negative language policy in education is supported most by people whose children are affected least, providing further evidence that the issue is about maintaining power. Unfortunately, those who promote negative language policies ignore the

---

[3] *Christian Science Monitor,* December 3, 2002.

historical record that demonstrates that "the endeavor to plan language behavior by forcing a rapid shift to English has often been a source of language problems that has resulted in the denial of language rights and hindered linguistic access to educational, social, economic, and political benefits even as the promoters of English immersion claim the opposite" (Wiley and Wright, 2004, p. 144).

Hispanics and other language minority groups in the states mentioned certainly face an uphill battle to reclaim their voices in educational policy, especially as concerns language. But the phenomenon of negative language planning is, sadly, not localized. Despite President George W. Bush's promise of smaller government, the passage of the No Child Left Behind (NCLB) Act in 2002 has ushered in unprecedented federal involvement in education policy. The term "bilingual" has been purged from federal vocabulary. For example, the Bilingual Education Act has been replaced with the "Language Instruction for Limited English Proficient and Immigrant Students" provision (Title III) of the Act. Similarly, the Office of Bilingual Education and Language Minority Affairs has been replaced with the Office of English Language Acquisition, Language Enhancement, and Academic Achievement for Limited English Proficient Students. While the Act permits bilingual education, a number of its provisions and requirements may make bilingual programs difficult to pursue. The requirements, for example, set a double standard which allows English Language Learners to pursue bilingualism as a legitimate goal only when sufficient numbers of English-speaking students share this goal. In short, the new language policies in NCLB have moved us away from the language policies to reform represented by the Bilingual Education Act and *Lau* and back to negative language policies to maintain the status quo, maintaining unearned privileges for language majority students. It is perplexing, therefore, that not a single member of the Congressional Hispanic Caucus voted against the legislation (Crawford, 2002). Without vigorous leadership—especially from the community that arguably has contributed most to the fight for progressive language policy—language policy and planning to transform a society handicapped by English monolingualism seem quite remote possibilities.

REFERENCES

Andersson, T. & Boyer, M. (1978). *Bilingual schooling in the United States* (2nd ed.). Austin, TX: National Educational Laboratory Publishers, Inc.

August, D. & Hakuta, K. (1997). *Improving schooling for language-minority children.* Washington, D.C.: National Academy Press.

Baron, D. (1990). *The English only question.* New Haven, CT: Yale University Press. Bilingual Education Act, Pub. L. No. (93-380), 88 Stat. 503 (1974).

Baugh, J. (1999). *Out of the mouths of slaves: African American language and educational malpractice.* Austin: University of Texas Press.

Castellano, D. (1983). *The best of two worlds: Bilingual-bicultural education in the U.S.* Trenton: New Jersey State Department of Education.

Chavez, L. (1991). *Out of the barrio: Toward a new politic of Hispanic assimilation.* New York: Basic Books.

Crawford, J. (2002). Obituary: The Bilingual Ed Act, 1968–2002. *Rethinking Schools, 16*(4). Retrieved from http://www.rethinkingschools.org/archive/16_04/Bil164.shtml.

Crawford, J. (2004). *Educating English language learners: Language diversity in the classroom* (5th ed.). Los Angeles: Bilingual Language Services.

Cubberley, E. (1919). *Changing conceptions of education.* Cambridge, MA: The Riverside Press.

del Valle, S. (2003). *Language rights and the law in the United States.* Clevedon, UK: Multilingual Matters, Ltd.

Ettinger, W. (1919). Americanization. *School and Society, 9*(214), 129–133.

Executive Order 12054. (April 21, 1978). President's commission on foreign language and international studies. Retrieved July 20, 2008, from http://www.presidency.ucsb.edu/ws/index,php?pid=30692.

Faust, A. (1969). *The German element in the United States.* Salem, MA: Arno Press.

Forty-ninth Annual Report. (1884, January). *The Pennsylvania School Journal, 32,* 262–268.

Herriman, M. & Burnaby, B. (1996). The implementation of corpus planning: Theory and practice. In J. Cobarrubias & J. A. Fishman (Eds.), *Progress in language planning* (pp. 269–289). Berlin: Mouton.

Immigrants and night schools. (1916, October 14). *School and Society, 592.*

Kaplan, R. B. & Baldauf Jr., R. B. (1997). *Language planning: From practice to theory.* Philidelphia: Multilingual Matters, Ltd.

Katz, M. B. (1987). *Reconstructing American education.* Cambridge, MA: Harvard University Press.

Keller, G. D. & Van Hooft, K. S. (1982). A chronology of bilingualism and bilingual education in the United States. In J. Fishman & G. D. Keller (Eds.), *Bilingual education for Hispanic students in the United States.* New York: Teachers College Press.

Kloss, H. (1977). *The American bilingual tradition.* Rowley, MA: Newbury House Publishers.

Labov, W. (1973). *Language in the inner city: Studies in the Black English Vernacular.* Philadelphia: University of Pennsylvania Press.

McNab, J. (2003). The Supreme Court's response to nativism in the 1920's. *Perspectives on International and Multicultural Affairs, 3*(1). Retrieved from http://www2.davidson.edu/academics/acad_depts/rusk/prima/Vol3Issue1/Nativism.htm.

Mujica, M. (2008). About U.S. English: Statement from the chairman. Retrieved August 7, 2008, from http://www.us-english.org/view/2.

National Committee of one hundred to promote school attendance of non-English-speaking immigrants. (1916, October 7). *School and Society, 557.*

Ovando, C. (2003). Bilingual education in the United States: Historical development and current issues. *Bilingual Research Journal, 27*(1), 1–24.

Petrovic, J. E. (2007). *Language policy*. In L. D. Soto (Ed.), *The Praeger handbook of Latino education in the U.S.* (pp. 239–243). Westport, CT: Greenwood Publishing Group.

Petrovic, J. E. & Majumdar, S. (in press). Language planning for equal educational opportunity in the multilingual states: The case of India. *International Multilingual Research Journal.*

Pratt, R. H. (1892). *"Kill the Indian, and save the man": Capt. Richard H. Pratt on the education of Native American.* Retrieved from http://historymatters.gmu.edu/d/4929/.

President's Commission on Foreign Language and International Studies. (1980). Strength through wisdom: A critique of U.S. capabilities. *Modern Language Journal, 64*(1), 9–57.

Ross, W. G. (1994). *Forging new freedoms: Nativism, education, and the constitution, 1917–1927.* Lincoln: University of Nebraska Press.

Spring, J. (2001). *The American school: 1642–2000* (5th ed.). Boston: McGraw-Hill.

Tanton, J. (1986). Memo to WITAN IV Attendees from John Tanton. Retrieved August 13, 2008, from http://www.splcenter.org/intel/intelreprot/article.jsp?sid=125.

Thompson, F. V. (1920). *Schooling of the immigrant.* New York: Harper & Brothers Publishers.

Tollefson, J. (1991). *Planning language, planning inequality.* New York: Longman.

Tyack, (1974). *The one best system: A history of American urban education.* Cambridge, MA: Harvard University Press.

Weinstein, B, (1990). Language Policy and Political Development: An overview. In B. Weinstein (Ed.), *Language policy and political development* (pp. 1–21). Norwood, NJ: Ablex Publishing Corporation.

Wiley, T. & Wright, W. (2004). Against the undertow: Language-minority education policy and politics in the "age of accountability." *Educational Policy, 18*(1), 142–168.

CHAPTER 2

LANGUAGE MINORITY RIGHTS AND EDUCATIONAL POLICY IN CANADA

Thomas Ricento and Andreea Cervatiuc
University of Calgary, Canada

INTRODUCTION

This chapter will provide a detailed description and analysis of the language policy framework for the learning and teaching of second, foreign, and heritage languages in Canada, focusing on the period from the 1960s to the present day. It will consider the factors that led to the passage of the Official Languages Act of 1969, the move to protect and promote French in Quebec in the 1970s, and the politics that led to passage of the Canadian Multiculturalism Act of 1988. The hope that individual bilingualism (principally in French and English) would become a reality for a large number of Canadians has not materialized. The preoccupation with the status of French and English has tended to dilute the resources allocated for the teaching of other so-called allophone languages. While nearly 20% of the Canadian population (6,186,950 people) was reported to be foreign-born (the vast majority being neither Anglophones nor Francophones) in 2006 (Statistics Canada, 2006), there has been little governmental support for

International Perspectives on Bilingual Education: Policy, Practice, and Controversy, pages 21–42
Copyright © 2010 by Information Age Publishing
All rights of reproduction in any form reserved.

the maintenance of non-official languages. In order to understand how and why the current policy landscape has evolved to its current form, we need to look at the historical context that led to the Quiet Revolution of the 1960s and 1970s, which gave rise to the current official bilingualism paradigm.

HISTORICAL BACKGROUND AND IMPACT
OF LANGUAGE POLICIES IN CANADA

The current linguistic landscape in Canada was already being shaped during the century that preceded the establishment of the Canadian Confederation. Although attempts were made after the British Conquest of 1760 to impose English as the language of government, the French language was given increased status through the Quebec Act of 1774 and the Constitutional Act of 1791 (Hayday, 2005, p. 16). The bilingual status for the federal government was formalized in section 133 of the British North America Act (BNA) of 1867. While the language of the BNA allowed either English or French to be used in debates in the Houses of Parliament and the Houses of the Legislature of Quebec (along with the written records and journals of those houses), it made no provisions allowing for federal government services in both languages in the courts or the legislatures of the other provinces. During the 100 years between passage of the BNA and the onset of the Quiet Revolution in the 1960s, which led to a much more expansive role for French in the federal civil service and opportunities for Francophone minority communities outside Quebec to be educated in French, the status of French varied from province to province, but the shift to English among Francophones outside Quebec continued apace. Immigration from non-English and non-French speaking countries complicated the supposed duality of the Canadian nation and tested the viability of educational language policies that had recognized only French and English as legitimate media for public education. In addition, First Nation groups had for many years objected to the "two founding races" ideology that had governed federal and provincial policy for more than 100 years. With the growing secularization of Quebec beginning in the 1960s, the maintenance of French became even more important as an identity marker. When the Liberals returned to power after the federal election of 1963, Prime Minister Lester B. Pearson established a commission to investigate the condition of Canada's French-speaking population and its relationship with the English-speaking population, as well as the status of other ethnic peoples in Canada (Mackey, 1998, p. 34). The Royal Commission on Bilingualism and Biculturalism (also referred to as the Laurendeau–Dunton Commission) was given the following charge:

To inquire into and report upon the existing state of bilingualism and biculturalism in Canada and to recommend what steps should be taken to develop the Canadian Confederation on the basis of an equal partnership between the two founding races, taking into account the contribution made by the other ethnic groups to the cultural enrichment of Canada and the measures that should be taken to safeguard that contribution (cited in Mackey, 1998, p. 34).

The commission held public hearings throughout Canada, received more than 400 formal briefs and commissioned 165 research studies. *A Preliminary Report* was published in 1965; it drew attention to serious divisions among Canadians and proved to be a harbinger of tensions that would not be resolved when the work of the B&B Commission was completed in 1971, tensions that continue to the present day. The final report appeared in six volumes between 1967 and 1970. The principal legislative outcome of the commission's work was the Official Languages Act of 1969, which made English and French Canada's official languages. It required that a range of external and internal documents, notices, decisions, and forms be published in both English and French; it established obligations for federal departments and agencies to provide services in both languages in the Ottawa–Hull area (the National Capital Region) and in a series of bilingual districts to be decided upon later (McRae, 1998, p. 66). The Act also created the position of Commissioner of Official Languages to oversee implementation of the Act and to serve as official languages ombudsman (Beaty, 1989, pp. 185–186). It was hoped that other provinces would protect the use of French in areas they controlled (e.g., education); however, the only province to follow the lead of the federal government was New Brunswick which, in 1969, declared itself to be officially bilingual.

As the Act dealt only with areas under federal jurisdiction, the recommendations in the area of language education, for example, were very general, because education falls primarily under provincial jurisdiction. Nonetheless, it was well understood by the members of the B&B Commission and the federal government that education would be central to the survival of French Canadian cultural identity. Book 2 of the B&B Commission's Report made detailed recommendations on minority-language schooling and second-language learning, emphasizing the importance of mother-tongue education and recommending that it be made available for official-language minorities in the proposed bilingual districts and in major metropolitan centers (McRae, 1998, p. 63). In 1970, following these recommendations, the Canadian government announced that it would provide financial assistance to the provinces to fund minority-language education for their official-language minorities (English in Quebec, French in the other nine provinces) and second-official-language instruction for the children of the majority-language communities. This was generally known as the Bilingualism in Education Program (BEP) until its name was changed in 1979 to the Official Languages in Education Program (OLEP), which exists to the present day (Hayday, 2005, p. 7). To achieve its objectives, the federal government has spent billions of dollars to support minority-language education programs and second-language instruction and to fund programs of grants and scholarships related to teacher training, student exchanges, and language training centers (pp. 7–8).

Because provinces differ with regard to their demographic profiles and political and economic priorities, the implementation of OLEP since 1970 has had mixed results. Eighteen months after implementation of OLEP (in 1973), the programs were evaluated. While minority-language education programs experienced growth in some provinces, secondary school instruction was decreasing, due in part to a shortage of second-language teachers and changes in university requirements (pp. 65–66). In addition, minority-language education programs cost more than had been anticipated, and the French-as-a-second-language programs (so-called core French programs) were found to be less than effective (although it has been argued that developing fluency in French was never the main objective of these programs) (Hayday, 2005, p. 180). While enrollments in English schooling in Quebec and French schooling in the rest of Canada (i.e., minority-language education) have not changed substantially since 1971, enrollments in second official language programs have increased, thanks in large measure to the development of French immersion programs. The first immersion class was opened in September 1965 in Quebec. The primary goals of the original program, which continue largely intact to the present day, are

1. To provide the participating students with functional competence in both written and spoken aspects of French
2. To promote and maintain normal levels of English-language development
3. To ensure achievement in academic subjects commensurate with the students' ability and grade level
4. To instill in students an understanding and appreciation of French-Canadians and their language and culture without detracting in any way from the students' identity with and appreciation for English-Canadian culture (Genesee, 1998, p. 310)

While students who graduate from French immersion programs do not generally achieve native-like proficiency in the minority language (French), they outperform students in other types of second-language programs in Canada (Genesee, 1998, p. 321). However, research has suggested that structural pressures render retention of French by immersion graduates difficult (Wesche & MacFarlane, 1995; Van der Keilen, 1995). One critic of these programs argues that "the entire effort was an interesting social experiment that did not work" (Veltman, 1998, p. 306). Census data also suggest that despite the successes of immersion programs, the number of fluent bilinguals in Canada has barely changed since the 1960s. Whereas in 1971 13% (2.9 million people) of the Canadian population could speak both official languages, in 1996 about 17% (4.8 million people) claimed fluency in both languages. The rate of bilingualism was nearly five times higher among Francophones (41%) than in Anglophones (9%). The rate of bilingualism of Francophones living outside Quebec was even higher (84%) than that of Anglophones living outside Quebec (7%). In contrast, the proportion of bilingual Anglophones living in Quebec (62%) was almost twice that of Francophones in that province (34%). Much of this variation is age-related. In the case of Quebec Francophones, the job market plays an important role in the learning of English as a second language. Hence, the rate of bilingualism reached a peak (48%) in the age group 20 to 24, ages corresponding to high labor market participation. For Anglophones outside Quebec, school is the main place for learning French as a second language. Consequently, the highest rate of bilingualism (16%) was in the age group 15 to 19, the secondary school years. The rate was lower in older age groups; French immersion was less popular or nonexistent during their school years (Statistics Canada, 1996).

Outside Quebec, the shift to English by both Francophone and allophone Canadians continues unabated. While facility in French can be an asset in certain sectors of the job market in English-speaking Canada (especially for federal jobs), nearly all Anglophone Canadians work and play in English-language institutions with English-speaking people (p. 306). Canadian legal scholar Joseph Magnet concludes that "Canada regulates language use in order to divert overheated competition between Canada's English- and French-speaking communities into manageable pathways where highly charged conflict may be blunted and controlled" (1998, p. 185). Thus, while Canada is an officially bilingual country, the vast majority of Canadians are not fluent in both official languages, although Francophones are far more likely to speak English than Anglophones are to speak French.

STATUS OF ABORIGINAL LANGUAGES IN CANADA

There are currently 50 aboriginal languages spoken by indigenous people in Canada, belonging to 11 major language families (Norris, 2007). Over the past 100 years, approximately 10 aboriginal languages in Canada have become extinct. The decline over the past 50+ years has been dramatic; in

1951, 87.4% of the aboriginal population had an aboriginal language as a mother tongue, while in 1981 it was only 29.3% (Burnaby & Beaujot, 1986, p. 36), and by 2001 it was 21% (Statistics Canada, 2001). Unfortunately, only 3 out of the 50 aboriginal languages in Canada are considered robust enough to have chances of survival in the long run, as the number of speakers has been constantly declining. Inuktitut, Cree, and Ojibway are the only flourishing or healthy languages, with over 20,000 speakers each, constituting a sufficient base to guarantee long-term viability (Norris, 1998). In contrast, most aboriginal languages face the risk of extinction unless serious language policy intervention is considered. The weakest ones are Kutenai, spoken by 120 indigenous people, and Tlingit, with a mother-tongue population of 145.

Passing a language from one generation to another by speaking it at home is the most effective way of ensuring its survival. Unfortunately, many of the Canadian indigenous people do not speak their language at home any more. In fact, according to 2001 census data, only 24% of the indigenous people in Canada can conduct a conversation in an aboriginal language, which indicates a sharp decline in use, as compared to 29%, recorded by the 1996 census. A number of factors have contributed to the decline in the use of aboriginal languages, including the pressure of the official languages, the prohibition of their use in residential (religious) schools, and the fact that most of them are predominantly oral (Norris, 1998). In addition, more and more aboriginal people leave the reserves, migrate to urban centers, and get into linguistic intermarriages (Petten, 2007).

The majority of public voices who advocate the preservation of endangered aboriginal languages view them as an integral part of Canadian society and as doors to the nation's collective memory (Saul, 2004). From an ideological perspective that would promote social justice, saving aboriginal languages is not a matter of charity, but of assuming responsibility for previous political stances that contributed to the erosion of endangered languages. Moreover, some analysts argue that aboriginal language preservation represents a protective factor against suicide in First Language younger generations (Chandler, 2006). Cultural and linguistic continuity may promote the self-esteem and well-being of indigenous people. Alienating aboriginal people from their cultural roots has been proven to be detrimental to their education achievement and sense of identity (McCue, 2008). A way to prevent this loss is to incorporate ancestral cultural values in the curricula for native people education and to offer instruction in their native language. A significant development in this regard was the creation of an aboriginal language and culture curriculum that was adopted by the provinces of Manitoba, Saskatchewan, Alberta, and British Columbia and by the three territories (Western Canadian Protocol for Collaboration in Basic Education, 2000).

HOW CAN ABORIGINAL LANGUAGES BE SAVED?

While it would be utopian to hope for the revival of dead aboriginal languages, investing in the revitalization of endangered languages may turn the tide and slow down their process of extinction. Historically, there have been some successful attempts of language revitalization by which imperiled languages have been rescued. Navajo is an example of a language that is today in good health, even though it was facing extinction until the 1940s, when the U.S. Marines decided to use it as a code in World War II to confuse the Germans and Japanese (Redish, 2001).

One way to revitalize endangered languages is to teach them as second languages. In fact, according to the 2001 census, 20% of the indigenous people in Canada who report that they can speak an aboriginal language learned it as a second language. For some aboriginal languages, the decline in the mother-tongue population has been offset by the rise in the number of second-language speakers (Norris, 2007). Even if learning an aboriginal language as a second language is not a substitute for acquiring it as a first language, Norris emphasizes that it may be the only viable option to revitalize and slow down the extinction of endangered languages for which intergenerational transmission is no longer available. For smaller languages such as Tlingit, Kutenai, and Haida, second-language speakers make the difference between survival and extinction (Petten, 2007). For instance, out of the 230 recorded Tlingit speakers, 130 report having learned it as a second language (Norris, 2007). The younger generation of indigenous people is increasingly more likely to acquire an aboriginal language as a second language rather than as a mother tongue. Therefore, investing in bilingual programs is one way to slow down or prevent aboriginal language loss. Currently, Inuktitut and Creed are used as languages of instruction, while other aboriginal languages are only taught as subjects. There are very few aboriginal immersion programs in Canada, and the curriculum support is still limited (McCue, 2008), despite the recent improvements mentioned above.

Can more policies be implemented in order to prevent the extinction of aboriginal languages? In an attempt to provide an answer to this question, we take a look at some of the measures that have already been put into practice and highlight some of the policies and priorities that can be addressed in the future. The past three decades have seen the creation of new structures and institutions to promote aboriginal languages, as well as the introduction of new legislation to foster their use and ensure their survival. Nine aboriginal languages have been made official languages in the Northwest Territories (along with English and French). In June 2007, the Nunavut legislative assembly read a new Official Language Act that would grant official language status to Inuit along with English and French (Suthers, 2007). If passed, the Act would promote Inuit use by creating the framework to introduce/implement various language programs and language policy measures. The goal is to make services to the public available in three languages and to establish Inuit as the working language of the local government by 2020. However, despite improvements in aboriginal language programs in schools, most programs are for the youngest children, are inadequately funded, and are transitional to fluency in an official language (Burnaby, 2008, p. 338). Based on current survey data, Burnaby (2002) found that aboriginal language programs give only lip service to pluralism and are in fact assimilationist in intent (cited in Burnaby, 2008, p. 339).

At the national level, some measures have been implemented to promote and protect aboriginal languages. In 1998, Heritage Canada contributed $20 million to the cause of aboriginal languages preservation (Black, 2000). The money was divided among the Assembly of First Nations (AFN), the Inuit Tapisarat of Canada, and the Metis National Council. The AFN established a Chiefs Committee on Languages and a Technical Committee on Languages to oversee and administer the funds from Heritage Canada and promote the protection of First Nation Languages. Perhaps more significant is the role of advocacy by First Nations political and cultural representatives. In December 1999, the Assembly of First Nations, the political driving force for the First Nations; and the First Nation Confederacy of Cultural Education Centres (FNCCEC), representing 77 cultural centers, partnered and signed a memorandum of understanding to coordinate language policy development and political advocacy for the preservation of aboriginal languages (Black, 2000). AFN and FNCCEC take the position that the government should accept responsibility for the destruction of aboriginal languages, create federal and provincial policies, and provide resources to correct the situation. AFN and FNCCEC have proposed some initiatives that would push forward the recognition of aboriginal languages through legislation such as the establishment of an aboriginal language foundation that would be funded partly by the federal government ($50 million) and partly by private money ($50 million). The other priority on their agenda is to create a list of Friends of Aboriginal Languages, which would include senators, members of parliament, and businesspeople who would lobby for legislation and assist with fundraising. It is clear that without immediate intervention, many aboriginal languages face the risk of extinction—and that from a language policy perspective, there are things that can be done to correct the situation.

CANADA AS A MULTICULTURAL NATION

Canada's linguistic landscape and approach to multiculturalism are unique in the world. One in five English-speaking Canadians was born in another country (Statistics Canada, 2006) and the immigration rate has been steadily increasing since the 1980s. Not only does Canada have a very diverse population, but it also has a distinctive multicultural paradigm that responds to three levels of diversity: (1) a high percentage of immigrants, (2) substate nationalism in Quebec, and (3) aboriginal people (Kymlicka, 2004). Other countries may face only one or two of these challenges, but not all three (e.g., New Zealand has immigrants and indigenous people, but no substate nationalism, while some European countries deal with immigration and substate nationalism but do not have indigenous people). Accommodating diversity has not been an easy road but an ongoing balancing act, the product of intense negotiations, hard work, and strategy-building. Canada's model of multiculturalism within a bilingual framework has been about reaching compromise and finding a happy medium. It may not have pleased all stakeholders, but it has at least managed to diffuse tensions and keep Canada united as a country.

While French achieved the same official status as English through the Official Languages Act (1969), less attention was paid to the status of non-official languages. Partly in recognition of this oversight, in 1971 the prime minister announced a policy of multiculturalism (Multiculturalism Act, 1971). John Berry (1998, pp. 84–85) identifies four elements of this policy enunciated in the Act. First, the policy seeks to avoid assimilation, a goal Berry identifies as "own group maintenance and development." A second purpose of the policy is to increase intergroup harmony in what Berry terms "other group acceptance and tolerance." Third, the policy argues that group development is not sufficient to lead to group acceptance; rather, "intergroup contact and sharing" is also required. Fourth, in order for cultural groups to attain full participation, a common language must be learned; thus, "learning of official languages" (French and English) is encouraged by the policy.

After 17 years of activities and programs, another multiculturalism act was passed in 1988. The Act recognized the importance of preserving and enhancing the multicultural heritage of Canadians, the importance of the rights of the aboriginal peoples of Canada, and the importance of the two official languages, and it espoused the equality of all Canadians, whether citizens by birth or by choice; equality of opportunity, regardless of race, national or ethnic origin, and color; freedom from discrimination based on culture, religion, or language; and the diversity of Canadians as a fundamental characteristic of Canadian society. The Canadian Multiculturalism Act (1988) requires all federal institutions to implement the multiculturalism policy and to report annually on their achievements, activities, and challenges in applying the Act through programs, initiatives, and services. Ethnic minorities continue to obtain financial support from the federal government through various projects initiated to implement the Canadian Multiculturalism Act (1988), and the commitments and treaties with the aboriginal people are stipulated in the Constitution Act (1982).

Controversies over and reactions to the federal government's policy of multiculturalism have come from several places. French nationalists perceived the bilingual and multicultural model initiated by Pierre Trudeau and his government as a diversion strategy aimed at eroding French-Canadian nationalism. Quebecoise nationalists claimed that the replacement of the policy of bilingualism and biculturalism by one of multiculturalism within a bilingual framework was a federal government plot (Cristopher, 1983), a Machiavellian strategy meant to undermine the perceived biculturalism of Canada and the historical contribution of French Canadians by reducing their status to "just one of the ethnic groups" (Kymlicka, 2004, p. 162). English-speaking assimilationists also reacted to the multiculturalism policy, but for different reasons. They consider it divisive and impractical and expect immigrants from different cultures to completely sever any ties with their countries of origin and fully embrace a Canadian identity and way of living:

> The waves of immigrants that arrived on the prairies early in the 20th century were quickly cut off from the old country. That doesn't happen to today's immigrants; many maintain intimate links to their homelands . . . . Only Canada, through its policy of official multiculturalism, actually encourages newcomers to cling to their original identities rather than fully embrace the identity of their new home (Stoffman, 2002, pp. 42–43).

The comments above convey an implicit lack of acceptance of visible minorities, who greatly contribute to today's immigration profile, and an idealization of the European immigrants who settled in Canada at the beginning of the 20th century. This view is reminiscent of the Anglo-conformists' stereotypical image of the "good" immigrant: a white, sturdy, easy-to-assimilate agriculturalist, suggestively depicted in the comments of Clifford Sifton, Canadian Minister of Interior at the beginning of the 20th century as "a stalwart peasant in a sheepskin coat, born on the soil, whose forefathers have been farmers for ten generations, with a stout wife and a half dozen children" (Sifton, 1975, p. 35). For today's assimilationists, even the advances of technology represent an obstacle to immigrants' immersion into Canadian culture, as they enable them to maintain their ties with the old countries:

> A different factor that has markedly slowed the integration of newcomers has been rapid developments in communication and technology. These developments have enabled immigrants to continue to be immersed in the culture and concerns of the countries they left, rather than having to concentrate on things Canadian and adapting to their new land. (Collacott, 2002, p. 30)

Immigrants who match old-timers' economic performance, give up their native languages, move away from ethnic enclaves, and adopt a Canadian way of life are considered "well-integrated." Such a view on integration is, in essence, based on assimilationist assumptions (Li, 2003, p. 8). Even relatively recent (1990s) documents produced by Employment and Immigration Canada reflect the view that ethnic enclaves eventually hinder immigrants' full participation in society:

> To the degree that ethnic enclaves restrict their members and shield them from alternative norms, values and behaviors, they can discourage immigrants from full participation in society and perpetuate segregation . . . . Ideally, in integrated society, immigrants move through ethnic enclaves, using its resources in order to enter the mainstream society. (Employment and Immigration Canada, 1993, pp. 4–5)

Most ethnic minorities approve of the multiculturalism policy in principle but are somewhat disappointed with its implementation. Some critics representing various ethnic minorities in Canada consider the "the multiculturalism paradigm within a bilingual framework" to be unfair, as it does not fully support the preservation of heritage languages. In their view, it is very difficult, if not impossible, to divorce culture from language. Language is seen as the vehicle that keeps culture alive. Promoting cultures without ensuring heritage language transmission translates into mere entertainment and pseudo-multiculturalism for decorative purposes.

In spite of some controversies and negative reactions, recent polls suggest that the vast majority of Canadians (74%) support the federal policy of multiculturalism (Dasko, 2004). However, a survey conducted in 1991 indicates a national paradox regarding the public acceptance of multiculturalism. Even if the majority of Canadians are in favor of multiculturalism, they do not support the idea of governmental funding of policies and programs intended to support ethnic (i.e., allophone or indigenous) communities (Garcea, 2004). In other words, Canadians embrace pluralistic and tolerant values in principle, but oppose the idea of using taxpayers' money to help non-indigenous ethnic groups preserve their culture and language. As long as these communities support their own activities, the majority of Canadians embrace multiculturalism.

The rate of national approval of multicultural values and policies may in fact be dependent on economic factors. For instance, in the early 1990s, when the economy was in recession and the unemployment rate high, polls indicate that Canadians were less likely to accept multiculturalism (54% approval rate) than in 2002 (74% approval rate), when the economy picked up (Dasko, 2004, p. 131). Younger and more educated people tend to be more appreciative of cultural and linguistic diversity, but a significant percentage considers that the Canadian multiculturalism policy empowers ethnic groups in excess. One in three university-educated Canadians under the age of 35 believes that aboriginal people have too much power, while one in seven considers that immigrants have too much power (Bibby, 2004).

The federal government does not directly fund heritage language classes, but it offers some support for ethnic programs to promote their culture and for communities to teach their languages using volunteers. The multiculturalism policy is less about promoting linguistic justice than it is about fighting and eliminating racism and discrimination. The federal government's stance is that the multiculturalism policy "aims to preserve and enhance the use of other languages, while strengthening the status and use of official languages" (Multiculturalism and Citizenship Canada, 1991, p. 20), but it is not clear how it supports other languages, since it does not directly fund heritage language teaching. A look at the Annual Report on the Operation of the Canadian Multiculturalism Act (Canadian Heritage, 2006–2007) reveals that the Multiculturalism Program of the Department of Canadian Heritage funds various initiatives in four activity areas: support to civil society, research and policy development, support to public institutions (including federal institutions), and public education and promotion. The stated goal of the Multiculturalism Program is to "support the removal of barriers related to race, ethnicity, cultural support or religious background that would prevent full participation in Canadian society" (Canadian Heritage, 2006–2007, p. 9). There is no mention of financial support for minority languages in particular.

The existing language policy framework may not truly reflect the linguistic composition of Canada and may not be in sync with its changing demographics. The policy of bilingualism was introduced to recognize the contribution of the founding nations of Canada, ignoring the rights of the aboriginal people. In 1867, when the Confederation was formed, 92% of the Canadian population was of British or French origin. Today, Canadian society is ethnically heterogeneous: 46% of the population belongs to ethnic groups that are not of British or French origin, 23% is of French origin, 20% British, and 11% mixed British and French (Gosh, 2004, p. 550). A policy that supports multiculturalism within a bilingual framework through programs that fund "multicultural days," song-and-dance routines, and workshops against discrimination may not do enough to promote and preserve allophone languages.

A multiculturalism paradigm that would promote linguistic justice should ideally give equal rights to all languages spoken in a country. It would probably be impractical to have more than two official languages, but more could be done to support the preservation of heritage languages. What kind of multiculturalism paradigm would ideally promote linguistic justice? Probably one in which all ethnic groups would have the right and financial support to preserve both their languages and cultures. Lupul (Cristopher, 1983, p. 116), a Ukranian Canadian writer, criticizes the implementation of the multiculturalism policy for divorcing culture from language and proposes a liberal language policy that would give all Canadians the possibility to choose their own linguistic program out of three available alternatives: unilingualism;

bilingualism, which could be either English/French or English/any other language; or trilingualism, meaning English/French/any other language. English and French would continue to be the official languages of the country, but all ethnic groups would have the opportunity at least to teach their children to read and write in their mother tongue. At first sight, the implementation cost of such a program might seem prohibitive, but it may not be necessarily so, as many Canadians may simply opt for unilingualism. Bilingualism and trilingualism, which include an allophone language, may seem impractical, but ethnic groups could provide their own teachers and curricula and the number of classes offered would depend on the percentage of potential students with an interest in studying some of the subject matter in their first language. It could mean that in a large city, only one school would offer a bilingual intake in English/Hungarian, for example.

A just multicultural and multilingual society could be built through educational programs based on the philosophical assumptions of critical pedagogy. A truly empowering curriculum would value and promote the preservation of various languages and cultures and would educate all learners, both old-timers and immigrants, to respect human rights, value diversity, fight racism and discrimination, and promote social equity.

HERITAGE LANGUAGE TEACHING IN CANADA

Although broad objectives of educational policy are covered in the Canadian Constitution, the formalizing and implementation of policy is primarily the responsibility of provinces and territories. There is no federal office of education or national educational policy and curriculum (Gosh, 2004). Provinces and territories have their own policies and curricula and cooperate through the Council of Ministers of Education in Canada (CMEC). The federal government supports bilingualism and multiculturalism, but national implementation of the Multicultural Policy in K–12 education is problematic due to the centralization of school systems only at the provincial level. Even if the Canadian Multiculturalism Act (1988) encourages ethnic groups to preserve their cultures and languages, heritage language teaching does not receive federal financial support. The funding is directed to programs that fight discrimination and promote cultural awareness. It should be noted that federal funding is available for some aspects of public education, such as support for teaching one of the official minority languages in geographical areas where the other one is dominant (e.g., English for Anglophones in Quebec and French for Francophones in other parts of Canada). Ironically, in the English-speaking parts of Canada for example, funding is provided to educate a student in French, but not in English (Early, 2008).

As a result of this fiscal division of responsibilities, provinces and territories vary considerably in the amount of funding they provide for heritage language teaching as well as in the languages offered and the grades in which they are offered. They also differ in educational goals and curricula, teacher certification requirements, and textbook authorization. Across the country, there are a few heritage/international programs that offer languages other than English, French, or aboriginal languages. In about 50% of the Canadian provinces, heritage language teaching is offered at the end of the school day or on Saturday (Early, 2008). In the Prairie Provinces (Alberta, Saskatchewan, and Manitoba) and in British Columbia, there are fully bilingual programs in which instruction in a heritage language is provided for at least 50% of the instructional time (Cummins, 2005). In Ontario, heritage languages are called "international languages" and are offered outside regular school hours.

Teaching heritage or international languages at public expense has been vehemently contested in some areas, especially in metropolitan Toronto, based on the assimilationist assumption that teaching languages other than the official ones would promote cultural division and hinder immigrants' integration into the Canadian mainstream society (Cummins & Danesi, 1990). There is a trend in education to indirectly blame language minority students for their academic failure (Ellwood, 1989), rather than critically examine the K–12 educational system to see whether it supports them to reach their full potential or to find ways in which they can be helped. Cummins (1988) argues that "Anglo conformity" and institutional racism still permeate the Canadian educational system. In his view, what is needed is not multicultural education but anti-racist education. Cummins's research (1979, 1982, 1988, 1995, and 1996) suggests that heritage language teaching might be an important step in supporting immigrant students to reach their academic potential.

In spite of the opposition to heritage language teaching and the lack of a coherent national policy, some provinces offer fully bilingual programs in English and a heritage language. Alberta, Manitoba, and Saskatchewan collaborated to develop the Common Curriculum Framework for Bilingual Programming in International Languages, Kindergarten to Grade 12 (Western Canadian Protocol for Collaboration in Basic Education, 1999) and the Common Curriculum Framework for International Languages, Kindergarten to Grade 12 (Western Canadian Protocol for Collaboration in Basic Education, 2000).

In addition, one can notice a progressive change towards the recognition of the benefits of teaching a second language to all children, regardless of their mother tongue. For instance, in Alberta, all K–12 students are expected to be able to communicate in two languages. Compulsory second-language teaching in Alberta was launched in 2006 and will be fully implemented by 2011–2012. In Calgary, there are public schools that offer English–Spanish, English–German, and English–Chinese/Mandarin bilingual programs and Japanese language and culture courses in addition to French immersion and French-as-a-second-language programs. The stated provincial rationale for making second-language learning compulsory is that "students gain both personally and academically by: developing cultural awareness, understanding differing perspectives, developing higher-level thinking skills, participating actively in the community, enhancing Alberta's influence and competitiveness, [and] helping to provide a multitude of services in the public and private sectors, including volunteer services" (Calgary Board of Education, 2008).

In Manitoba, the official provincial philosophy declares that "the study of heritage languages within the regular school day strengthens Manitoba's linguistic and cultural heritage, maintains a valuable economic resource, and promotes intercultural and cross-cultural understanding" (Manitoba Education and Training, 1993). Manitoba school divisions offer bilingual programs in English–German, English–Hebrew, and English–Ukrainian, as well as Spanish language courses.

Even if allophone languages have slowly made their way into some public schools, most heritage language teaching in Canada is still done in community-based language schools that do not receive funding from the government. For instance, the Saskatchewan Organization for Heritage Languages (SOHL) is funded mainly through SaskLotteries. The mission of the SOHL is to financially support heritage language schools, offer professional development opportunities for heritage language teachers, and provide resource materials (Reilly, 2006). All over Canada, there are regional non-profit heritage language associations, such as the Northern Alberta Heritage Language Association, that support international language teaching outside the public system. Some representatives of these associations (Pallard, Shakille, Embaie, Gretton, Ricard, & Roncucci, 2004) argue that heritage/allophone languages are not foreign to Canada but should be considered Canadian languages, not international or foreign languages. This view inspired the name of the Canadian Languages Association (CLA), established in 1994 as a national organization dedicated to the preservation and promotion of international/heritage languages in Canada. The mission of the CLA is "to increase public awareness and understanding as well as create a platform for informed public dialogue about multiculturalism, racism and cultural diversity in Canada through a focus on heritage/international language education" (CLA, 2008).

CANADA AND THE UNITED STATES: DIFFERENCES AND SIMILARITIES

While it is true that the federal government in Canada has played a much more active role in managing languages than has the federal government of the United States, it is also the case that it did so, in large measure, to ensure national security and not because of a philosophical or moral commitment to language minority rights. Absent the Official Languages Acts and initiatives taken by Quebec to make French the only official language of the province and to restrict access to English education among newly arrived immigrants, it is possible that the attempts made in Quebec to spearhead its separation from the rest of Canada could have succeeded. Those in the United States who seek to avoid what they consider to be a fragile accommodation achieved between French- and English-speaking Canadians by declaring English the only official language of the United States fail to understand that the Francophone population constitutes the overwhelming majority of the population in Quebec (25% of the Canadian population). It also controls the provincial government, and French (especially in rural areas) is the daily and customary language of education, work, and social life. There is nothing really comparable to this set of facts in the United States. No U.S. state, for example, is controlled by a large percentage of Spanish-speakers desirous of establishing a separate country. For more than 200 years, French has been recognized as a legitimate language of government in Canada, and with passage of the British North America Act of 1867 (the beginning of the Canadian Confederation), the bilingual status of the federal government was officially recognized. No language in the United States has been considered to have co-equal status at the federal level with English (although Spanish was recognized in the state constitution of New Mexico, and laws are published in both Spanish and English; Hawaii recognizes Hawaiian Creole, along with English, as an official language; French and English are official languages in Louisiana; and Spanish and English have official status in the Commonwealth of Puerto Rico). While all federal offices in Canada are required to have signage, forms, and services available in both French and English, and while all commercial products sold in Canada are required by law to have bilingual labeling as a result of language legislation, the absence of such laws in the United States has not prevented a substantial increase in Spanish language services and signage in the private sector. This underscores the fact that patterns of language use and acquisition cannot be predicted simply by analyzing language policies or the stated goals of governments or politicians. The situation in Canada, as noted by Joseph Magnet (1998, p. 203), is one in which "duality and accommodation strive to keep language activists committed to the Canadian state. Duality and accommodation provide the operators of the language rights system with doctrine that history teaches best serves to keep language conflict manageable." In the United States, activists for Spanish and English are engaged in an ideological, or more accurately, a symbolic struggle whose roots can be traced back two hundred years (see Ricento, 1998a; Schmidt, 1998 for extended discussion), and that continues in large measure because of the proximity of Spanish-speaking countries and high levels of immigration, especially over the past 40 years. Granting rights to particular peoples, whether based on linguistic or ethnic/cultural identities, is anathema to the dominant political culture in the United States. Conflicts between language/ethnic groups are usually dealt with at the local and state level—for example, by passage of laws and ordinances that mandate English as the only official language of government and education. The federal government has been involved only (and often reluctantly) when individual civil rights recognized in the constitution or by federal statute are abrogated, as determined by federal court decisions. Businesses are generally free to require English only in the workplace, so long as this is claimed to be a business necessity (Miner, 1998). While bilingual education was briefly supported by the U.S Federal government (Bilingual Education Act of 1968) as a means for improving the educational attainment of (mostly) Spanish-speaking students in the Southwest, the policy was never designed to promote or protect minority languages or minority language communities per se or to enhance the status of languages other than English. To the extent that bilingual education has succeeded in the United States, it has mostly been as a result of community involvement and support, and not as a result of governmental promotion or assistance.

In both Canada and the United States, language remains a source of political conflict and often serves as a proxy for ongoing animosities among groups that have co-existed in the same geographical space, often for many generations. The Canadian response to these conflicts has been to enshrine official-language minority rights in education at the federal level through acts of Parliament, especially the Canadian Charter of Rights and Freedoms (1982) and the Official Languages Act (1969), as well as by providing a role for the Supreme Court of Canada to enforce these rights. The approach to managing languages in the United States has been far more ad hoc and responsive to political pressures brought by aggrieved parties to state and national (congressional) legislatures and through state referenda. The tensions and conflicts between the two "founding races" in Canada will likely never be resolved, because the approach taken was a compromise that managed conflict rather than addressing the aspirations and needs of all Canadians. The duality of Francophone and Anglophone Canada (with allophones often marginalized) persists, despite stipulated protections in the legal, educational, and governmental sectors. Yet the approach that has developed beginning in the 1960s has somehow managed to keep the country together and has enhanced the status of French as a Canadian language. In contrast, the approach taken in the United States has been a battle of attrition and power politics; language/ethnic minority groups who seek to gain recognition in the political culture, improved access to education, and enjoyment of civil rights afforded all Americans do so largely through political activism, which has rarely resulted in major/sustained legislative involvement. Dominant/majority groups who view such activism as a threat to "American" identity and the hegemony of the English-speaking majority and its purported "American values" (vaguely defined but symbolically potent) react with their own brand of political activism, which has included a movement to declare English the (only) official language of the United States as well as the promotion of legislation to eliminate any federal support for other languages in education, voting, government/public services, and to restrict immigration from non–English-speaking countries (Ricento, 1998b). While the Canadian approach has not eliminated conflict and controversy (referenda in support of Quebec sovereignty in 1980 and 1995 attest to the fragility of the current arrangement), the American approach has failed to manage diversity in a pro-active, supportive manner. Rather than recognizing Spanish and Native American languages as American languages, which they demonstrably are, the federal government has generally promoted and supported policies designed to eradicate these languages under the guise of "assimilation," while giving lip service in the form of unfunded legislation and other symbolic gestures for the "protection and promotion" of "heritage languages" (mainly Native American languages).

In both Canada and the United States, intergroup conflict began early in national history. In both countries, political activism in the 1960s by disenfranchised (including language minority) groups was perceived by dominant groups as a threat to national stability and led to passage of major legislation at the federal level. In Canada, the legislative/constitutional changes in the area of language policy were more dramatic than in the United States, because an aggrieved party (Quebecois Francophones) had the numbers and political power to threaten national stability. Issues related to *language* minorities in the United States were dealt with in legislation that sought, primarily, to redress civil rights violations of *racial* minorities and language minority groups based on national origin grounds (Ricento 2005). There was no sweeping legislation on language rights/policies and government responsibility in this area comparable to what occurred in Canada in the 1960s and 1970s. In Canada, the principal focus was on Francophone issues—their access to education, political power, and employment—and much less on the interests of other (allophone) languages or ethnic groups. In both Canada and the United States, attempts to deal with the broad range of policy issues in the area of language education on a national level have been much less effective, in part because of the decentralized nature of education in both countries but also in part because powerful/majority groups do not want to cede their power and privilege. In place of concrete and properly funded programs and meaningful accountability measures, we have seen that language policies directed towards non-dominant—i.e., politically less-powerful—groups tend to take the form of political or moral statements that have little chance to influence behavior or policies, such as unfunded mandates in support of anti-racist (Canada) or aboriginal (Canada)/Native American (U.S.) language education. In this sense, neither the Canadian nor the United States federal government can be said to have embraced in any principled way linguistic human rights as a framework for dealing with the ethnic and linguistic diversity that exists in their respective countries, a situation that will likely continue into the foreseeable future.

REFERENCES

Beaty, S. (1989). A new official languages act for Canada: Its scope and implications. In P. Pupier & J. Woehrling (Eds.), *Language and law: Proceedings of the first conference of the international institute of comparative linguistic law* (pp. 185–193). Montreal: Wilson and Lafleur.

Berry, J. (1998). Official multiculturalism. In J. Edwards (Ed.), *Language in Canada* (p. 84–101). Cambridge, UK: Cambridge University Press.

Bibby, R. (2004). Beyond the prosaic mosaic: Canadian inter-group attitudes, 1975–2000. In M. Zachariah, A. Sheppard, & L. Barratt (Eds.), *Canadian Multiculturalism: Dreams, realities, expectations* (pp. 224–240). Edmonton, Alberta: Canadian Multicultural Education Foundation.

Black, J. (2000). Fight is on to preserve Aboriginal languages. *Windspeaker, 17,* 1–2.

Burnaby, B. (2008). Language policy and education in Canada. In S. May & H. Hornberger (Eds.), *Encyclopedia of Language and Education 1* (2nd ed.) (pp. 331–341). New York: Springer Science, Business Media LLC.

Burnaby, B. (2002). *Provincial governments' initiatives in aboriginal language and cultural education.* Ottawa: Department of Indian and Northern Affairs.

Burnaby, B. & Beaujot, R. (1986). *The use of aboriginal languages in Canada: An analysis of 1981 census data.* Ottawa: Social Trends Analysis Directorate and Native Citizens Directorate, Department of the Secretary of State.

Calgary Board of Education. (2008). *International Language and Culture Courses.* Retrieved July 15, 2008, from http://www.cbe.ab.ca/programs/languages/intlanguages.asp.

Canadian Heritage. (2006–2007). *Promoting Integration: Annual report of the Canadian Multiculturalism Act 2006–2007.* Quebec: Canadian Heritage.

Chandler, M. J. (2006). *Cultural continuity in the face of radical social change: Language preservation as a protective factor against suicide in First Nations Youth.* Paper presented at Raising our Voices, Language Conference, Cornwall, Ontario.

CLA. (2008). *Canadian Languages Association.* Retrieved July 17, 2008, from http://www.sahla.ca/cla1.htm.

Collacott, M. (2002). Canada's immigration policy: The need for major reform. *Public Policy Sources, 64,* Vancouver: Fraser Institute.

Cristopher, C. (1983). *Multiculturalism and Nation Building.* Unpublished master's thesis. University of Calgary, Calgary, Alberta, Canada.

Cummins, J. (1979). Linguistic interdependence and the educational development of bilingual children. *Review of Educational Research, 49,* 222–251.

Cummins, J. (1982). *Bilingualism and minority language children.* Toronto: Ontario Institute for Studies in Education.

Cummins, J. (1988). From multicultural to anti-racist education: An analysis of programmes and policies in Ontario. In T. Skutnabb-Kangas & J. Cummins (Eds.), *Minority education: From shame to struggle* (pp. 127–157). Philadelphia: Multilingual Matters LTD.

Cummins, J. (1995). Heritage language teaching in Canadian schools. In O. Garcia & C. Baker (Eds.) *Policy and practices in bilingual education: A reader* (pp. 134–138). Clevedon, UK: Multilingual Matters.

Cummins, J. (1996). *Negotiating identities: Education for empowerment in a diverse society.* Ontario, CA: California Association for Bilingual Education.

Cummins, J. (2005). Language issues and educational change. In A. Hergreaves (Ed.). *Extending educational change* (pp. 160–179). Netherlands: Springer.

Cummins, J. & Danesi, M. (1990). *Heritage languages: The development and denial of Canada's linguistic resources.* Toronto: Our Schools/Our Selves and Garamond Press.

Dasko, D. (2004). Multiculturalism by Canadian numbers. In M. Zachariah, A. Sheppard, & L. Barratt. (Eds.). *Canadian multiculturalism: Dreams, realities, expectations* (pp. 129–134). Edmonton, AB: Canadian Multicultural Education Foundation.

Early, M. (2008). Second and foreign language education in Canada. In S. Van Scholl Deusen & N. H. Hornberger (Eds.). *Encyclopedia of Language and Education 1* (2nd ed.) (pp. 331–341). New York: Springer Science + Business Media LLC.

Ellwood, W. (1989). Learning by root. *New Internationalist, 191.* Retrieved July 15, 2008, from http://www.newint.org/issue191/root.htm.

Employment and Immigration Canada. (1993). *Strategies for immigrant integration.* Ottawa: Public Affairs, Employment and Immigration Canada.

Garcea, J. (2004). Reflections on institutional responses to multiculturalism in light of terrorism. In M. Zachariah, A. Sheppard, & L. Barratt. (Eds.). *Canadian multiculturalism: Dreams, realities, expectations* (pp. 141–150). Edmonton, AB: Canadian Multicultural Education Foundation.

Genesee, F. (1998). French immersion in Canada. In J. Edwards (Ed.), *Language in Canada* (pp. 305–325). Cambridge, UK: Cambridge University Press.

Gosh, R. (2004). Public education and multicultural policy in Canada: The special case of Quebec. *International Review of Education, 50*(5–6), 543–566.

Hayday, M. (2005). *Bilingual today, united tomorrow: Official languages in education and Canadian federalism.* Montreal: McGill-Queen's University Press.

Kymlicka, W. (2004). Canadian Multiculturalism in Historical and Comparative Perspective. In M. Zachariah, A. Sheppard, & L. Barratt. (Eds.). *Canadian multiculturalism: Dreams, realities, expectations* (pp. 157–172). Edmonton, AB: Canadian Multicultural Education Foundation.

Li, P. (2003). *Deconstructing Canada's discourse of immigrant integration.* PCERII Working Paper No. WPO4-03. Edmonton: Prairie Centre of Excellence for Research on Immigration and Integration. Retrieved June 15, 2008, from http://www.pcerii.metropolis.net.

Mackey, W. F. (1998). The foundations. In J. Edwards (Ed.), *Language in Canada* (pp. 13–35). Cambridge, UK: Cambridge University Press.

Magnet, J. (1998). Language rights theory in Canadian perspective. In T. Ricento & B. Burnaby (Eds.), *Language and politics in the United States and Canada: Myths and realities* (pp. 185–205). Mahwah, NJ: Lawrence Erlbaum.

McRae, K. (1998). Official bilingualism: From the 1960s to the 1990s. In J. Edwards (Ed.), *Language in Canada* (pp. 61–83). Cambridge, UK: Cambridge University Press.

Manitoba Education and Training. (1993). *Policy for heritage language instruction.* Retrieved from http://www.edu.gov.mb.ca/k12/cur/languages/index.html.

McCue, H. (2008). Native people, education. *The Canadian Encyclopedia Historica.* Retrieved June 1, 2008, from http://www.thecanadianencyclopedia.com/PrinterFriendly.cfm?Params=A1ARTA0005646.

Miner, S. (1998). Legal implications of the official English declaration. In T. Ricento & B. Burnaby (Eds.), *Language and politics in the United States and Canada: Myths and realities* (pp. 171–184). Mahwah, NJ: Lawrence Erlbaum.

Multiculturalism and Citizenship Canada. (1991). *Multiculturalism: What is it really about?* Canada: Government Publications.

Norris, M. J. (1998). Canada's aboriginal languages: Canadian social trends. *Statistics Canada, 11*(008), 8–16.

Norris, M. J. (2007). Aboriginal languages in Canada: Emerging trends and perspectives on second language acquisition: Canadian social trends. *Statistics Canada, 11*(008), 19–27.

Pallard, J., Shakille, A., Embaie, M., Gretton, M., Ricard, F., & Roncucci, S. (2004). International heritage languages: The very heart of a multicultural state. In M. Zachariah, A. Sheppard, & L. Barratt. (Eds.). *Canadian multiculturalism: Dreams, realities, expectations* (pp. 301–302). Edmonton, AB: Canadian Multicultural Education Foundation.

Petten, C. (2007). Knowledge of aboriginal languages in decline. *Windspeaker, 7,* 22.

Redish, L. (2001). *Native languages of the Americas: Endangered language revitalization and revival.* Retrieved June 2, 2008, from http://www.native-languages.org/revive.htm.

Reilly, J. (2006). Saskatchewan organization for heritage languages. *The Encyclopedia of Saskatchewan.* Retrieved on July 17, 2008, from http://esask.uregina.ca/entry/saskatchewan_organization_for_heritage_languages_sohl.html.

Ricento, T. (1998a). National language policy in the United States. In T. Ricento & B. Burnaby (Eds.), *Language and politics in the United States and Canada: Myths and realities* (pp. 85–112). Mahwah, NJ: Lawrence Erlbaum.

Ricento, T. (1998b). Partitioning by language: Whose rights are threatened? In T. Ricento & B. Burnaby (Eds.), *Language and politics in the United States: Myths and realities* (pp. 317–330). Mahwah, NJ: Lawrence Erlbaum.

Ricento, T. (2005). Problems with the "language-as-resource" discourse in the promotion of heritage languages in the USA. *Journal of Sociolinguistics, 9,* 348–368.

Saul, J. R. (2004). Strength in diversity. *Education Canada, 44*(2), 43.

Schmidt, R. (1998). The politics of language in Canada and the United States: Explaining the differences. In T. Ricento & B. Burnaby (Eds.), *Language and politics in the United States and Canada: Myths and realities* (pp. 37–70). Mahwah, NJ: Lawrence Erlbaum.

Sifton, C. (1975). Only farmers need apply. In H. Palmer (Ed.). *Immigration and the rise of multiculturalism* (pp. 34–38). Toronto: Copp Clark Publishing.

Statistics Canada (2001). Aboriginal peoples of Canada: A demographic profile, 2001 Census. Retrieved from http://www.statcan.gc.ca/bsolc/olc-cel/olc-cel?lang=eng&catno=96F0030X2001007.

Statistics Canada. (2006). *Immigration in Canada: A portrait of the foreign-born population, 2006 Census.* Retrieved April 23, 2008, from http://www12.statcan.ca/english/census06/analysis/immcit/index.cfm.

Stoffman, D. (2002). *Who gets in.* Toronto: Macfarlane Walter & Ross.

Suthers, L. (July 2007). Legislation introduced to promote Inuit language. *Windspeaker, 7,* 22.

Van der Keilen, M. (1995). Use of French, attitudes and motivations of French immersion students. *The Canadian Modern Language Review, 51,* 287–304.

Veltman, C. (1998). Quebec, Canada, and the United States: Social reality and language rights. In T. Ricento & B. Burnaby (Eds.), *Language and politics in the United States and Canada: Myths and realities* (pp. 301–315). Mahwah, NJ: Lawrence Erlbaum.

Wesche, M. & MacFarlane, A. (1995). Immersion outcomes: Beyond language proficiency. *The Canadian Modern Language Review, 51,* 250–274.

Western Canadian Protocol for Collaboration in Basic Education. (1999). *The common curriculum framework for bilingual programming in international languages, kindergarten to grade 12.* Retrieved July 15, 2008, from http://www.wncp.ca/languages/internat.html.

Western Canadian Protocol for Collaboration in Basic Education. (2000). *The common curriculum framework for international languages, kindergarten to grade 12.* Retrieved July 15, 2008, from http://www.wncp.ca/languages/internat.html.

CHAPTER 3

EDUCATION POLICY AND LANGUAGE SHIFT IN GUATEMALA

Ivonne Heinze Balcazar
California State University–Dominguez Hills, USA

GEOGRAPHIC, DEMOGRAPHIC, LINGUISTIC, AND HISTORICAL BACKGROUND OF GUATEMALA

The Republic of Guatemala is a constitutionally representative democracy located on the Central American Isthmus, with a territory of 108,889 square kilometers. Its population comprises 11,450,000 inhabitants (Instituto Nacional de Estadística, 2002). Over 60% of Guatemalans live in rural areas, and most are indigenous peoples. The republic is one of the poorest countries in the Western Hemisphere, with an annual GNP of approximately $31.7 billion dollars (2005). Guatemala spends 1.7% of its GNP on public education and is one of the least literate countries in the Americas, with an illiteracy rate of 55%.

Regarding Guatemala's linguistic background, Campbell and Terrence (1990) proposed that the predecessor of the modern Mayan languages was spoken about 4,200 years ago in the region of the Cuchumatán Mountains of Guatemala. Since then, speakers of Mayan languages have come

International Perspectives on Bilingual Education: Policy, Practice, and Controversy, pages 43–66

into direct and indirect contact with other language groups, including the Mixe-Zoquean groups that contributed loanwords to the Mayans, influenced their writing system, and created bilingual communities. Appel and Muysken (1987) proposed a typology of bilingualism and described five dominant language contact situations. One of these contact situations results from colonialism, creating societies in which high-prestige European languages "coexist with the native languages of the conquered peoples" (p. 5). Guatemala's bilingualism and multilingualism result from precisely this language contact situation; the country's linguistic context is the direct outcome of Spanish colonialism. Speakers of Garifuna, Xinca, and 21 Mayan languages have coexisted, and still coexist, as speakers of low-prestige languages, with *Ladinos*, who are generally the descendants of Spanish colonizers and indigenous women and who speak the high-prestige Spanish language. According to the 1996 figures of the *Proyecto de Educación Maya Bilingüe Intercultural* (PEMBI), there are 6,176,126 speakers of the 21 Mayan languages of Guatemala. The various Mayan groups have had different levels of language contact—mostly with Spanish, but also with other languages, including American English and English Creole from Belize (Garzon, 1998).

According to Garzon (1998), language contact in the indigenous communities of Guatemala reflects a "continuum in their relations with the other language groups. At one end, communities have virtually no bilingual speakers, while at the other, widespread multilingualism is the norm" (p. 10). Garzon asserts that for some communities, language contact and economic and social pressures have resulted in language shift toward Spanish—i.e., speakers in indigenous communities are becoming Spanish monolinguals.

EDUCATION POLICY: A HISTORICAL ACCOUNT FROM THE SIXTEENTH TO THE NINETEENTH CENTURIES[1]

In 1512, King Fernando II established the 32 "Laws of Burgos" to formalize governance for both the colonizers and the indigenous peoples. In essence, these laws regulated the colonial economy and the teaching of religion, which became the respective responsibilities of the *encomenderos*[2]

---

[1] The subsections of this historical overview owe to Orellana, 2006.

[2] An *encomendero* administered the *encomienda*, which was a royal trusteeship of land. The *encomienda* was established to control and exploit the peoples and resources of the Americas. Conquistadors were granted *encomiendas*, up to 300 indigenous people to work the land, and became *encomenderos* for the Spanish Crown. This system had characteristics of slavery; indigenous people were branded, sold, and forced to work for the *encomendero*.

and the friars. One of these laws specifically mandated that each *encomendero* select one boy to be taught reading and writing, so that he could teach others. However, formal education was not seen as of primary importance for the indigenous people, because in the ideology of exploitation and acculturation of the conquistadors and the *encomenderos*, educating indigenous people would not improve their work on the land, in the mines, or in commerce (Orellana, 2006). Thus, the history of colonial education in Guatemala began with Catholic conversion. The first lessons taught were religious, beginning with the arrival of the first contingent of Franciscan friars in 1524. Dominicans, Augustinians, and Jesuits soon followed the Franciscans to further this objective.

These friars needed to indoctrinate, preach, and take confession from indigenous people who did not speak Spanish. This linguistic challenge caused these religious orders to adopt the policy that conversion efforts be conducted in the native languages. They found it necessary to master the native languages of the people, particularly the languages of the groups considered to be numerically important, which resulted in the writing of numerous *doctrinas* (catechisms), *confesionarios* (manuals for confession), *sermonarios* (collections of sermons), *artes* (grammars), and *vocabularios* (vocabularies). More than a hundred of these were written for ten languages spoken in the Viceroyalty of New Spain between 1524 and 1572 (Suárez, 1983).

According to Suárez (1983), the use of native languages for religious indoctrination was a response to the theological and missionary formulations of the Council of Trent (1545–1564) that consolidated the use of vernacular languages *(vulgares lingus)* for religious instruction and for writing and publishing of catechisms. Nevertheless, religious instruction in indigenous languages was not fully accepted, and in 1596, the Council of the Indies, the administrative organ of the Spanish Empire, recommended to Philip II that Castilian Spanish be used as the language of instruction of the indigenous people specifically in order to hasten the disappearance of their languages, which the Council deemed to be sources of idolatry and superstition. However, Philip II rejected this recommendation and ordered the priests to continue to evangelize the indigenous peoples through their native languages. Responding to later economic and religious interests, Charles III reversed course to enforce the acceptance of Spanish by ordering the exclusive use of Spanish in religious instruction through his famous 1770 *Cédula* of Aranjuez (Suárez, 1983). Thus, Charles III legalized the *castellanización* (acquiring Castilian Spanish through formal instruction) for the purpose of evangelizing the indigenous peoples.

Under the previous royal policy that favored teaching religious doctrine in native languages, some of the friars had taught indigenous people to write in their own languages, a process that produced texts that preserved some of the history, culture, and traditions of their cultures. Books were written in indigenous languages including Nahuatl, Yucatec, K'ichee', and Kaqchikel (Suárez, 1983). Important texts were produced, particularly during the sixteenth and seventeenth centuries. Some of the original works are still extant, but others are available only in Spanish translation; for example, the books of *Chilam Balam* comprise religious texts, explanations of the calendar, historical accounts, prophecies, descriptions of rituals, and treatises on astrology and medicine. The songs of *Dzitbalché* consist of 15 lyrical songs, prayers, and a description of the sacrifice of a captive. The *Popol Vuh*, written in the sixteenth century, is based on an earlier hieroglyphic code. (The original was lost, but fortunately it had been copied in the seventeenth century). This book is about the K'ichee' people and provides mythical, historical, and ethnographic information. The only preserved example of a preconquest drama is the *Rabinal Achí*, which resembles theatrical activities known to have been practiced by the Aztec and Yucatec peoples. The *Annals of Cakchikels* relate the mythology and history of this Maya group, as well as the history of Spanish colonization. Five centuries would pass before the indigenous peoples, particularly the Mayans, would again write so prolifically about their culture and languages.

Education as a Colonial and Evangelizing Project

Education, like religion, was implemented by the clergy, and both the Spanish clergy and the aristocracy determined its pedagogy and content. The Laws of Burgos did not specify the importance of educating the indigenous peoples, and there were no schools for indigenous children during colonial times, except for those that served the *caciques*[3] and the sons of the indigenous nobility. As a result, Christianization through *castellanización* was the first and essentially the only type of formal education that the indigenous people received during colonial times. Thus, systematic public education in Guatemala began with the intention of benefiting primarily the sons of the *peninsulares* (Spanish colonizers) and the clergy, as well as those children born from the (often forced) unions of the conquistadors and indigenous women, euphemistically described as *irregular unions*.

Dominicans, Franciscans, and Jesuits established, mostly within their convents, the first primary and middle schools and the first college in Guatemala, but these schools were few in number. Few students learned

---

[3] "Cacique" or "Cazique" is a term in the Taíno-Caribe culture applied to forms of government that facilitated the formation of alliances or federations. The colonizers adopted and applied it to indigenous men who had many wives and economic power. The Spanish Crown, through its 1538 *Cédula*, restricted the term to describing men with political authority.

literacy, and even fewer advanced to secondary or college levels of education. From 1534 to 1763, four convents and three orders carried out Catholic indoctrination. In 1534, in the city of Santiago, Bishop Francisco Marroquín founded the first *Escuela de Primeras Letras* (School of First Letters), where writing, reading, basic arithmetic, and religion were taught to the Spanish aristocracy and clergy. In 1653, the religious order of Betlén founded the first school for poor children in Santiago, where religion, basic literacy, and arithmetic were taught. The first Guatemalan University, *La Universidad de San Carlos*, was founded in 1676 by mandate of the Spanish Crown, and some of its priest–professors were bilingual. The University of San Carlos accepted indigenous students and mandated the creation of college scholarships for them in the seventeenth century.

Education as a National and Assimilatory Project

Public education as a national project surfaced as a necessity to consolidate the birth of the new independent nation of Guatemala, which officially declared itself no longer subject to the Crown on September 15, 1821. Later, on August 3, 1823, Guatemala declared independence from Mexico as well, and, together with El Salvador, Nicaragua, Costa Rica, and Honduras, formed the *Federación de Estados Centroamericanos* (Central American Federation), which dissolved in civil war between 1838 and 1840.

At the dawn of Guatemalan independence, ignorance among Ladinos and indigenous peoples prevailed, and public education became a concern of liberal political leaders such as Mariano Gálvez, who saw it as an important aspect of the cultural and social integration of these diverse groups into the new independent nation and its republican democratic ideals. On August 31, 1835, Gálvez decreed the Statute of Elementary Education, which stipulated that Sunday schooling would be provided to adults, and that special programs for indigenous people would be provided in their own languages, to elevate their cultures. It was the first time since the *Cédula de Aranjuez* that any type of education was provided in the indigenous languages of the Guatemalan students.

Gálvez, following the democratic spirit of the time, made education secular, free, and mandatory. However, in 1852, Carrera's Pavón Law overturned Gálvez's educational reforms and returned to the Church the authority over education it had enjoyed in colonial times. Thus, Carrera's government brought back to Guatemala the concept of the divine origin of the State, which was already a moot question in Europe and many other states, including some in America. With no provision for education in the state budget, responsibility for local schools fell to municipalities. By 1867, the population of Guatemala was 1,250,000, but the primary schools together accommodated only 8,074 students, less than 1% of the total population.

Liberal Reform and the Educational System

Supported by the growing capitalist class, Don Justo Rufino Barrios and Congressman Miguel García Granados led the liberal revolution of 1867–1871 and triumphantly entered into the city of Guatemala on June 30, 1871. The revolution brought about a liberalization of the nation's politics, culture, commerce, economy, and educational system. The Pavón Law was abolished and replaced with liberal educational reforms influenced by Europe's dominant positivist philosophy. Subsequently, the 1879 Constitution allowed nonclergy to teach and required uniformity in the curricula of private and public schools. Additionally, this constitution again mandated free secular elementary education. As a result, the Jesuits, who had written the Pavón Law and had ruled the educational system for 30 years, were expelled from Guatemala, and convents and religious schools were turned into secular schools.

The 1875 law made education mandatory for children between the ages of 6 and 14 and established a commission to ensure that parents obeyed. Its Article XCV addressed, for the first time, some of the educational needs of Guatemala's indigenous peoples by establishing permanent and temporary schools in rural areas. Remarkably, the teachers had addressed the educational needs of the indigenous people by insisting, among other things, that indigenous people be trained as primary school teachers in an 1852 testimony to the *Comisión de Escuelas de la ciudad de Guatemala* (School Commission of the City of Guatemala).

THE EDUCATIONAL SYSTEM DURING THE TWENTIETH CENTURY: CASTELLANIZACIÓN AND BILINGUAL EDUCATION[4]

In the first four decades of the twentieth century, Guatemalan education lacked continuity, objectives, and a program. Undemocratic presidents successfully clung to power, sometimes through *coups d'etat*, each time destroying the educational system built by the previous president. The first president of the century, Manuel Estrada Cabrera, governed from 1898 to 1920, but was seen as a pawn of foreign investors. Calling himself the *protector de la juventud estudiosa* (protector of studious youth), Cabrera militarized education by decree on June 16, 1900, ordering that all students in elementary and secondary schools be taught military tactics.

After 20 years of continued dictatorships, Major Francisco Javier Arana and Captain Jacobo Arbenz Guzmán led a *coup d'état* on October 20, 1944.

---

[4] This review owes to Orellana, 2006.

A military junta of Arana, Arbenz, and Jorge Toriello Garrido then led the country into Guatemala's first free election, which was won by the prominent writer and teacher Juan José Arévalo Bermejo, with a majority vote of 85%. Arévalo, who had lived in exile in Argentina for 14 years, became the first democratically elected president of Guatemala to complete the term for which he was elected.

At the time Arévalo was elected president, Guatemala was a poor country that lacked such basic infrastructure as hospitals, homes, roads, agricultural land, and schools. Three-fourths of the population was illiterate, and half the school-aged children did not have access to elementary schools. The new administration's reforms impacted favorably on the economy, agriculture, culture, the availability of land, and education. Popular education was a priority for Arévalo, and his cabinet planned a literacy campaign and a number of cultural initiatives and began to address rural education by building technical schools.

Elementary education was reformed, its structure and pedagogy modernized. Schools held morning and evening sessions, giving student laborers the opportunity to continue their education in the evenings. In some cases, an industrial center or a school for adults was annexed to the new elementary schools. At the secondary-school level, new structural organization, curriculum, and a three-year cycle of study were implemented. Advisory committees of teachers and students were convened to oversee the improvement of student learning.

With regard to popular education, Arévalo's government initiated a national literacy campaign, dispatched mobile cultural workshops, opened evening elementary schools, and reopened the *Universidad Popular* (Popular University). Moreover, for the first time since independence, an *Instituto Nacional Indigenista* (National Indigenous Institute) was established, and cooperated in the production of bilingual materials in K'ichee', Mam, Kaqchikel, and Q'eqchi'. Nevertheless, the government's intention was not to promote or create biliterate and bilingual communities, but to facilitate the study and learning of Spanish. In other words, the study materials were bilingual, but their underlying pedagogical purpose was the same as in the past—i.e., the *castellanización* of the indigenous peoples, who were not taught to write their indigenous languages. From 1945 to 1950, the government carried out seven literacy campaigns in which 82,278 people were taught to read and write. However, Guatemala's first serious twentieth-century literacy initiative barely changed the cultural landscape; according to 1950 census, there were 1,552,847 illiterate Guatemalans. In other words, 89.2% of the population had not attended school—and 90.3% were illiterate.

This period was also the beginning of the Cold War between the United States and the USSR, which was to have considerable influence on Guatemalan history. From the 1950s through the 1990s, the U.S.

government directly supported Guatemala's military establishment with training, weapons, and money. In 1954, the U.S. Central Intelligence Agency (CIA) and the Guatemalan army overthrew Arévalo's freely-elected successor, Jacobo Arbenz. The CIA and the Guatemalan army installed Colonel Carlos Castillo Armas as president the same year, and he ruled until a member of his personal guard assassinated him.

After 1954, a succession of military governments relegated education to secondary status, and many of the schools and projects of Arevalo's government were closed or discontinued. Although movements known as *Alianza para el progreso* (Alliance for Progress) and the *Acción Católica* (Catholic Action) promoted educational projects in rural areas, a new program of *castellanización* was implemented in indigenous zones in 1965 with the usual professed goal of integrating indigenous groups into the national culture. According to Chiodi (1990), the government expected that if the communicative abilities of these groups were channeled into Spanish, it would be easier to assimilate them into the national culture. Thus, the new program's method utilized the home languages of the indigenous students as instruments of transition to the learning of Spanish and trained indigenous bilinguals to implement and to promote this program.

The *Proyecto de Educación Bilingüe* (PROEBI) (Bilingual Education Project) functioned as a pilot program from 1980 to 1984. The government implemented it in ten schools serving the four principal Mayan language groups: K'ichee', Mam, Q'eqchi', and Kaqchikel. After 1984, the PROEBI became the PRONEBI—the *Programa Nacional de Educación Bilingüe* (National Bilingual Education Program). PRONEBI joined the Ministry of Education's Directorate of Rural Social Education (*Dirección Socio-Educativo Rural*), which was responsible for all rural primary education. According to Menéndez (2002), PRONEBI was supported by USAID through the Rural Primary Education Improvement Project (1984–1989) and the Basic Education Strengthening (BEST) Project (1990–1997). PRONEBI expanded its programming and an intercultural component was developed, although never implemented. PRONEBI's goal was the promotion of bilingual education, although the program was offered only to indigenous groups. These projects were intended to provide a relevant bilingual education to rural indigenous boys and girls and to build the capability of the Ministry of Education to provide this service.

Menéndez (2002) pointed out that PRONEBI did not approve of the transition model and favored instead a model that supported the development of students' mother languages, promoting the learning of Spanish as a second language from preschool to fourth grade. PRONEBI was transformed in 1995 through Governmental Decree No. 726-95 into DIGEBI, the *Dirección General de Educación Bilingüe Intercultural* (General Directorate of Bilingual Intercultural Education). Some of its objectives were (1) to develop bilingual education scientifically, for all students in all areas, at all educational levels, (2) to strengthen the ethnic and cultural identities of all the country's linguistic groups, (3) to develop, implement, and evaluate its curriculum, and (4) to develop, consolidate, and preserve bilingualism within the Mayan-speaking student population.

Interestingly, according to Heckt (2004), it was the 1954 program of *castellanización*, the PRONEBI, and the DIGEBI that created the impetus toward bilingual education. The teachers that received training and worked in these programs developed into an intellectual group that criticized the government's educational policies. They also became protagonists in the Mayan movement and have continued to participate in governmental educational institutions, as well as in nongovernmental ones.

THE MAYAN MOVEMENT, THE 1996 PEACE ACCORDS, AND EDUCATIONAL REFORM

Particularly after the 1996 Peace Accords, the state, together with indigenous social movements such as the Mayan movement, created a new context for social interactions. The Mayan movement surfaced in the 1970s and gained impetus after the end of the civil war (Zapeta, 2005). This movement promotes Mayan cultural values, seeking to open a new political space through the revitalization of their culture and language. This movement was vital to the passage of the 1995 Accord on Identity and Rights of Indigenous Peoples, which amended the national constitution to redefine Guatemala as a multiethnic, multicultural, and multilingual nation. The government made commitments to make official the use of indigenous languages in the public domain and to promote training programs for judges and legal interpreters. The Accord also mandated profound reforms in the country's educational, judicial, and political systems, and it formalized the indigenous peoples' legal right to make claims upon the state.

The Peace Accords of 1996 ended Guatemala's 36-year civil war, the longest and bloodiest of Latin America's Cold War civil wars, which left between 150,000 and 200,000 civilians dead or "disappeared." Parts of the Accords that addressed issues of public education affirmed—among other things—that the national educational system should respond to the cultural and linguistic diversity of the population by recognizing and fortifying indigenous identities and values, that the system would facilitate the indigenous peoples' access to formal and informal education, and that the government would create a Mayan University, among other new educational entities (Menéndez, 2002).

The government committed itself to promote educational reforms that would (1) decentralize and regionalize education to address local cultural and linguistic conditions, (2) concede to the indigenous communities an active role in defining their local school curricula, school calendars, and the hiring and firing of teachers, to advance their own cultural and educational interests, (3) integrate the educational philosophies of the indigenous peoples into all social venues (i.e., philosophical, scientific, artistic, pedagogical, historical, linguistic, and sociopolitical), (4) expand and promote bilingual intercultural education, valuing the study and knowledge of indigenous languages at all levels of education, (5) improve the socioeconomic life of the communities, (6) include in all educational curricula content that strengthens national unity and respect for cultural diversity, (7) hire and train bilingual teachers and administrators from the indigenous communities to develop new educational programming, institutionalizing mechanisms of consultation and participation in the educational process by representatives of indigenous communities and organizations, (8) enforce the constitutional right to education in all communities, particularly indigenous communities, and create legal mechanisms to enforce this right, and (9) to increase the education budget to implement these reforms (Menéndez, 2002).

The Maya movement continues to demand that the government continue promoting bilingual education and the revitalization of Mayan languages. Mayas continue their efforts to prevent language shift and loss and to revitalize Mayan languages, particularly through the ALMG, *Academia de Lenguas Mayas de Guatemala* (the Academy of Mayan Languages of Guatemala), which they administer and govern. The ALMG was established in 1990 and became the first governmentally approved and financed indigenous language academy in Guatemala.

The Mayan movement and the ALMG see language as the center of their culture and identity and continue to advocate for their indigenous languages to become official; despite the language of the 1996 Accords, the state has not yet amended the Constitution to officially recognize the indigenous languages.[5] Nonetheless, Maya indigenous linguists have continued to train themselves to read and write their own languages and to promote bilingual education and the use of indigenous languages in all possible domains of language use, including the workplace, the courts, government offices, schools, and public spaces. These linguists are active in the community, teaching, translating, participating in language planning, and collaborating in the production of grammars and other educational materials relating to indigenous languages. After more than 400 years, the Mayas are again prolifically writing in and about their indigenous languages. They are also producing materials in Spanish, including political essays, descriptive and pedagogical grammars, articles, and books on dialects.

The Maya movement, with its cultural and political aspirations, continues to consider the use of indigenous languages essential to the promotion of

---

[5] The constitutions of 1945, 1956, and 1965 declared Spanish the official language.

Mayan political and economic mobility. They regard language as both the principal symbol of their identity and the essential medium through which their identity is transmitted. The movement continues to reject the stereotyping of indigenous languages and cultures as mere folklore, demanding, among other things, that the government make indigenous languages official, establishing programs to prevent language shift and language loss.

LANGUAGE SHIFT

The Mayas are not alone in this experience of language shift and language loss. In recent decades, documentation of the rapid loss of many of the world's languages has contributed to the efforts of linguists, including Maya linguists, to direct their attention to the preservation and maintenance of minority languages. Krauss (1992) estimated that half of the world's 6,000 spoken languages will vanish in the next century, and also that children are not speaking 20–50% of these languages—partly because their parents choose not to transmit their own languages to their children when, under social and economic pressure, the parents decide to abandon a minority language and shift to the language of prestige. Hale (1992) estimated that 90% of these 6,000 languages will die and proposed that languages spoken by a million or fewer people will survive only if they are supported by government policy. This decline in the number of the world's languages is due to various factors, including parental decision-making regarding language transmission; government policy; economic and social changes, such as industrialization and urbanization; and the availability and quality of bilingual education.

The Role of Adolescents and Children in Language Shift

Children and adolescents play a vital role in maintaining and transmitting their native languages, but it cannot be assumed that they will speak or transmit their native languages, particularly if they are low-prestige languages. Children and adolescents often decide to abandon their native languages to speak exclusively in the official, prestigious language. Williamson and Van Eerde (1980) reported that adolescents tend to use official languages with their parents, and even more so with their own children. In some cases, animosity toward the persistent use of the low-prestige language results in an intergenerational communication breakdown. According to Trudgill and Tzavaras (1977), older speakers of Arvanitika reported that their attempts to transmit the language were obstructed by their children. The children did not want their parents to speak to them in Arvanitika, which upset the parents. In some cases, intergenerational communication occurs with one person speaking the low-prestige language and the other the prestigious one. Kroskrity (1982) reported that adolescents in Arizona Tewa families respond in English when their parents address them in Tewa. Similarly, House (2002) reported that Navajo children refuse to learn or use the Navajo language.

The Role of Bilingual Education in Language Shift

Regardless of the multilingual realities of many nations, many modern public school systems utilize only a single language as the medium of instruction, which is generally the official language of the country. This has been the case in Guatemala since colonial times; the society's multilingual reality has historically been ignored by the state and its educational systems. The fact that Spanish has been Guatemala's official language and the medium of its public educational instruction has been detrimental to the survival of the country's indigenous languages. Spanish monolingual education has been one of the most important factors in language shift toward Spanish.

The Mayan Movement proposed that expanding the use of indigenous languages in school instruction, bilingual education programs, and other social domains would dramatically alter the patterns of language use in Guatemala, bringing the indigenous languages into new, official, and previously all-Spanish domains (Zapeta, 2005). The indigenous languages would gain prestige through these affiliations, which would reduce the negative social stigma that these languages carry. Indigenous students and their families might then be motivated to use their languages in additional new domains and reverse the language shift to Spanish, especially in light of Fishman's (1966) suggestion that prestige contributes to language maintenance, and the use of indigenous languages in school would tend to mitigate the negative assumptions that these languages are not "civilized," or not adequate for scientific and academic expression. In sum, then, the instruction and use of languages in the school domain, and the associated increased status of the language, can be factors that would reverse language shift.

Reported Patterns of Kaqchikel-Maya Communities in Guatemala

Several studies demonstrate that although language shift varies across individual indigenous communities, language loss and language shift are clear and measurable in Guatemala's Kaqchikel communities. For instance, Richards (1998) examined the increasing use of Spanish in Guatemalan communities and their school systems. In the early 1980s, the San Marcos

La Laguna community was monolingual, but over the next twenty years, it gradually moved to bilingualism as knowledge of Spanish became a prerequisite for economic, social, and political survival. To Richards (1998), it remained unclear whether the community's nascent bilingualism would become additive or would move rapidly toward language shift, as has occurred in other Kaqchikel highland communities.

Brown (1998) surveyed four communities in the Quinizilapa Valley that were in intermediate to late stages of language shift. His research focused on the central role of Kaqchikel-speaking parents who shifted to Spanish to communicate with their offspring. He found that in 444 homes, people over 40 years old—the oldest group surveyed—were most fluent in Kaqchikel, which they had acquired during childhood. Brown also found that communities in the Quinizilapa Valley were becoming progressively less fluent in Kaqchikel. In all the towns of the Valley, half the respondents did not speak Kaqchikel with their children, and Spanish was spoken to some degree in over two-thirds of Valley households. He concluded that if present patterns of language use continue in the next generations, Kaqchikel will cease to be spoken in the Valley.

Garzon (1998) investigated language shift in San Juan Comalapa and found that some parents spoke Spanish with their children, who were learning both Spanish and Kaqchikel at home. She also conducted interview-style proficiency tests in Kaqchikel and Spanish in Comalapa's primary school, and her findings indicated that although many children still acquired Kaqchikel, Spanish served as the common medium of communication among school-age children. One-fourth of the children tested failed to respond adequately in Kaqchikel, while nearly all the children were able to converse in Spanish. She pointed out that Kaqchikel has lost its hegemony in San Juan Comalapa, and that the majority of young adults were Kaqchikel–Spanish bilinguals.

RESEARCH ON LANGUAGE SHIFT IN KAQCHIKEL–MAYA ADOLESCENTS OF TECPÁN

In order to investigate the language patterns and attitudes of Kaqchikel-Maya adolescents in the municipality of Tecpán, Guatemala, I designed a 16-question survey to investigate and detect language shift and characterize the language attitudes of Kaqchikel Maya adolescents in Tecpán. The survey's design took into consideration some of the findings of De Vries (1992), who pointed out that a Canadian General Survey had utilized two questions that were unreliable:

1. Which languages do you, yourself, speak at home?
2. Do you speak this language at home more than 90% of the time?

De Vries (1992) also pointed out that these questions proved too general in that they tended to focus on a single speaker in a potentially multiple-speaker dialogue at home. Thus, the investigator designed a 16-question survey only in Spanish, because of illiteracy in Kaqchikel, that posed questions about intergenerational and intragenerational language use to determine the extent of language shift in adolescents. In other words, the survey addressed the question of who spoke what language, with whom, and where? In this chapter, I report results on 12 of the 16 questions.

The municipality of Tecpán has nine high schools: three in rural areas and six in Tecpán proper. All of these high schools were visited, and a total of 1,069 students took the survey. Of these, 187 were from rural schools and 882 from urban ones. The first survey question inquired about the languages that the high school students spoke and found that far more of the rural students were bilingual. Of the rural students, 92 percent of these students reported speaking both Kaqchikel and Spanish, while less than half of the urban students (35%) reported that they spoke both languages. Of the urban students, 65 percent of these students indicated that they spoke only Spanish, while 8 percent of the rural students so reported. Thus, of the 1069 students, 45 percent reported speaking both languages, and 55 percent reported speaking only Spanish.

The investigator used questions about language knowledge, language preference, and intragenerational patterns of language use to detect language loss and language shift among those students who indicated that they spoke only Spanish. These questions and their English translations are as follows:

1. ¿Qué idiomas entiende usted, pero no habla? [What languages do you understand but not speak?]
2. ¿Si sus padres son bilingües, en qué idioma les gusta hablar más? [If your parents are bilingual, in what language do they prefer to speak?]
3. ¿Qué idioma usan sus padres cuando se hablan? [In what language do your parents speak with each other?]
4. ¿Si sus abuelos son bilingües, en qué idioma les gusta hablar más? [If your grandparents are bilingual, in what language do they prefer to speak?]
5. ¿Qué idioma usan sus abuelos cuando se hablan? [In what language do your grandparents speak with each other?]

These questions allowed the investigator to detect language loss and shift among these high school adolescents. Responses to the first question divided the 588 Spanish monolingual students into those who did not understand Kaqchikel and those who did. That is, students were monolingual in Spanish and bi-audial in Spanish and Kaqchikel. An important finding for this monolingual group was that of the 588 Spanish monolinguals, 292 students

	Did not understand Kaqchikel		Understood Kaqchikel	
	+ Kaqchikel Family	− Kaqchikel Family	+ Kaqchikel Family	− Kaqchikel Family
Urban (*n*=573)	229	57	71	216
Rural (*n*=15)	3	3	0	9
	Language loss	Ladino students	Passive bilinguals with language shift	Ladinos as passive bilinguals

Figure 1. Monolingual Students who Represent Language Loss, Language Shift, and Passive Bilingualism.

(49.6%) did not understand Kaqchikel, while 296 students (50.3%) did. These two groups are represented in Figure 1. Additionally, the monolingual students who did not understand Kaqchikel and those who did were divided into two subgroups: those with Kaqchikel families and those without.

As highlighted in Figure 1, approximately 79 percent (229) of the students from the group that did not understand Kaqchikel came from Kaqchikel-speaking families: that is, their parents or grandparents spoke Kaqchikel. This means that of these 292 students, 79 percent have experienced language loss. Moreover, language loss is occurring more rapidly in urban students (39.9%) than in rural students (2%). Additionally, I suggest that the 60 students who did not understand Kaqchikel and did not have Kaqchikel families most likely represented students of Ladino background.

Of the 296 students who understood Kaqchikel, 23.9 percent had Kaqchikel-speaking families. These were the urban students, who could be classified as passive bilinguals, but most important, they represented language shift phenomena, for they understood Kaqchikel and had Kaqchikel-speaking parents or grandparents. Interestingly, the survey did not detect passive bilingualism or language shift in the rural areas. Furthermore, those students who understood Kaqchikel but did not have a Kaqchikel-speaking family also represented passive bilinguals; I suggest that this group represented Ladino students who had learned Kaqchikel from their peers. Notably, this type of passive bilingualism was occurring in both urban (37.6%) and rural areas (6%).

With regard to patterns of language use of the 481 bilingual students, the survey explored their language use with parents, grandparents, and siblings. The students responded to the following questions:

6. ¿Qué idioma usa usted cuando habla con sus padres? [What language do you use when you speak with your parents?]
7. ¿Qué idioma usa usted cuando habla con sus abuelos? [What language do you use when you speak with your grandparents?]

Of the urban bilingual students, 89 percent reported speaking Kaqchikel with their parents or grandparents, as did 91 pecent of the rural bilingual students. In contrast, the percentage of bilinguals who spoke Spanish to their grandparents or parents was small. Of the urban bilinguals, only 11 percent spoke Spanish with their elders, and only 9 percent of the rural bilinguals did so. Thus, of the 481 students who reported speaking both languages, 89 percent were actively using Kaqchikel with their elders, and 9 percent were not. This latter group represented a tendency toward language shift since they did not speak Kaqchikel with their elders. The other 2 percent of these students did not answer these two questions or indicated that their elders were no longer living.

With regard to sibling communication, there was greater contrast between speaking with the elders and siblings. Students responded to the following question:

8. ¿Qué idioma usa usted cuando habla con sus hermanos? [What language do you use when you speak with your siblings?]

Of the 481 bilingual students, 53.8 percent reported speaking Spanish with their siblings, while 39.2 percent spoke Kaqchikel with their siblings. The differences between the rural and the urban students was also striking; 63 percent of the urban bilinguals spoke Spanish with their siblings, while just 37 percent of the rural bilinguals did so. There was a stronger tendency for the rural bilinguals to speak Kaqchikel with their siblings than for the urban bilinguals, with 60 percent of the 172 rural students reporting use of Kaqchikel, but only 27 percent of the 309 urban bilinguals doing so. Small percentages of students reported that they used both languages with their siblings; 9 percent of the urban students used both languages, and just 2 percent of rural students did so. Additionally, of these three patterns of language use with siblings, it is the Spanish pattern of language use that may be the greatest threat to the survival of Kaqchikel and that provides evidence that these students were at the early stages of language shift.

The nine high schools of the Tecpán municipality have not yet implemented bilingual education programs; consequently, speaking Kaqchikel has been limited to informal peer conversation. Students were asked the following question about the school domain:

9. ¿Qué idiomas usa en la escuela? [What languages do you use at school?]

Of the 172 rural students, 12.7 percent spoke Kaqchikel at school, as did 7.4 percent of the 309 urban students. In contrast, the percentages of students who spoke Spanish at school were much higher. Of the urban students, 85 percent reported using Spanish, while 77 percent of the rural students did so. The percentage who reported using both languages at school was 7 percent for the urban students and 9 percent for rural. These results indicated that Spanish predominated in the school domain, with 82.5 percent of the 481 bilinguals using it. I suggest that the tendency of the bilingual students to speak mostly Spanish at school also indicated that they were at the early stages of language shift.

I found similarities between the bilingual students' patterns of language use at school and at the market. Of the 481 bilingual students, 470 responded to the question:

10. ¿Qué idiomas usa en el mercado? [What languages do you use at the market?]

For these respondents, of the urban bilinguals, 77 percent reported using Spanish at the market, as did 74 percent of the rural bilinguals. Rural bilinguals used Kaqchikel at the market at a slightly higher percentage (19%) than urban ones (13%). Only 9 percent of all students reported using both languages at the market. The overall results for the market domain indicated that 76 percent of bilingual students used Spanish at the market. In contrast, 16 percent used Kaqchikel in this domain. Therefore, Spanish clearly dominated in the public domains of the school and market.

Language Transmission and Bilingualism

Also collected in this study were data on language transmission and the motivations surrounding parental decision-making, since Hale (1992) suggested that language shift is closely linked to parents' decision to speak to their children in the prestige language. Students were asked the hypothetical question:

11. ¿Si es bilingüe, qué idiomas le enseñará a hablar a sus hijos? [If you are bilingual, what languages will you teach to your children?]

Significantly, 40 percent of the bilinguals indicated that they would raise future children as Kaqchikel–Spanish bilinguals; 39 percent would raise them as Spanish monolinguals. Another important finding was that 12 percent of the entire bilingual group indicated that they would raise their children using Kaqchikel. Nevertheless, the data indicate that speaking in Kaqchikel to one's parents or grandparents is not a decisive factor in the choice to transmit Kaqchikel as a first language, given that 89 percent of the bilinguals reported active use of Kaqchikel with their parents or grandparents. It is significant that the 15 percent of the bilingual students responded that they would choose to teach only English to their future children. This is especially interesting because there was no indication that these students could speak English. Moreover, this percentage is slightly higher than the 12 percent of the bilingual students who indicated that they would transmit only Kaqchikel to their future children.

Identity and Language Ideology

Economic, cultural, and social factors impact speakers' decisions about language transmission, especially in multilingual communities where low-prestige languages coexist with a prestigious language. Adolescents are also motivated by these factors, and those who participated in this study seemed to be motivated by the same factors. Students were asked the following follow-up question:

> 12. ¿Por qué quiere enseñarle estos idiomas a sus hijos? [Why would you want to teach these languages to your future children?]

Students responded that they thought that the economic factor strongly impacted their decision to transmit Spanish. Interestingly, they also indicated that language rights, social communication, and culture were also important factors in choosing to transmit either Spanish or Kaqchikel.

These adolescents indicated that Kaqchikel was part of their ancestral culture, for example, characterizing Kaqchikel as "the language of our ancestors" or "the language of our grandparents." With these statements, they made direct connections between their ancestral inheritance and their cultural identities. They highlighted the cultural importance of Kaqchikel to them, with statements such as, "It is part of the Mayan culture" or "I want to teach my children Kaqchikel so they will value our culture." Many characterized Kaqchikel as a beautiful language, noting that its survival was threatened and insisting they would transmit Kaqchikel so "it won't disappear." In contrast, other adolescents reported that they would teach only Spanish to their children, because Spanish was "more modern" and Kaqchikel was "not civilized." They associated modernity with Ladino culture and the Spanish language, and Kaqchikel with their ancestral culture, family, aesthetics, and linguistic survival.

Obviously, clear and proper oral communication has been historically a problem in Maya and Ladino interaction. Like other indigenous peoples, the Mayans had difficulty communicating with the Spanish colonizers. The colonizers—and, later, the Ladinos—imposed the Spanish language on the Mayans, but by and large, neither the colonizers nor the Ladinos learned to speak in a Mayan language (Lerner, 2000). Thus, responsibility for effectively producing and receiving messages was placed on the Mayans and the other indigenous groups.

The adolescents' responses indicated a preoccupation with proper communication: that is, they showed concern with effectively producing and understanding messages. They recognized the value of producing messages efficiently and saw Spanish as the language with appropriate efficiency and reach; for instance, they said that with Spanish, "You can express yourself in different places." For them, efficient communication with teachers and Ladinos was essential, and they saw Spanish as the most effective language for that purpose. Students said they would transmit Spanish so their children "could communicate with Ladinos" and "understand Ladinos and teachers." For these students, failure to transmit Spanish would contribute to future detrimental misunderstandings. One adolescent reported the she "wouldn't want [her] kids to be insulted in a language they don't speak." For her, a message in Spanish must be understood, even—perhaps particularly—if it is offensive. In general, the students projected the view that communication problems can be mitigated only if Spanish is the language of communication between Mayas, teachers, and Ladinos. For them, Spanish had a broader scope of use and was less likely to create social confusion. Thus, for these adolescents, it is a "good thing to speak Spanish."

Two other values that can be deduced from the adolescents' responses concern their concepts of language equality, and the value of language itself. With regard to the equality of languages, the bilingual students responded that they would transmit Kaqchikel because "It is my right and the right of my children." They believed that the use and transmission of Kaqchikel was their linguistic right. Furthermore, they expressed their belief that acquiring Spanish would make them the equals of Ladinos. Spanish, for them, is "the language of the majority" that "everybody uses." Spanish, then, functions for these students as a social equalizer, allowing them a point of entry into Ladino society. Thus, for them, language equality may be achieved through the framework of citizenship; thus, they intend to teach Spanish to their future children because it "is the language of Guatemala" and the Mayas are also "Guatemalan."

Interestingly, their insistence on their linguistic rights contrasts with their acknowledgment that Spanish is a significant social and economic asset as well as a marketable commodity in itself. Spanish, if transmitted, would provide "a good job" and "more opportunities for progress," since it is an "international language." This contrasts sharply with the monetary value attributed to Kaqchikel, which according to these adolescents, "doesn't get you a job." It is clear that knowledge of English was also considered economically valuable. The students expressed the view that "to learn English is to make huge progress," and English permits them "to communicate with tourists." In sum, the students' answers shed light on the complex sociolinguistic conditions of the Tecpán community and of Guatemala as a whole. The future looms large to adolescents, which motivates them to favor the language or languages that seem to be associated with the future; thus, they reported that "Spanish and English are the languages of the future." Economic and social conditions pressure students to endorse either or both Spanish and English as part of their planning for their economic and social futures. They perceive these two languages as the languages of the future and, indeed, of modernity itself.

CONCLUSION

The indigenous languages of Guatemala have been assaulted from several directions. Spanish colonial policies aimed to eliminate them; the postcolonial governments imposed *Castellanización* programs and curricula that ignored their multilingual realities. In the school domain, the indigenous languages have been prohibited and restrained, pushing language shift toward Spanish in the indigenous communities. However, after the 1996 Peace Accords, the efforts of the Mayan movement precisely targeted the school domain as one in which the indigenous languages have a chance to survive and be maintained, particularly through bilingual education. The Mayan movement has endorsed bilingual education as an important educational system that can play an important role in reversing language shift and revitalizing indigenous languages and cultures. Bilingual education would make official the use of indigenous languages as instruments of instruction, which would rebalance the prestige relations between Spanish and the indigenous languages and alter the patterns of language use among school officials, teachers, and students in a domain that has historically been limited to Spanish.

The concept that school is the principal domain where prestige relations between languages are reinforced has also been discussed by Kloss (1966) and Fishman (1966). Kloss indicated that students were apparently motivated to maintain their home languages by attending schools that provide instruction in those languages. Kloss proposed that changing language pattern use in the school domain would augment the status of the low-prestige languages, which would result in students' holding more positive attitudes toward these languages and toward their use in this domain. Furthermore, Fishman suggested that prestige is a factor that contributes to language maintenance, and that augmenting the prestige of low-prestige languages would undermine the notion that these languages do not belong in the school domain.

With the support of the government, NGOs, the Academy of Mayan Languages, and the Mayan movement, bilingual education in Guatemala has made tremendous strides. An evaluation of the years 1986–1991 demonstrated that children in bilingual programs outperform students in comparison schools on 7 of 10 measures of academic achievement; on the 3 other measures, average scores were about the same. Moreover, according to Dutcher (2004) a 2003 study showed that bilinguals entered school at an earlier age—before the age of seven (39.2%), compared to those entering Spanish-only school programs (33.9%). In terms of language use, teachers in bilingual programs used an indigenous language 30 percent of the time, Spanish 28.9 percent of the time, and both languages 39.5 percent of the time. In comparison, 52.5 percent of students spoke a Mayan language to teachers, 42.9 percent spoke Spanish, and 5.7 percent spoke both languages.

Another important benefit associated with the implementation of bilingual education is the 50 percent decrease in the school dropout rate from 2000 to 2003. According to Dutcher (2004), the Directorate for Intercultural Bilingual Education successfully provided bilingual education to rural indigenous children, which was widely accepted by parents and the community because of the combination of the economic benefits associated with Spanish and the cultural benefits associated with the indigenous languages. The problem is that intercultural bilingual education has not been implemented completely throughout the country. A case in point is the municipality of Tecpán, where bilingual education has not been implemented, which is a factor that contributes to the language shift and loss that is occurring in this Kaqchikel community. Moreover, the data reported in this chapter indicate that future parents are unlikely to choose a bilingual school due to economic pressures to learn Spanish. The results of this study also support Hale (1992) in that the adolescents who participated responded that as future parents they would choose to transmit to their children their society's prestigious languages—English and Spanish. The implementation of bilingual education in the municipality of Tecpán could potentially reverse the language shift and loss patterns of the younger generations.

After 500 years, the implementation of bilingual education for the indigenous peoples of Guatemala still represents a notable transformation in the educational system. The 1996 Peace Accords and the Mayan movement successfully channeled the focus of the Ministry of Education to issues of bilingual education, particularly to educational quality and its cultural relevance in the rural curriculum. For the first time in the country's history, bilingual education has legitimized and validated the use of the students' indigenous languages. Moreover, those indigenous communities where bilingual education has been implemented have been notably empowered. These indigenous communities and bilingual teachers have become important voices and essential players in the Guatemalan educational and political arena. Bilingual schools are more accessible to historically marginalized indigenous groups. Most importantly, the Mayan movement argues that because the goal of the educational system is to achieve literacy in both the students' indigenous languages and Spanish, these indigenous languages can and should be used as media of instruction in all subject areas. Indigenous children need, and should have, the opportunity to learn the content of subject areas in their own languages. In sum, diminishing language shift in Guatemala's indigenous communities can still be achieved, but only through the implementation of bilingual education programs throughout the entire country. Bilingual education can succeed, but only with firm governmental commitment and substantial economic investment, well-designed programs and curricula, well-trained teachers, and institutionalized community involvement.

REFERENCES

Appel, R. & Muysken, P. (1987). *Language contact and bilingualism.* New York: Routledge.

Brown, R. McKenna. (1998). Case study two: San Antonio Aguas Calientes and the Quinizilapa Valley. In S. Garzon, R. McKenna Brown, J. B. Richards, & W. Ajpub (Eds.), *The life of our language: Kaqchikel Maya maintenance, shift, and revitalization* (pp. 101–128). Austin: The University of Texas Press.

Campbell, L. & Terrence, K. (1990). Lingüística mayance: ¿Dónde nos encontramos ahora? [Mayan linguistics: Where are we now?]. In N. England & S. Elliot (Eds.), *Lecturas sobre la lingüística maya* [Readings about Mayan linguistics] (pp. 51–58). Guatemala City: CIRMA.

Chiodi, F. (Ed.) (1990). *La educación indígena en América Latina* [Indigenous education in Latin America] (Vol. 1). Quito: Abya-Yala.

De Vries, J. (1992). Language maintenance and shift: Problems of measurement. In W. Fase, K. Japaert, & S. Kroon (Eds.), *Maintenance and loss of minority languages* (pp. 211–222). Amsterdam: John Benjamins.

Dutcher, N. (2004). *Expanding educational opportunity in linguistically diverse societies.* Washington, D.C.: Center for Applied Linguistics.

Fishman, J. (1966). *Language loyalty in the United States: The maintenance and perpetuation of non-English mother-tongues by American ethnic and religious groups.* The Hague: Mounton de Gruyter.

Garzon, S. (1998). Case study three: San Juan Comalapa. In S. Garzon, R. McKenna Brown, J. B. Richards, & W. Ajpub (Eds.), *The life of our language: Kaqchikel Maya maintenance, shift, and revitalization* (pp. 129–154). Austin: The University of Texas Press.

Hale, K. (1992). Endangered languages. *Language, 68,* 1–42.

Heckt, M. (2004). *Guatemala: Pluralidad, educación y relaciones de poder* [Guatemala: Plurality, education, and power relations]. Guatemala City: Asociación para el Avance de las Ciencias Sociales en Guatemala.

House, D. (2002). *Language shift among the Navajos: identity politics and cultural continuity.* Tucson: The University of Arizona Press.

Instituto Nacional de Estadística. (2002). *XI Censo nacional de población y VI de habitación* [XI national population census and the VI for census of housing] (Censo 2002). Retrieved March 15, 2008, from http://www.ine.gob.gt/index.php/demografia-y-poblacion/42-demografiaypoblacion/75-censo2002.

Krauss, M. (1992). The world's languages in crisis. *Language, 68,* 6–10.

Kroskrity, P. V. (1982). Language contact and linguistic diffusion: The Arizona Tewa speech. In F. Barkin, E. Brandt, & J. Ornstein-Galicia (Eds.), *Community, bilingualism and language contact: Spanish, English, and Native American Language* (pp. 51–72). New York: Teachers College Press.

Kloss, H. (1966) German-American language maintenance efforts. In J. Fishman (Ed.), *Language loyalty in the United States: The maintenance and perpetuation of non-English mother-tongues by American ethnic and religious groups* (pp. 355–387). The Hague: Mounton de Gruyter.

Lerner, I. (2000). Spanish colonization and the indigenous languages of America. In E. G. Gray & N. Fiering (Eds.), *The language encounter in the Americas, 1492–1800* (pp. 281–293). New York: Berghahn Books.

Menéndez, L. A. (2002). *La educación en Guatemala 1954–2000: Enfoque histórico-estadístico.* [Education in Guatemala 1954–2000: A historic and statistical focus]. Guatemala City: C.J.C. Computación.

Orellana, C. G. (2006). *Historia de la Educación en Guatemala* [History of education in Guatemala]. Guatemala City: Editorial Universitaria de la Universidad de San Carlos.

Richards, J. B. (1998). Case study one: San Marcos La Laguna. In S. Garzon, R. McKenna Brown, J. B. Richards, & W. Ajpub (Eds.), *The life of our language: Kaqchikel Maya maintenance, shift, and revitalization* (pp. 62–100). Austin: The University of Texas Press.

Suárez, J. A. (1983). *Las lenguas indígenas mesoamericanas* [The indigenous languages of Mesoamerica]. Mexico City: Instituto Nacional Indigenista: Centro de Investigaciones y Estudios Superiores en Antropología Social.

Trudgill, P. & Tzavaras, G. A. (1977). Why Albanian-Greeks are not Albanians: Language shift in Attica and Biotia. In H. Giles (Ed.), *Language, ethnicity and intergroup relations* (pp. 171–184). London: Academic Press.

Williamson, R. & Van Eerde, J. (1980). "Subcultural" factors in the survival of secondary languages: A cross-national sample. *International Journal of the Sociology of Language, 25,* 59–83.

Zapeta, J. A. (2005). *El movimiento maya: Sus tendencias y transformaciones* [The Mayan movement: Its tendencies and transformations]. Guatemala City: Asociación Maya Uk'u'x B'e.

SECTION II

PRACTICE

CHAPTER 4

TRANSITIONS TO BILITERACY: CREATING POSITIVE ACADEMIC TRAJECTORIES FOR EMERGING BILINGUALS IN THE UNITED STATES

Kathy Escamilla and Susan Hopewell
University of Colorado, USA

POLICY AND CONTROVERSY

Language policy debates in the United States have been raging over the past several decades. The nature, tone, tenor, and substance of these debates is complex, but at their core, these debates focus on what role (if any) a non-English language should play in the education of language minority children[1] in U.S. schools. Advocates for English-only or English-medium schools have argued that using the minority language as a vehicle for instruction slows the acquisition of English (Rossell & Baker, 1996), and

---

[1] Language Minority Children are defined in the United States as children who come from a home where a language other than English is spoken (Ovando, Combs, & Collier, 2006).

International Perspectives on Bilingual Education: Policy, Practice, and Controversy, pages 69–94
Copyright © 2010 by Information Age Publishing
69

delays overall academic progress (Baker & DeKanter, 1983). This position has been labeled the language-as-interference, or language-as-a-problem, paradigm (Ruiz, 1984). While there is little support in the extant academic research for this point of view, it has become the major educational policy in many U.S. states, with three states in particular (California, Arizona, and Massachusetts) having educational policies that mandate English-only instruction almost exclusively. To illustrate the predominance of the belief that non-English languages are problems to be solved, one need look no further than the label of English Language Learner (ELL).[2] At all levels of the educational spectrum, from the federal government to university researchers to policymakers and practitioners, Emerging Bilingual children are routinely labeled ELLs as if learning English is their single most (or only) defining characteristic. Aligning with definitional issues that label Emerging Bilingual children solely by the fact that they are learning English, it is also noteworthy that nationally, 87 percent of children who carry the label English Language Learner (ELL) are in English-medium instructional programs with no instructional support in their native language (Kindler, 2002; NCES, 2006). ELL is the reference term for this population in the United States, even in schools where bilingual or dual language approaches are implemented.

On the other side of the debate is the viewpoint that all languages are resources that can be used in building and implementing academic programs for Emerging Bilingual children, and that the development of bilingualism and biliteracy are desirable outcomes of schooling for all children, including those who are native English speakers (Ruiz, 1984). Contrary to being a source of interference or a problem, proponents of language-as-a-resource paradigms posit that non-English languages can serve as scaffolds to facilitate English language acquisition and that there are linguistic, cognitive, and academic benefits from learning in and through two languages (Cummins, 1981, 1986; August & Hakuta, 1997; August & Shanahan, 2006; Genesee, Lindholm-Leary, Saunders, & Christian, 2005). There is a plethora of theoretical and empirical research that supports the language-as-a-resource paradigm. In addition to a broad research base, the growth in dual language programs in the United States over the past decade provides further evidence that the language-as-a-resource paradigm

---

[2]English Language Learner (ELL) is defined as a child who is in the process of learning English but whose English is so limited that he or she would have difficulty understanding instruction in a classroom where English is the medium of instruction. While this term is more neutral than the historical and more pejorative term Limited English Proficient (LEP), it is still problematic in that it focuses on the need to learn English without acknowledging the value of the child's proficiency in L1 or the child's potential to become bilingual (Crawford, 2004).

is gaining in momentum and support. For example, in 1997 there were 149 existing dual-language programs, but by 2007 this number had increased to 335 (CAL, 2008a). This growth includes 12 programs in Arizona and 107 programs in California, states with English-only mandates (CAL, 2008b). Despite this movement, the vast majority of children labeled as Language Minority Children or English Language Learners continue to be schooled in English-medium or very short-term bilingual education programs (Kindler, 2002; NCES, 2006).

It will come as no surprise to readers of this chapter that the authors concur with the language-as-a-resource paradigm. But a central argument in this chapter is that for far too long, the field of bilingual education in the United States has been mired in arguments about language of instruction, and that this focus has detracted policymakers, practitioners and researchers from engaging in other areas of inquiry, such as how best to use one or more languages to create, implement, and evaluate the quality of instructional programs for emerging bilingual children. We concur with a number of researchers (Genesee, Lindholm-Leary, Saunders, & Christian, 2005; Slavin & Cheung, 2003; August & Shanahan, 2006) who have concluded that the 35-year debate over language of instruction in the United States has been settled (a child's native language *is* a resource). However, the field is in dire need of new theories and innovative instructional approaches about how best to teach the approximately 5 million children who are labeled as ELLs but who will be referred to hereafter in this chapter as Emerging Bilinguals. To reiterate, it is not only important that Emerging Bilinguals have opportunities to learn in their native languages, but it is also important that the quality of instruction in both the native language and English be effective, grounded in research, contextualized, and based on the reality of schools and schooling for U.S. Emerging Bilinguals.

NEEDED: NEW PARADIGMS FOR DEVELOPING LITERACY PROGRAMS FOR EMERGING BILINGUALS

The population of Emerging Bilingual children in the United States is growing quickly. While this population in its entirety is diverse, nearly 80 percent of Emerging Bilinguals speak Spanish as a first language and are ethnically Latino (60% are from Mexico) and poor and attend schools that are highly segregated (Kindler, 2002; NCES 2006). To have the potential to be successful, an educational intervention must be developed with an understanding of the population to be served by the intervention as well as the context in which the intervention is being implemented. The Literacy Squared® intervention program was developed especially for Spanish-speaking children attending schools in communities where the majority is poor and Latino. Moreover, these children reside in a country where the Spanish language has little status and where school districts and schools view any non-English language largely as a problem in need of remediation by the school.

In designing the Literacy Squared® intervention, we decided to utilize theories of bilingualism in the program design (Grosjean, 1989; Valdés & Figueroa, 1994), rather than the dominant and pervasive theories of parallel monolingualism. Theories of bilingualism examine the totality of the bilingual experience as a unique and unified whole rather than as a fractional representation that perpetuates the idea that the bilingual resembles two monolinguals in one person. The coexistence of two or more languages contributes to a uniquely endowed human being whose experiences and knowledge can never be measured or understood as independently constrained by each language separately. A theory of bilingualism better captures the attributes of the children in the program, who are, for the most part, simultaneous bilinguals. The exact ways in which theories of bilingualism have been applied in the program will be further illustrated in the chapter.

Simultaneous bilingualism is a concept that is not well understood or widely used in the United States in the development and implementation of either bilingual or dual-language programs, yet it is a term that fits a vast majority of Emerging Bilinguals. Briefly defined, simultaneous bilinguals are children aged 0–5 who have been exposed to and are acquiring two languages (Baker, 2001). Emerging Bilinguals who were born in the United States are likely to be simultaneous bilinguals, for many live in homes where two languages are used or attend preschools where English is the medium of instruction. The Urban Institute reports that 77 percent of the ELLs in grades K–5 and 56 percent in grades 6–12 were born in the United States (Capp, Fix, Murray, Ost, Passel, & Herwantoro, 2005). As will be illustrated below, simultaneous bilinguals have attributes and behaviors that may be misunderstood by teachers, policymakers, and others who have only learned about sequential bilingual theories. For example, assessments that are designed to assess developing bilingualism vis-à-vis monolingual assessments in two languages frequently conclude that simultaneous bilinguals are "limited in both of their languages" or "semilingual" (MacSwan, Rolstad, & Glass, 2002; Escamilla, 2006). Consequently, many proponents of bilingual education and bilingualism view simultaneous bilingual behaviors as problems to be corrected. We propose that this view is, in essence, a different iteration of the language-as-a-problem paradigm.

In contrast to the above, sequential bilinguals are persons who began the process of second language acquisition after the age of six with a well-established first language base (Baker, 2001). Notions of sequential bilingualism are embedded in the majority of decisions relating to the current implementation of bilingual and dual language programs in the United States, including identification and labeling of students, student placement in instructional programs, the design and implementation of these programs, and the methods used to evaluate program effectiveness.[3] In short, the majority of bilingual programs in the United States were created for children and contexts assuming sequential bilingualism and with lenses on bilingual development that privilege parallel monolingualism. Ironically, the majority of Spanish-speaking Emerging Bilingual children in the United States are now simultaneous bilinguals (Capp, Fix, Murray, Ost, Passel, & Herwantoro, 2005). Table 1 is meant to illustrate how traditional bilingual programs have been designed and implemented using sequential bilingual frameworks and how these frameworks pose problems with regard to serving simultaneous bilinguals. Additionally, an alternative paradigm is suggested.

The Literacy Squared® program reported in this chapter was created to serve children who are simultaneous Spanish–English bilinguals who attend schools where there are few native English speakers. At the beginning of the study, teachers and administrators in the study schools were outspoken and ardent advocates for bilingual programs for the Emerging Bilingual children in their schools; however the majority largely perceived the children they were serving as semilingual, in need of remediation in both languages. Most had been schooled in theories of sequential bilingualism. Further, both formal and informal assessments[1] (particularly in the area of literacy) were based on assumptions of parallel monolingualism in combination with bilingual instructional programs that were short and transitional in nature, allowing only limited use of Spanish. Moreover, literacy programs in Literacy Squared® schools were based on a one-size-fits-all approach, both in English and in Spanish.

As a result, when the study began, we found ourselves working with dedicated and talented teachers and administrators who were outspoken advocates for the development of bilingualism and biliteracy in their Emerging Bilingual children, however, these colleagues, who had been educated exclusively in paradigms of sequential bilingualism, were also frustrated at what they perceived as lack of progress or success with Emerging Bilingual children. This situation was exacerbated because these colleagues worked

---

[3] To illustrate this point further, many of the foundational books on bilingual education and dual language use the terms L1 and L2 throughout the book, with L1 referring to a child's first language and L2 to the second language that the child is learning (cf. Ovando, Combs, & Collier, 2006; Crawford, 2004; Cloud, Genesee, & Hamayan, 2000).

[1] Informal assessment, as used in this study, consists of an informal reading inventory which consists of graded passages with comprehension questions. Results of informal assessments provide data on students' relative reading levels and provide diagnostic information to help teachers develop instructional lessons (Peregoy & Boyle, 2001).

TABLE 1. LANGUAGE ATTRIBUTES OF SEQUENTIAL AND SIMULTANEOUS BILINGUALS

	Problematic Assumptions from the Sequential Bilingualism Paradigm	Attributes of Simultaneous Bilingual Student	Erroneous Solutions from the Sequential Bilingualism Paradigm	Preferred Paradigm
Pedagogy 1	All children have an identifiable L1.	Students may enter school with no clear L1.	Either L1 or L2 should be the basis of initial literacy instruction, but not both.	Paired literacy instruction capitalizes on bilingualism.
Pedagogy 2	Children without an identifiable L1 are limited in two languages.	Students may know different concepts and have different strengths in each of their languages.	Teachers choose only one language for initial literacy instruction, usually English.	Paired literacy instruction enables children to use both of their languages to become biliterate.
Pedagogy 3	Languages must be strictly separated. Children are taught to keep the two languages separate.	Bilinguals use all of their linguistic resources to communicate.	Children are denied access to opportunities to work across languages.	Teaching children to connect their two languages has cross-language benefits.
Program Design 1	After transition to an English-only environment, students learn like monolinguals.	Students' total academic language repertoire may still require access to and development of both languages.	After transition, no further Spanish literacy or ESL instruction is required.	There should be recognition that the development of biliteracy is a long-term endeavor.
Program Design 2	Spanish literacy serves solely as a bridge to English.	Simultaneous bilinguals use two languages to process information and to make sense of their worlds.	Spanish literacy is temporary and is discontinued as soon as possible.	Linguistic resources in are mutually reinforcing, and children are capable of bidirectional transfer.

TABLE 1. *(Continued)*

	Problematic Assumptions from the Sequential Bilingualism Paradigm	Attributes of Simultaneous Bilingual Student	Erroneous Solutions from the Sequential Bilingualism Paradigm	Preferred Paradigm
Program Design 3	ESL instructions should be focused on oral language or sheltered in content areas.	Bilingual children are immersed in oral language as well as print literacy across two languages.	Children are denied opportunities to read in English.	One linguistic system need not be in place (e.g., oral language) before another is begun (e.g., reading).
Assessment	Bilingualism is parallel monolingualism.	Students will codeswitch in a variety of ways, because knowledge is distributed across languages.	Assessment should be administered and analyzed in each language separately.	Assessment documents bilingual trajectories. Comparison to monolinguals is inappropriate.

in districts and cities that view "language as a problem," and bilingual education as a component of that problem.

THE LITERACY SQUARED® PROGRAM: CONCEPTUAL FRAMEWORK AND INSTRUCTIONAL COMPONENTS

The Literacy Squared® program was created using theories of bilingualism created by Grosjean (1989) and Valdés and Figueroa (1994) as a basis for developing a literacy intervention to serve simultaneous Spanish–English Emerging Bilinguals. The program and research project had two major purposes. The first was to examine the potential of a simultaneous (Spanish–English) literacy intervention designed for Emerging Bilingual children. The second was to develop new paradigms and lenses through which to examine and describe literacy development in emerging Spanish/English bilinguals. We propose that Trajectory toward Biliteracy is a more valid means of assessing the progress of Emerging Bilingual children and a more effective way to evaluate the efficacy of bilingual programs.

The conceptual framework for this study utilized the work of recent syntheses of research in the field (August & Shanahan, 2006; Slavin & Cheung, 2003; Genesee, Lindholm-Leary, Saunders, & Christian, 2005) as the underpinnings for the intervention. In short, these syntheses posit that development of biliteracy requires that programs pay attention to the language of instruction, the quality of instruction, and to making explicit cross-language connections for children. This framework was explicitly created for simultaneous Spanish–English Emerging Bilinguals.

We consider quality of instruction to include such things as utilization of effective language-specific teaching methods, strategies, and organizational structures and routines, particularly methods and techniques that have been developed especially for second language learners. In this study, Literacy Squared® (the intervention) is the independent variable that was studied vis-à-vis its impact on the dependent variables of English and Spanish reading and writing achievement, and children's progress toward becoming biliterate.

The Development of a Trajectory toward Biliteracy

The foundation of the program consisted of developing a framework that could be utilized by the research team and project teachers to document and observe children's literacy development in Spanish and English. While we are well aware that foundations for literacy begin prior to formal schooling, academic school-based literacy for this program begins in first grade in both English and Spanish. This framework is key to the project for several reasons. First, although the research is clear that there is a strong and positive correlation between Spanish and English literacy, there has never been clear articulation for teachers and practitioners about how literacy in the two languages might develop concurrently. Such a framework would require attention to the following unanswered questions: Should literacy development in two languages be parallel? Should there be a lag between Spanish and English? If there is a lag, how large or small should it be? And, should Spanish literacy skills be fully developed before English literacy instruction is begun?

For the purposes of this project, the research team developed a theoretical trajectory toward biliteracy hypothesizing that literacy development in English need not be delayed while children are learning to read and write in Spanish. Moreover, we hypothesized that Spanish development would provide the foundation and scaffold for English literacy development, meaning that literacy development in Spanish would likely be ahead of English development, but only slightly. In short, we intended to examine if effective instruction in both Spanish and English could result in a positive biliteracy trajectory.

Instructional Components

The Literacy Squared® program was created as a way to operationalize the study's conceptual framework into a Spanish/English biliteracy program for grades 1–5. It is founded upon the premise that a biliteracy trajectory can be described and measured. The Literacy Squared® intervention in this study has four major components: assessment, instructional program, professional development, and research.

Assessment

A foundational component of the study was the identification of formal and informal reading and writing assessments in English and Spanish. Informal assessments included the Spanish *Evaluación del Desarrollo de Lecto-escritura* (EDL) and the English *Developmental Reading Assessment* (DRA) (Celebration Press, 2007a, 2007b). These tools were identified because they were available in both Spanish and English and because they were useful for addressing the research questions. Moreover, in addition to being informative for researchers, these tools are teacher-friendly. Their results yield concrete information about children's strengths and needs in reading that can help teachers design and deliver instruction. The EDL/DRA leveling system was the basis for the hypothetical trajectory to biliteracy we created. The trajectory proposes that a student's Spanish reading scores should be only slightly ahead of a student's English reading scores, and that scores in *both* Spanish and English inform text selection in either language.

The Literacy Squared® Instructional Program

The instructional components of this intervention constitute the heart of the intervention and its unique elements. They include

1. *Spanish literacy instruction*
   Students participate in daily instruction in literacy in Spanish. Intervention teachers are encouraged to use direct and explicit teaching methods that have been demonstrated to be effective in literacy instruction for Emerging Bilinguals (August & Shanahan, 2006; Genesee & Riches, 2006) and to use methods that are authentic to teaching literacy in Spanish rather than methods that had been developed in English and translated into Spanish (Vernon & Ferreiro, 1999; Smith, Jiménez, & Martínez-Leon, 2003). Literacy in Spanish includes reading and writing.
2. *Literacy-Based ESL*
   Literacy-based ESL begins in grade 1 and is implemented a minimum of three days per week. Literacy-based ESL involves direct, explicit, literacy lessons designed specifically for emerging bilingual children (Genesee & Riches, 2006; Slavin & Cheung, 2003). Over the years of project development, demonstration lessons for literacy-based ESL were designed and compiled into a booklet that each intervention teacher received (Escamilla, Hopewell, Geisler, &

Ruiz, 2006b). Literacy-based ESL does not duplicate literacy instruction in Spanish, but rather is specially designed to complement and build on Spanish literacy instruction. It includes writing as well as reading.

3. *Oral ESL (focus on oracy)*

Oral language instruction consists of explicit instruction in ESL with a focus on oracy. For the purposes of this project, oracy is defined as the skills and structures of oral language that correlate highly to literacy acquisition (Gentile, 2004a, 2004b; Vaughn, Cirino, Liñan-Thompson, Mathes, Carlson, Hagan, Pollard-Durodola, Fletcher, & Francis, 2006; Hickman, Pollard-Durodola, & Vaughn, 2004). Oracy work in literacy-based ESL includes the following: scaffolded dialogues, targeted language structures, and opportunities to rehearse, use, reuse, and apply language structures in the context of reading and writing. It is important to note that this intervention was designed to focus the teaching of ESL on language arts and literacy. Literacy-based ESL was added to the program but did not eliminate oral ESL.

4. *Explicit Cross-Language Connections*

Rather than follow a strict separation of languages framework, this project encourages teachers to design and teach lessons that make explicit cross-language connections for children. Cross-language connections enable children to develop metacognitive abilities and metalinguistic knowledge about their two languages and how each language is similar and different. Further, cross-language connections are bidirectional (Hernández, 2001). This project uses two types of cross-language connections. The first cross-language connections refer to specific literacy methods that the program has adapted from Mexico and modified for use in Spanish and English. Appropriate cross-language methods assist children in using their knowledge of literacy events in one language to do the same or a similar event in a different language. In contrast to cross-language methods, the second type of connection, cross-language strategies, focuses on teaching children the metacognitive linguistic skills of cross-language expression in reading and writing. Cross-language strategies may include carefully orchestrated work in translation and interpretation. Research support for cross-language connections comes from the work of Zentella (1997), Manyak (2002), Kennedy (2006), and Kenner (2004).

In sum, the instructional components were tied to the theoretical framework and to a set of assessment tools (EDL/DRA and writing samples), but not to any particular set of instructional materials. Teachers and schools were free to utilize any materials they felt were appropriate or that they were mandated to use.

The Professional Development Component

Critical to the successful implementation of the Literacy Squared® program was the need for regular and scaffolded professional development. The intervention implemented two types of professional development. The first was for school leadership and site coordinators. This involved four days of professional development per year so that leaders in Literacy Squared® schools fully understood the theoretical frameworks of the project, the data collection and analysis techniques, and the proposed methods, allowing them to successfully monitor full implementation of the intervention. The second type of professional development was for intervention teachers. This development consisted of six days of professional development per year so that teachers understood the theoretical underpinnings of the intervention, learned the teaching strategies and techniques required to implement the intervention, and were grounded in how to administer, score, and use the assessment instruments in the intervention to guide and inform their instructional decisions, allowing them to better observe student progress.

It is important to note that the Literacy Squared® intervention is different from other bilingual instructional approaches in several significant ways. First, the Literacy Squared® intervention provides specific benchmarks for literacy development in both Spanish and English and a concrete framework for scaffolding the development of biliteracy. Second, the intervention does not choose to develop Spanish literacy at the expense of English literacy, or vice versa, but rather seeks to explore how both can be developed simultaneously. Third, the intervention does not delay the introduction of English literacy until some arbitrary transition criteria have been attained. Biliteracy is developed beginning in grade 1. Finally, the intervention has created a special instructional program that acknowledges the need for bilingual/biliterate development for Emerging Simultaneous Bilinguals beginning in grade 1.

THE LITERACY SQUARED® PROGRAM: RESEARCH RESULTS

Research on this program has had two major purposes. The first was to examine the potential of the simultaneous literacy intervention designed for emerging bilingual children. The second was to develop new paradigms and lenses through which to examine and describe literacy development in Emerging Spanish/English Bilinguals.

Research Questions

With regard to this chapter, the following research questions were addressed:

1. What gains have been made in Spanish and English reading and writing achievement by intervention students in grades 1–5 across the three-year intervention program, as measured by informal reading measures?
2. Is there a relationship between Spanish EDL reading outcomes and English DRA reading outcomes for intervention students?
3. Is there a relationship between Spanish writing outcomes and English writing outcomes?
4. What is the trajectory toward biliteracy that is demonstrated by the first- through fifth-grade students in the study?

Methods and Data Collection

The research design for this study was a single subject's longitudinal design that utilized an intervention and used informal reading and writing measures to address the four research questions. Seven school districts and 16 schools volunteered to participate in the study as Literacy Squared® schools. In 2007–2008, program schools included more than 1,500 students in grades 1–5 and 120 teachers. Data for the research questions posed above were analyzed only for students who had complete data sets. In other words, to be included in the grade 4 data sample, a student had to be in the project for its entirety and had to have a complete data set in reading and writing for all of these years. Data analysis included both descriptive and inferential statistics.

Study Subjects and Schools

The vast majority (99%) of study subjects are Latino (Mexican American), poor, labeled by their schools as English Language Learners, and, for our purposes, considered to be Emerging Bilinguals in Spanish and English. Most critical to this study is that all program schools committed to the Literacy Squared® framework in which children would begin the paired literacy instruction in Spanish and English in grade 1 and continue to grade 5. Furthermore, all schools in the study were highly motivated to better serve their emerging bilingual students. Table 2 provides descriptive statistics with regard to study schools.

**TABLE 2. DEMOGRAPHIC CHARACTERISTICS OF LITERACY SQUARED®
SCHOOLS, 2007–2008**

School	Total Students	Latino	ELL	Percent Free/ Reduced Lunch
CO-1	432	79%	56%	71%
CO-2	369	83%	77%	84%
CO-3	459	85%	38%	82%
CO-4	548	86%	44%	79%
CO-5	396	55%	37%	70%
CO-6	564	45%	25%	49%
CO-7	451	74%	64%	74%
CO-8	629	95%	65%	76%
CO-9	472	67%	49%	71%
CO-10	574	95%	56%	75%
CO-11	618	94%	76%	78%
CO-12	693	77%	77%	80%
CO-13	449	89%	52%	84%
CO-14	412	90%	53%	85%
TX-1	686	90%	35%	82%
TX-2	889	58%	54%	58%

Data Collection and Instrumentation

Study subjects were assessed using the DRA2 (*Developmental Reading Assessment*) (Celebration Press, 2007a) and the EDL2 (*Evaluación del Desarrollo de Lecto-escritura*) (Celebration Press, 2007b) in the spring of every year since 2006. The DRA2 assesses English, and EDL2 assesses Spanish. They are parallel instruments and are informal measures of reading in both languages. Together, they provide information on student progress in each language. We used them to examine students' trajectories toward biliteracy.

Writing samples in Spanish and English were solicited and collected on all students in the project schools in December/January each project year. Children were given a writing prompt and 30 minutes to respond to the prompt. Writing samples were rated on a rubric developed by Literacy Squared® researchers and determined to have high rates of interrater reliability in scoring (Escamilla, Hopewell, Geisler, & Ruiz, 2006b). Writing prompts varied by grade level and by language. Data analyses included both descriptive and inferential statistics. Only children who had complete data sets in reading and writing were included in the analyses.

Findings

As discussed above, Literacy Squared® had its inception in 2004. For research purposes, 2004 was considered to be exploratory and developmental, and 2005 was considered to be a pilot year. Therefore, data for the longitudinal research project began to be collected in 2006. Data reported below present longitudinal findings for the years 2006–2008 for three different cohort groups of students. Cohort 1 students were in grade 1 in 2006 and finished grade 3 in 2008, Cohort 2 students were in grade 2 in 2006 and finished grade 4 in 2008, and Cohort 3 students were in grade 3 in 2006 and finished grade 5 in 2008.

Research Question 1 explored the gains in Spanish and English reading and writing achievement by program students in each of the cohort groups across the three-year intervention as measured by informal reading and writing measures. Table 3 presents these data with regard to growth in Spanish reading (EDL) and English reading (DRA). The EDL and DRA have numbering systems that utilize both letters and numbers. The level ranges go from A to 60 for the EDL2 and from A to 80 for the DRA2. Each assessment also has a benchmark level that is considered to be indicative of being on grade level at the end of an academic year. Benchmark levels for grades 1–5 are as follows: grade 1 = 18; grade 2 = 28; grade 3 = 38; grade 4 = 40; grade 5 = 50. Lower grades are represented by multiple levels of text. For example, grade 1 has 12 distinct levels, while grades 2 and 3 each have 3 levels, and grades 4 and 5 have 1 level. Early levels assess various decoding challenges, whereas upper levels assess comprehension skills including recall and inference.

Using the Literacy Squared® Emerging Bilingual framework, the following findings are noteworthy. Children in all cohort groups made

TABLE 3. MEAN LEVEL SCORES AND CROSS–GRADE LEVEL GROWTH IN SPANISH/ENGLISH READING FOR LITERACY SQUARED® COHORT GROUPS (2006–2008)

	Assessment	2006 $\bar{X}$ (SD)	2007 $\bar{X}$ (SD)	2008 $\bar{X}$ (SD)
Cohort 1	EDL2	17.0 (5.2)	25.9 (7.0)	34 (8.2)
Grades 1–3 n = 52	DRA2	6.0 (4.0)	14.8 (7.2)	27.1 (10.5)
Cohort 2	EDL2	22.2 (9.8)	29.2 (7.9)	37.9 (10.5)
Grades 2–4 n = 72	DRA2	8.8 (6.3)	17.9 (9.0)	29.5 (11.1)
Cohort 3	EDL2	29.9 (9.8)	38.2 (12.7)	46.8 (13.5)
Grades 3–5 n = 19	DRA2	17.3 (7.8)	27.1 (11.9)	40.5 (17.3)

cross–grade level growth in both Spanish and English reading across three years. Growth in Spanish for all cohort groups ranges from 7 to 8 EDL levels over the three-year period. Growth in English reading was 8 to 9 levels for all cohort groups during the first year of the project and 12 to 13 levels for all cohort groups during the second year of the project. These findings are important for several reasons. First, simultaneous literacy instruction does not seem to have a negative impact on either Spanish or English literacy acquisition. Furthermore, simultaneous literacy acquisition seems to accelerate English literacy acquisition. As an example, the results on Table 3 indicate that Cohort 1 children who received the Literacy Squared® intervention beginning in grade 1 have grade 3 Spanish literacy outcomes of 34 and English literacy outcomes of 27.1. In contrast, students who began Literacy Squared® in grade 3 in spring 2006 had outcomes of 29.9 and 17.3 in Spanish and English, respectively. Participating in the intervention results in increased literacy achievement in both Spanish and English.

Writing results show a similar pattern to reading results. All children in the project were given a grade and language specific writing prompt during December/January of each project year. Writing prompts were scored by researchers and teachers in the project using the writing rubric developed for Literacy Squared®. The quantitative part of this rubric is divided into four criteria (content, punctuation, spelling, and overall). A maximum score on the rubric is 14 (content = 7; punctuation = 3; and spelling = 4). Table 4 illustrates the mean overall scores for Spanish–English writing from 2006 to 2008. It is significant to note that the program emphasized writing as well as reading instruction in the creation of the literacy programs in both languages; most U.S. literacy programs privilege reading over writing. Results in writing, as in reading, demonstrate that students in all cohort groups grew in their writing development over time. Writing growth from 2006–2007 ranged from 0.6 to 1.2 levels of growth in Spanish writing and from 0.2 to 2 levels in English. In 2007, the growth ranged from 0.2 to 0.7 in Spanish and –0.2 to 1.7 in English. As with reading, the findings indicate that simultaneous writing instruction was having a positive impact on both Spanish and English writing growth. As an example, the results on Table 4 indicate that Cohort 1 children who began the Literacy Squared® intervention in grade 1 have Spanish writing outcomes of 8.7 and English writing outcomes of 7.2 for the spring of 2008. In contrast, students who began Literacy Squared® in grade 3 in spring 2006 had outcomes of 8.5 and 6.6 in Spanish and English, respectively, thereby demonstrating increased literacy achievement in both Spanish and English.

Just as with reading outcomes, there is a need to use a bilingual lens when assessing the writing of Emerging Bilinguals. The writing rubric used in this program asked raters to note bilingual strategies that children were using

TABLE 4. MEAN LEVEL SCORES AND CROSS-GRADE LEVEL GROWTH IN SPANISH-ENGLISH WRITING FOR LITERACY SQUARED® COHORT GROUPS (2006–2008)

	Language	2006 $\overline{X}$ (SD)	2007 $\overline{X}$ (SD)	2008 $\overline{X}$ (SD)
Cohort 1	Spanish	7.2 (2.5)	8.4 (1.9)	8.7 (1.8)
Grades 1–3 $n = 52$	English	4.9 (2.3)	6.6 (2.1)	7.2 (2.1)
Cohort 2	Spanish	7.8 (2.3)	8.9 (1.7)	9.6 (1.6)
Grades 2–4 $n = 72$	English	5.7 (2.3)	7.2 (2.1)	8.9 (3.6)
Cohort 3	Spanish	8.5 (2.3)	9.1 (2.0)	9.3 (2.5)
Grades 3–5 $n = 19$	English	6.6 (2.3)	8.6 (2.4)	8.4 (2.8)

as they wrote in either Spanish or English. Bilingual strategies may include the following: codeswitching (no puedo hablar in just one language), cross-language word borrowing (I love my new ropa; aprendí a hacer divide), syntax (the bike of my sister), bidirectional phonics transfer (japi/happy), and others. Consider the writing sample below:

The Tree Piks

My story is about of tree piks and 1 lobo feroz. The lobo tiro dawn the house of paja. Den the little pik go roning to the huse of jis brotter a sai guat japen to the house. (*My story is about the three pigs and the ferocious wolf. The wolf tore down the straw house. Then the pig went running to his brother's house and says, "What happened to the house?"*)

A monolingual interpretation of this child's writing may lament the codeswitching. Further, the reader may not be able to read many of the words or understand that the child is using phonetic principles from both of his languages to spell words. In fact, the child is quite adept at cross-language invented spelling. The monolingual reviewer, however, may conclude that the child is a poor writer and his Spanish skills are interfering with his ability to write in English. In short, even at the classroom level this writing could be seen as evidence of language as a problem.

Using the writing rubric developed for Literacy Squared® and the analytic procedures, we would come to a very different conclusion about this child's writing. We propose that the child is using some very powerful strategies to express himself in English. Specifically, the child uses the Spanish phonetic system to write some of the words (e.g. piks for pigs; jis for his; guat for what). This illustrates knowledge that language is rule governed and that sounds can be heard in your mind and then recorded on a page. He is using what he knows in one language to communicate in a second language. Further, his approximations for words like den (for then) and brotter (for brother) illustrate his emerging knowledge of English as these words represent frequent approximations for spelling used by native English speakers. His use of Spanish syntax (the house of paja instead of the straw house) indicates a knowledge of word order, and his lexical borrowing (lobo for wolf; paja for straw; and feroz for ferocious) again illustrates a stage of interlanguage in which he is using what he knows in his first language to communicate in a second. In short, a major finding in this study has been that developing biliterate children use multiple strategies when learning to write in Spanish and English. Further, valid assessments must assess Emergent Bilingual children vis-à-vis both of their languages taking into consideration cross-language transfers. Monolingual rubrics developed in English and then adapted into Spanish that assess only one language at a time are based on parallel monolingual paradigms. These rubrics may be underestimating the writing strengths of Emergent Bilinguals.

Figures 1 and 2 present a visual representation of the children's Emerging Biliteracy. Figure 1 relates to reading and Figure 2 to writing. Significant to the findings are that children are making gains in both Spanish and English reading across grade levels and that they are developing as biliterate learners. In short, they are on a trajectory toward biliteracy.

Research Questions 2 and 3 addressed further the question of the relationship between reading and writing in English and Spanish. To examine this relationship, correlation coefficients were calculated for reading and writing for each cohort group in the project. Results are presented in Table 5. It is noteworthy that there are strong and positive correlations between reading in Spanish and reading in English and writing in Spanish and English for all cohort groups and that these correlation coefficients increase in both reading and writing as children move up in grade levels.

The final research question addressed the overall trajectory toward biliteracy of children in the project. The chart below illustrates this trajectory for 2008 for grades 1–5. In setting up this program, we theorized that Emerging Bilingual children developing literacy simultaneously would develop biliteracy in both similar and dissimilar ways and possibly not at equivalent speeds. We hypothesized a potential discrepancy between Spanish and English but were hopeful that a well-articulated cross–grade level program would minimize this discrepancy. We used the EDL and DRA reading levels to develop a range of expected reading levels for students making good progress in both languages. The range is a slightly staggered leveling for biliteracy development. Students' achievements in Spanish and English

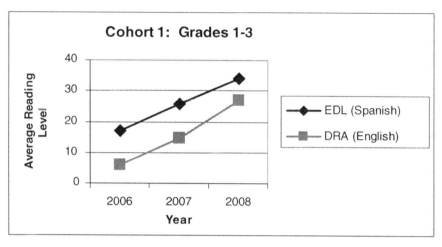

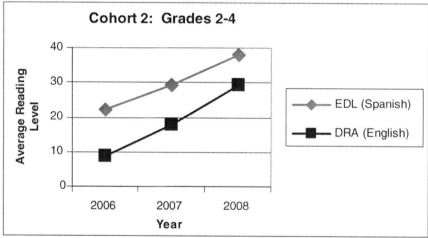

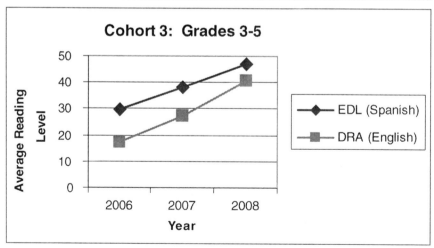

Figure 1. Trajectories toward Biliteracy in Reading (2006–2008)

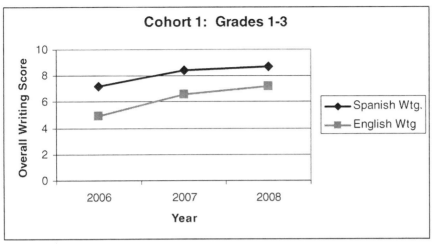

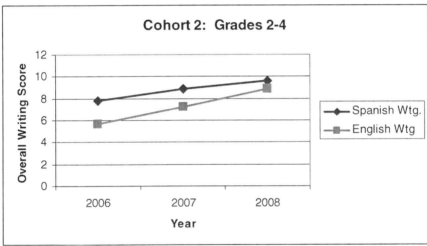

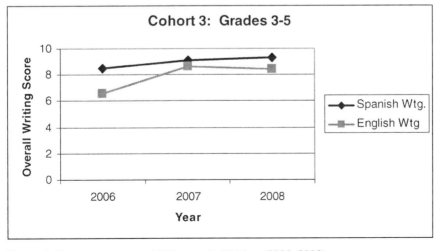

Figure 2. Trajectories toward Biliteracy in Writing (2006–2008)

TABLE 5. CORRELATION COEFFICIENTS BETWEEN SPANISH AND ENGLISH READING AND WRITING FOR CHILDREN IN LITERACY SQUARED® (2006–2008)

	2006 Reading/Writing	2007 Reading/Writing	2008 Reading/Writing
Cohort One (Grades 1–3)	0.57/0.49	0.45/0.56	0.52/0.73
Two (Grades 2–4)	0.55/0.64	0.44/0.60	0.64/0.72
Three (Grades 3–5)	0.42/0.38	0.48/0.56	0.69/0.92

are not expected to be at the same level, but they should be in a "zone" of biliteracy.

These data are indicative of the increasing number of children whose literacy development in Spanish and English are proportional to the hypothetical trajectory we predicted. While they are not evidence of meeting a grade level benchmark, we argue that they are a valid way of assessing whether Emergent Bilingual children are developing literacy in Spanish and English. The graph below demonstrates that the majority of children in all cohort groups (over 80%) are on positive trajectories toward biliteracy.

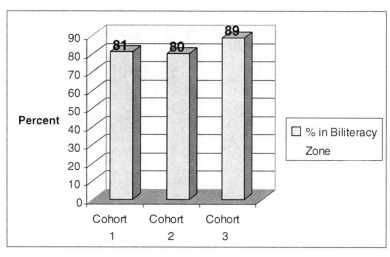

Figure 3. Biliteracy Zones for Those with Three Years of Complete Data (2008)

IMPLICATIONS FOR POLICY AND PRACTICE

This chapter will end where it began. Current policy in the United States at the federal, state, and local levels serves to discourage (and in some cases restrict) local schools from implementing bilingual education programs. We argue that these policies are, among other things, based on paradigms that assume that the presence of multiple languages in a community presents a problem and that the school's role is to rectify this problem with English-only policies and English-medium schools. There is no question that the narrow and restrictive language policies mentioned above mitigate against the ability of researchers and teachers to conceptualize, implement, and study bilingual education programs including structures and strategies to improve their quality.

Federal and state policy aside, however, we further argue in this chapter that there are other dynamics at play that limit how bilingual education is conceptualized and practiced in the United States. We suggest that the there are two pervasive paradigms that govern the implementation of bilingual education programs that have also limited the ability of policymakers and practitioners to move the field forward. The twin paradigms of sequential bilingualism and parallel monolingualism as guideposts of program implementation are problematic and have led to an unconscious but nonetheless powerful perception of language as a problem—a perception unfortunately often shared by bilingual teachers, administrators, and those policymakers who support bilingual education.

Throughout this chapter, and indeed through the course of the Literacy Squared® project, we have come to believe that while we struggle to change federal and state policy and perception, we must also change the perceptions of bilingual educators. Our research has indicated to us that parallel monolingual views with regard to assessment, curriculum, instruction, and program evaluation will most likely only serve to confirm notions that some children can be semilingual, that Spanish interferes with English, and that bilingual programs result in low levels of performance in both languages. All of these beliefs held by bilingual educators and others serve to perpetuate the language-as-a-problem paradigm.

If bilingual education programs are to be successful for the ever-increasing number of simultaneous Emerging Bilinguals, we must build programs around a new paradigm that sees bilingual development holistically and that has as its center the development of trajectories to biliteracy. We suggest the following implications for program development and practice:

1. Program development needs to view children as Emergent Bilinguals and opportunities to develop literacy in both Spanish and English need to begin in kindergarten.

2. Assessment systems need to be developed that are sensitive to and that can measure bilingual development, unlike current systems that measure parallel monolingualism.

3. Success for children needs to be measured by looking at bilingual–biliterate development, rather than by comparisons with monolingual peers in either Spanish or English.

4. There is a need for teacher education and preparation in order to help teachers and others develop bilingual interpretive lenses with which to examine the reading, oral language, and writing of Emerging Bilingual children.

5. There is a need to study, in depth, structures and strategies in the area of literacy to better understand how to propel children in their acquisition of biliteracy. Too little attention is currently paid to this; often, reading and writing instruction in Spanish and English is parallel but not connected. Instruction must be coordinated and connected. Systematic scheduling must accommodate teachers' need to meet and plan together. The theoretical foundation from which we work depends entirely on understanding that Spanish and English do not develop separately and in isolation but in a coordinated and mutually beneficial manner. Program models and teaching must be reconceptualized so that coordinated instruction happens for all Emergent Bilingual children. The bottom line is that we need to look at these children as literate human beings and not continue to try to dissect their literacy into language-specific pieces.

6. Similarly, there is a need to create spaces where children are encouraged to be bilingual and where language mixing is not censored.

7. There is a need to practice biliteracy and explicitly develop cross-language metalinguistic skills and strategies.

In conclusion, one of the greatest sources of joy in this project was working with the many talented and dedicated bilingual teachers in our research schools. These teachers instinctively believe in children's ability to become biliterate, and they are committed to helping them. They are also committed to their own professional development and are eager to try new approaches and techniques. With or without drastic changes in federal and state policy, we believe that classroom-based research and applications can help us move the field forward.

REFERENCES

August, D. & Hakuta, K. (Eds.). (1997). *Improving schooling for language minority children: A research agenda.* Washington, D.C.: National Academy Press.

August, D., & Shanahan, T. (2006). *Developing literacy in second-language learners: Report of the national literacy panel on language-minority children and youth.* Mahwah, NJ: Lawrence Erlbaum Associates.

Baker, C. (2001). *Foundations of bilingual education and bilingualism* (3rd ed.). Clevedon, UK: Multilingual Matters.

Baker, K., & de Kanter, A. (1983). *Bilingual education: A reappraisal of federal policy.* Lexington, MA: Lexington Books.

Capp, R., Fix, M., Murray, J., Ost, J., Passel, J. S., & Herwantoro, S. (2005). *The new demography of America's schools: Immigration and the No Child Left Behind Act.* Washington, D.C.: Urban Institute.

Celebration Press. (2007a). *Developmental reading assessment.* Parsippany, NJ: Celebration Press.

Celebration Press. (2007b). *Evaluación del desarrollo de la lectura.* Parsipanny, NJ: Celebration Press.

Center for Applied Linguistics. (2008a). TWI Directory Tables. Retrieved December 17, 2008, from http://www.cal.org/twi/directory/table.htm.

Center for Applied Linguistics. (2008b). Directory of Two Way Immersion Programs in the U.S. Washington, D.C. Retrieved December 17, 2008, from http://www.cal.org/jsp/TWI/SchoolListing.jsp.

Cloud, N., Genesee, F., & Hamayan, E. (2000). *Dual language education: A handbook for enriched education.* Boston: Heinle & Heinle.

Crawford, J. (2004). *Educating English learners: Language diversity in the classroom.* (5th ed.). Los Angeles: Bilingual Education Services.

Cummins, J. (1981). The role of primary language development in promoting education success for language minority students. In Office of Bilingual Bicultural Education, *Schooling and language minority students: A theoretical framework* (pp. 1–49). Los Angeles: Evaluation, Dissemination and Assessment Center, California State University.

Cummins, J. (1986). Empowering minority students: A framework for intervention. *Harvard Educational Review, 56*, 18–36.

Escamilla, K., Hopewell, S., Geisler, D., & Ruiz, O. (2006a). *Literacy Squared®: Report of a pilot intervention.* Paper presented at the annual conference of the National Association for Bilingual Education, Phoenix, AZ.

Escamilla, K., Hopewell, S., Geisler, D., & Ruiz, O. (2006b). *Transitions to biliteracy: Literacy Squared® literacy-based ESL sample lessons.* Paper presented at the annual conference of the Colorado Association for Bilingual Education, Denver, CO.

Escamilla, K. (2006). Semilingualism applied to the literacy behaviors of Spanish-speaking emerging bilinguals: Bi-illiteracy or emerging biliteracy? *Teacher's College Record, 108*(11), 2329–2353.

Genesee, F., Lindholm-Leary, K., Saunders, W., & Christian, D. (2005). English language learners in U.S. schools: An overview of research findings. *Journal of Education for Students Placed At Risk, 10*(4), 363–385.

Genesee, F. & Riches, C. (2006). Literacy instruction issues. In F. Genesee, K. Lindholm-Leary, W. Saunders, & D. Christian (Eds.), *Educating English language learners: A synthesis of research evidence* (pp. 109–176). Cambridge, UK: Cambridge University Press.

Gentile, L. (2004a). *The Oracy Instructional Guide.* Carlsbad, CA: Dominie Press, Inc.

Gentile, L. (2004b). The *Oral Language Acquisition Inventory (OLAI).* Carlsbad, CA: Dominie Press, Inc.

Grosjean, F. (1989). Neurolinguists, beware! The bilingual is not two monolinguals in one person. *Brain and Language, 36*, 3–15.

Hernández, A. (2001). The expected and unexpected literacy outcomes of bilingual students. *Bilingual Research Journal, 25*(3), 251–276.

Hickman, P., Pollard-Durodola, S., & Vaughn, S. (2004). Storybook reading: Improving vocabulary and comprehension for English language learners. *The Reading Teacher, 57,* 720–730.

Kennedy, E. (2006). Literacy development of linguistically diverse first graders in a mainstream English classroom: Connecting speaking with writing. *Journal of Early Childhood Literacy, 6*(2), 163–189.

Kenner, C. (2004). Living in simultaneous worlds: Difference and integration in bilingual script-learning. *Bilingual Education and Bilingualism, 7*(1), 43–61.

Kindler (2002). Survey of states' limited English proficient students available educational programs and services: 2000–2001 summary report. Prepared for OELA by National Clearinghouse for English Language Acquisition and Language Instruction Programs. Washington, D.C.

Manyak, P. (2002). "Welcome to salón 110": The consequences of hybrid literacy practices in a primary-grade English immersion class. *Bilingual Research Journal, 26*(2), 213–234.

MacSwan, J., Rolstad, K., & Glass, G. (2002). Do some school-age children have no language? Some problems of construct validity in the pre-LAS Español. *Bilingual Research Journal, 26,* 395–420.

National Center for Education Statistics. (2006). The condition of education 2006: Indicator 7: Language minority school age children. U.S. Department of Education: Institute of Education Sciences. Retrieved May 10, 2008, from http://nces.ed.gov/programs/coe/2006/pdf07_2006.pdf.

Ovando, C., Combs, M.C., & Collier, V. (2006). *Bilingual and ESL classrooms.* Boston: McGraw Hill.

Peregoy, S. & Boyle, O. (2001). Reading, writing, and learning in ESL. New York: Longman.

Rossell, C., & Baker, K. (1996). The educational effectiveness of bilingual education. *Research in the Teaching of English, 30*(1), 7–74.

Ruiz, R. (1984). Orientations in language planning. *NABE Journal, 8,* 15–34.

Slavin, R. & Cheung, A. (2003). *Effective reading programs for English language learners: A best-evidence synthesis.* Washington, D.C.: Center for Research on the Education of Students Place at Risk (CRESPAR).

Smith, P. H., Jiménez, R. T., & Martínez-León, N. (2003). Other countries' literacies: What U.S. educators can learn from Mexican schools. *The Reading Teacher, 56*(8), 772–781.

Valdés, G. & Figueroa, R. (1994). *Bilingualism and testing: A special case of bias.* Norwood, NJ: Ablex Publishing Corporation.

Vaughn, S., Cirino, P., Liñan-Thompson, S., Mathes, P., Carlson, C, Hagan, E., Pollard-Durodola, S., Fletcher, J., & Francis, D. (2006). Effectiveness of a Spanish intervention and an English intervention for English-Language Learner at Risk for Reading Problems. *American Education Research Journal, 43*(3), 449–487.

Vernon, S. & Ferreiro, E. (1999). Writing development: A neglected variable in the consideration of phonological awareness. *Harvard Educational Review, 69*(4), 395–415.

Zentella, A. (1997). *Growing up bilingual: Puerto Rican children in New York.* Boston: Blackwell Pub.

Kathy Escamilla, School of Education, University of Colorado at Boulder; Susan Hopewell, BUENO Center for Multicultural Education, University of Colorado at Boulder.

We wish to thank Olivia A. Ruiz for her conceptualization of the trajectory toward biliteracy. We also wish to thank Diana Geisler for her work developing literacy-based ESL and Sandra Butvilofsky and Wendy Sparrow for their work in gathering and analyzing data for this project.

Correspondence concerning this chapter should be addressed to Kathy Escamilla, School of Education, University of Colorado, UCB 247, Boulder CO 80309-0247. E-mail: kathy.escamilla@colorado.edu.

CHAPTER 5

BILINGUALISM AND BILITERACY IN INDIA: IMPLICATIONS FOR EDUCATION

Prema K. S. Rao, Jayashree C. Shanbal,
and Sarika Khurana
All India Institute of Speech and Hearing, India

INTRODUCTION

The diversity in cultural and linguistic heritage of India is well known. For centuries, this diversity has been viewed both as a problem and an asset in sociocultural, political, and educational domains. The bilingualism and multilingualism that are highly prevalent in the Indian population have been interesting but challenging to the educational policymakers and practitioners. In order to address the issue of perspectives on bilingual education, this chapter enunciates the many facets of bilingualism and biliteracy in India and their implications for educational practice.

Section I gives an overview of India to the reader, covering linguistic status, linguistic diversity, and literacy development in India. Section II describes the national policies for education that have been framed in light

International Perspectives on Bilingual Education: Policy, Practice, and Controversy, pages 95–130
Copyright © 2010 by Information Age Publishing
95

of the bilingual/multilingual status of India. Section II details educational practice in India, challenges posed by this unique population, strategies adopted to face these challenges, and empirical research in this direction, as well as their implications. The chapter concludes with a few recommendations for teaching practices designed to enhance the success of literacy in bilingual–biliterate children of India.

INDIA IN BRIEF

India, a union of states, is a sovereign socialist secular democratic republic with a parliamentary system of government. The republic is governed in terms of the constitution, which was adopted by the Constituent Assembly on November 26, 1949, and came into force on January 26, 1950. The Constitution of India distributes legislative powers between the parliament and state legislatures. The parliament is bicameral—the lower house is known as the Lok Sabha (House of the People) and the upper house as the Rajya Sabha (Council of States). At the state level, some legislatures are bicameral and are run along the lines of the two houses of the national parliament.

India is comprised of 28 states and 7 union territories spread over an area of 3.28 million square kilometers. The States Reorganization Act of 1956 was a primary force in reorganizing the boundaries of India's states along linguistic lines. Each state/UT of India has unique demography, history and culture, dress, festivals, and languages. India is one of the oldest civilizations in the world, with a variety of cultural heritage. India has achieved phenomenal socioeconomic and educational progress during the last 61 years of its independence.

LINGUISTIC STATUS OF INDIA

India is a multilingual, multicultural nation with a population of over a billion people. The Indian linguistic landscape presents a picture of coexistence of more than one, and often more than two or three, languages almost throughout the country. It has 1,576 rationalized mother tongues grouped into 114 languages. The 114 language groups of modern India genetically belong to 5 different language families. Among these, 22 languages (Assamese, Bengali, Bodo, Dogri, Gujarati, Hindi, Kannada, Kashmiri, Konkani, Maithili, Malayalam, Manipuri, Marathi, Nepali, Oriya, Punjabi, Sanskrit, Santhali, Sindhi, Tamil, Telugu, and Urdu) are included in the Constitution of India (Mallikarjun, 2001a). Eighteen Indian languages are spoken by 96.29 percent of the population of the country, and the remaining 96 languages are spoken by 3.71 percent of the population. As per the Third All India Education Survey (Sharma, 2001b), 58 languages find a place in the school curricula, and 47 are used in public administration at various levels. Newspapers are published in 87 languages, and there are radio broadcasts in 91 languages. With India being one of the most linguistically and culturally diverse nations in the world, the overall literacy rate of 65.38 percent (Census India, 2001) is a commendable achievement.

For more than a hundred years, Census India[1] reports have taken notice of the increase in bilingualism. Some of the important results of the multilingual picture of India emerging from the 1991 census are that in the case of major languages, 19.44 percent are bilinguals and 7.22 percent are trilinguals; bilinguals among minor languages represent 38.14 percent and trilinguals 8.28 percent. Significantly, among major-language speakers, the spread of bilingualism in English is greater (than in Hindi, the national language)—8 percent second-language and 3.15 percent third language, as opposed to Hindi bilingualism at 6.15 percent and 2.16 percent. Furthermore, among the bilinguals reported in the 1991 census, 70 percent are forced bilinguals in groups of people who speak languages that have no scripts of their own (Census India, 1991). Census India also reports a gradual increase in the population of bilinguals: 9.7 percent in 1961, 13.04 percent in 1971, 13.34 percent in 1981, and 19.44 percent in 1991.

LINGUISTIC DIVERSITY IN INDIA

India has been characterized as a sociolinguistic giant (Pandit, 1972) whose nerve system is multilingualism (Annamalai, 1986). It is not simply the presence of many languages in a geographical region but the ethos of multilingualism that makes the Indian society so different from the dominant monolingual countries of the West[2] (Mohanty, 1994). In India,

---

[1] Bilingualism is defined in the Indian census thus: If the respondent knows only one language, the name of that one language is recorded. If the respondent has knowledge of more than one language, the names of two languages in the order of proficiency self-assessed by the respondent are recorded. These two languages are recorded one after the other. Between these two languages, whichever language the respondent knows how to speak, comprehend, and communicate is recorded first and the other language second. The individual need not know how to read and write these languages; it is enough if he speaks and communicates in these two languages. However, the number of languages thus recorded will not exceed two.

[2] The West or Western countries refers to those countries that are geographically on the western side of India (such as European countries and the United States of America).

language diversity is an intrinsic part of the culture, unlike in the West, where bilingualism means another language in addition to another culture.

Each state and union territory within India is multilingual, thereby making the entire country multilingual in nature. A considerable number of people in each state speak the dominant language of the neighboring state. Being bilingual, they continue to use their mother tongue while they learn and use the dominant language of the state in which they are settled. For example, in the state of Andhra Pradesh, although Telugu is the dominant state language, there are speakers of Kannada language (519,507), Marathi language (503,609), Oriya language (259, 947), and Tamil language (753,484) (Sharma, 2001b).

A significant feature of Indian bilingualism is that it is complementary, as linguistic diversity is inherited in the process of acquiring the composite culture of the nation. Thus an individual may use a particular language at home, another in the neighborhood and the market, and a third in certain formal domains such as education, administration, and other situations. An individual usually has some mastery of his home language and the regional/state language (when the home language is different from the regional/state language). In addition, the languages of national and international communication, Hindi and English, are also part of the linguistic repertoire of a majority of Indians (Sharma, 2001b).

The mobility of population within the country has further strengthened the traditionally strong constituencies of multilingual groups. Additionally, the introduction of formal education in all parts of the country that insists on learning at least two languages until the end of higher secondary education has contributed to multilingualism in India. Children in India sometimes acquire two or more languages informally from their early childhood and thus are bilinguals or multilinguals well before they begin their schooling. This happens because they are exposed to many coexisting languages in the market, in the media, and in their day-to-day surroundings. Here learning more than one language is integrated as a natural process in their life.

The picture of linguistic diversity suggests that India is made of many "mini-Indias" (Mallikarjun, 2004). The dialectal variations in the cultural groups compound the linguistic diversity. More than 2,000 dialects are reported to exist in the country. Therefore, the language policy of India relating to the use of languages in administration, judiciary, legislature, mass communication, and education is pluralistic in its scope. The language policy is both language development– and language survival–oriented. The language policy of India elucidated in the constitution since 1950 and implemented through various executive orders and judicial pronouncements has directed the way the languages should be used in various domains, including the domain of literacy development through the process of education.

OVERVIEW OF DEVELOPMENT OF LITERACY IN INDIA

"When India became independent, it was still plagued with illiteracy" (Kothari & Joshi, 2002). At the beginning of the 20th century, India's literacy rate was only 5.3 percent. It was not until 1922 that a mass movement inspired by Mahatma Gandhi addressed this challenge, establishing education programs such as night schools and literacy classes that covered urban areas, villages, and remote areas. Despite these consistent efforts, illiteracy in rural areas persisted. The 2001 census results indicate a literacy rate of 64.8 percent for the total population (75.3 percent males; 53.7 percent females), while CIA findings (www.cia.gov/india) indicate 59.5 percent literacy for the total population (70.2 percent males and 48.3 percent females). Hence, the factors contributing to low success rate in the literacy movement, including the system of education, were examined by various bodies and councils in India. One of the major factors reported was lack of provision for early childhood education until the turn of the 20th century (Aggarwal, 1992). Although there is no policy for early childhood education, the government of India felt a need to take care of children in their preschool years. Hence, the Integrated Child Development Scheme (ICDS) was launched in 1975. Although the scheme covers many domains of child development such as basic hygiene, health, and nutrition, the scheme does not spell out any formal methods and approaches to meet the requirements of bilingual/multilingual population of India.

In addition to the lack of policy for early child education, the organizational system in the government also could be another reason for lack of success in the outcome of literacy development programs. While education for the younger children has been under the interests of the Department of Child Development under the Ministry of Social Justice and Empowerment, that of older children rests with the Department of Education under the Ministry of Human Resource Development. Thus, there is a "clear divide between the Department of Education and the Department of Child Development, each being largely unaware of the work done by the other" (Kaur, 2004).

Once children enter the formal schooling system, there are broadly four stages of school education in India: primary, upper primary, secondary, and higher secondary. Overall, schooling lasts 12 years, following the "10 + 2 pattern." In India, the main types of schools are those controlled by the state government boards like Secondary School Leaving Certificate (SSLC), the Central Board of Secondary Education (CBSE), the Council for the Indian School Certificate Examinations (CISCE), the National Open School (NOS), and the international schools, which mimic the schools in the West in pattern and syllabi and which are considerably more expensive than regular schools. The exams conducted by these schools have the syllabus of any one of the above-mentioned councils or boards.

Apart from the state schools and private schools, there are 500 central schools with the bilingual medium (English and Hindi) in addition to a compulsory language, Sanskrit. There are 500 Navodaya Vidyalayas, where some competence in English and Hindi is imparted simultaneously. Overall, according to the latest government survey undertaken by the District Information System of Education (DISE, 2005–2006) of the National University for Education Planning and Administration (NUEPA), there are 1,124,033 schools in the country. But the students who graduate from these schools go to the English-medium colleges, because there is no college in the country that offers a bilingual medium of instruction. Therefore, although the primary and higher primary education system promotes multilingualism in children, the system of higher education does not promote multilingualism in India (Sharma, 2001b). A majority of the courses for higher education, such as medicine, engineering, and other professional courses, are taught in English, thus restricting the scope for those children who study in non–English-medium schools. The paradox of this situation in India should be viewed with greater attention by the department of higher education.

EDUCATIONAL POLICIES

The enormous variety of languages and dialects, the different school systems, the disparities in the curricula and its practices, and inadequacy in teacher training protocols and methods of teaching created an urge to evolve national policies for education. As a result, in the second half of the 20th century a number of educational policies were proposed by the government of India in view the diverse population of children. Before moving on to the specifics of educational policies, a few terminological clarifications are offered in the following paragraphs to help the reader appreciate the information from the context of a country with linguistic diversity.

Language Acquisition and Language Learning

While language acquisition and language learning are generally viewed as two distinct terms in the predominantly monolingual countries, it need not be so in the Indian context. Many Indian children have acquired languages apart from their mother tongue by virtue of exposure and experience in their early childhood long before they enter formal schooling. Hence the typical definitions of language acquisition[3] and language

---

[3] Language acquisition refers to a less deliberate, subconscious process of mastering a language that is often associated with the manner in which children acquire their native or first language.

learning[1] may not be directly applicable to the Indian situation. It is important to consider this aspect when understanding educational policies and teaching practices for bilingual children in India.

The commonly held image of a bilingual individual is that he or she is brought up in a culture in which there is exposure to two languages from birth. However, not all bilinguals acquire the languages in a similar manner. The nature of bilingualism depends on the contexts in which the two languages are learned. An individual who learns the two languages in the same environment so that he or she acquires one notion with two verbal expressions is a compound bilingual, whereas an individual who acquires the two languages in different contexts (e.g., home and school), with the words of the two languages thus belonging to separate and independent systems, is a coordinate bilingual. In the third type, the subordinate bilingual, one language dominates the other.

Bialystok and Hakuta (1994) describe bilingualism from the perspective of the time of acquisition of the two languages during the developmental phase. They make a distinction between simultaneous (L1 and L2 learned about the same time), early sequential (L1 learned first and L2 learned before adolescence) and late (L2 learned from adolescence onward) bilingualism. Early sequential bilinguals form the largest group worldwide, with an increase in number over the decades. Biliteracy/multiliteracy also depends on various factors that include characteristics of language systems; characteristics of orthographic systems considered independently of the languages they represent (e.g., direction of reading, ideographic vs. phonologic scripts), and factors in the course of second-language acquisition, such as the age and manner (oral, written, translation) of learning the second language, the order of acquisition of different scripts, and the attitude toward language and the use of language (Obler, 1984).

While the terms *language acquisition, language learning,* and *bilingualism* relate to the context of verbal communication, in education the term *second language* is commonly used to mean a language that is learned after the first or native language is relatively established. Learning to read and write in a second language can mean different things in different situations and settings. For instance, the situation of a bilingual child learning to read English as a second language (ESL) is qualitatively different from that of an adult ESL learning to read English for literacy purposes (Pang & Kamil, 2004). In the literature, one can find different terms for describing children developing literacy in more than one language: "bilingual students," "English language learners (ELL)," "language minority students," "English-as-a-second-language students," "second-language learners," "limited-English-proficient students," "limited-English-speaking (LES) students," and so on.

---

[1] Language learning is the result of direct instruction in the rules of language.

The linguistic heritage of India gives a mixed picture of many of the above types of bilingual children that often necessitates operational definitions to describe the bilingual status of a given child/individual. People in India acquire bilingualism from their early childhood. They do not have to go to school to learn to use two or more languages. Since India has a multilingual/multicultural status, none of the definitions and descriptions of bilingualism given in the previous paragraphs seem to apply, in a strict sense to the Indian population.

However, in the majority of instances, bilingualism relating to English is a different category altogether. Most often it is a "government-sponsored, institutional arrangement" (Mallikarjun, 2001b). It is driven by formal necessities and is not an acquisition in early childhood. But in the recent decades, many families in urban areas prefer English as the first language for their children, a trend that may lead to emergence of a different kind of bilingualism not defined/documented in the Western literature. As a result, there is a great need for conceptual thinking on the terminologies in order to frame policies and strategies for educational practice. Framing the educational policies and planning for educational practice with children are highly challenging tasks in the Indian context.

National Policies for Education

India's independence on August 15, 1947, led to the formation of a full-fledged Ministry of Education on August 29, 1947. Given the peculiar linguistic situation in India, the responsibility of educational programs was exclusively assigned to the states. The Department of Education under the Ministry of Human Resource Development shares with the states the responsibility for educational planning in addition to formulating policies for education such as the National Policy on Education (University Grants Commission, 1968, 1986), the Program of Action (POA, 1986), and the revised NPE and POA (1992). The National Policy on Education (NPE, 1986) envisages "Free and Compulsory Education" for all children of India aged 6–14. The NPE was reformulated in 1986 and further updated in 1992 (www.Departments .India.org). The National Policy on Education is concerned with quality improvement, expansion of educational facilities, and education of girls. In order to achieve this goal, the government of India proposed several policies, of which the Three Language Formula (TLF) is an important proposition to the multilingual context of India.

The Three Language Formula (TLF)

Language diversity and plurality is the hallmark of India. Because of this, promotion of linguistic and cultural diversity is crucial to equip children to think and operate globally and to deal effectively with linguistic and cultural diversity. The linguistic character of a particular country determines the issues of language rights, language empowerment, language promotion, language planning, and language policy. It is directly related to the use of language or languages in education at different levels (Koul, 2006). In a dominant monolingual approach to education, the dominant language is assigned the prominent role, ignoring the mother tongues of the linguistic minorities. In a multilingual approach, all the languages spoken in the region, state, or country are given equal importance as far as their use in different domains is concerned. This approach promotes the development of all the languages and encourages their use in the domain of education too. Language policy in general ensures the teaching of the mother tongues at the elementary level and their use as media of instruction in early school education. Children may learn other languages at the higher levels of their education. Multilingual countries face various problems in the formation and implementation of their language policies in education. The multilingual and multicultural status of India, along with its high rate of illiteracy (approximately 33 percent), however, poses problems for the use of languages in education. Yet, while the analyses of Indian multilingualism during the 19th and 20th centuries viewed multilingualism as a problem, the systematic language policy initiatives of the past half-century view it as a resource.

Since the constitution of India did not make explicit statements regarding the languages to be taught in education or the languages through which education has to be imparted, in September 1956 the All India Council for Education recommended the adoption of the Three Language Formula (TLF). The responsibility of formulation of language policy per TLF and its implementation was left to the state governments under the constitutional safeguards and broad guidelines of the Union Government. In order to promote the TLF, the National Policy on Education stipulated that the school children study three languages—the regional language (state language), the national language (Hindi), and English in the non-Hindi speaking states and one of the modern South Indian languages, Hindi (the regional language), and English at the secondary stage in the Hindi-speaking states.

In addition to the initiatives of the Central Government, the National Council for Educational Research and Training, a statutory body at the national level, proposed the National Curriculum Framework for School Education: 2000 (National Council of Educational Research and Training, 2005). The specific section of this document relating to language states that the Three Language Formula is highly relevant and that sincere efforts should therefore be made to implement it in all states and union territories. According to this document, the three languages are the mother tongue/regional Language, English, and Hindi (in non–Hindi-speaking states) or any other modern Indian language (in Hindi-speaking states).

Furthermore, according to NCF, children study one language (either the regional language—the mother tongue, in the majority of cases) at the primary level (standards I and V) and three languages (a modern Indian language and English in addition to the mother tongue/regional language) at the upper primary level and secondary level (standards VI–VIII and IX–XII, respectively).

With all these provisions for education in multiple languages and mother tongues, different languages are used as media of instruction at different levels of education. As the members of the National Curriculum Framework were also of the opinion that learning more languages in the process of schooling may not be an undue burden for a child, the framework encouraged inclusion of another language, Sanskrit, as part of a composite course of Hindi and the regional languages at a suitable point of the primary or the upper primary stage. Furthermore, the framework provides the option of learning other foreign languages, such as Chinese, Japanese, Russian, French, German, Arabic, Persian, and Spanish, at the secondary level, depending on the demand and availability of infrastructure for teaching. In a nutshell, the NCF proposed multilingualism at the school level.

The NCF further proposed that in cases where mother tongue and regional language are one and the same for the learners, the medium of instruction should be in the mother tongue at all levels, or up to the end of the elementary stage. But in the case of learners whose mother tongue and regional language are different, the regional language may be adopted as the medium of instruction from the third standard. However, as one goes up the ladder to higher education, the options for languages and the medium of instruction become fewer. Although many languages are offered as media of instruction at the lower level, only English is offered in the technical and management education.

EDUCATIONAL PRACTICE

Traditionally India was known for oral transmission of knowledge. Hence, the spread of literacy was rather sporadic in the past. The post-independence period witnessed significant changes in the system of education, including bilingual educational policies for states and union territories. Bilingual education is a broad term that refers to the presence of two languages (or more, as in the context of India) in instructional settings in which bilingual education programs may be either additive or subtractive in terms of their linguistic goals, depending on whether students are encouraged to add to their linguistic repertoire or to replace their native language with the majority language.

Owing to the oral tradition of teaching and learning that existed in the past, the need to reduce the emerging languages to writing was not achieved in several of the Indian languages. As a result, many potential languages remained as oral languages without developing scripts of their own. While the normal convention for any language is to use a single script for visual rendering, the pluralistic tradition of India introduced the practice of using different scripts to write the same language and using the same script to write different languages.[5] Whenever an unwritten language was to be given a script, the Devanagari script was the first choice. Hence, by tradition, script has never become a boundary among the Indian languages.

The Writing Systems

Classification of the writing system on the basis of the relationship between sound and print was proposed by Katz and Feldman (1983). If the sound of a word can be easily predicted, then the orthography is said to be a shallow orthography. On the other hand, if the sound–print relationship is not very regular, then it is a deep orthography. The variety of scripts employed to denote the languages of India appear to fall under different writing systems, although very few studies of this are reported. The scripts of Indian languages are reported to be semisyllabic/alphasyllabary in nature (Karanth, 1992)—or shallow and transparent, unlike English.

The difference in sound–print relationship in orthographies may trigger different processing strategies to achieve reading proficiency. Crosslinguistic studies on reading in different orthographies have found that orthographic differences influence processing of scripts (Tzeng & Hung, 1981). Owing to the influence of a script on learning to read and write, the system of writing employed for Indian languages would have a significant effect on children learning languages with different writing systems. Therefore, the inherent differences in the linguistic structure as well as the script features of the languages introduced in schools may compound the problems in implementing and achieving the goals of the national policies for education in India. Evidences for this premise are offered in this section, along with a review of empirical studies carried out on monolingual and bilingual children in India.

In India, the languages of instruction cannot be equated with those in countries where educational policies are framed within a monolingual

---

[5] Kannada script for Kannada, Kodagu, Tulu, Banjari, Konkani, and Sanskrit. Sanskrit is written using the Devanagari, Kannada, Telugu, Tamil, and Malayalam, among many other, scripts. Kashmiri is written using the Perso-Arabic, Sharada, and Devanagari scripts. Sindhi in India is written both in the Perso-Arabic and Devanagari scripts. In Nagaland and Meghalaya, Roman script is used to write some tribal languages. Rabha language uses Assamese script in Assam and Bengali script in West Bengal.

perspective. As said earlier, the schools have to ensure a transition from the mother tongue to the regional/state language at the primary and secondary levels (in case they are different in children) and then to the national link language (in India, either Hindi or English). They also have the task of bridging the gap between the language or dialect spoken at home and the language of the school. The complexity of deciding the language of instruction is further enhanced by the presence of many minority languages, differences between many dialectal, nonstandard, and standard varieties of language, and the necessity of providing links from one level to the other. From among a thousand or so mother tongues, only 58 languages find a place in the school curricula (Sharma, 2001a). A large number of speakers of other mother tongues do not have any opportunity for literacy in their native language. Therefore, over the decades, educational practice has gone through several phases of modification in India. The modifications are mainly focused on educational policies, curricular framework and language of instruction, teaching and evaluation strategies, and strengthening teacher training programs. Despite a fair amount of consensus on most of these concerns, the languages of instruction are highly debated across the country by education authorities as well as the public.

Bilingualism and Language of Instruction

Since most of the languages are used in an overlapping manner in India—both geographically and socially—a majority language in one context becomes a minority language in another (Mohanty, 1994). In this multilingual milieu, bilingualism is a strategy toward maintenance of minority mother tongues and integration in language contact situations. For example, Hindi may be a national language in one context but a minority language in states where other languages are dominant. While there are several educational models adopted in countries with bilingual or multilingual populations, the Indian education system follows a combination of these models based on situational needs and necessities.

a) Transitional bilingual education: This model involves education in a child's native language, typically for no more than three years, to ensure that students do not fall behind in content areas like math, science, and social studies while they are learning English. The ultimate goal is to help students transition to mainstream English-only classrooms as quickly as possible, and the linguistic goal is English acquisition only.

b) Two-way/dual language bilingual education: This model is designed to help both native and the nonnative English speakers become bilingual and biliterate. In this program, when the children are enrolled in a school with English as the medium of instruction, a variety of academic subjects are taught in the students' second language.

c) Late-exit or developmental bilingual education: In this type of model, education is in the child's native language for an extended duration, accompanied by education in English. The goal is to develop bilingualism and biliteracy in both languages.

The transitional bilingual education program is quite common in most of the semirural and rural schools, because a majority of parents—as a result of their limited literacy skills—find it difficult to support the children in second- and third-language literacy-building. Two-way/dual language education has intensified in recent years. But in this program, students learn reading, writing, and higher-order language skills in their mother tongue/regional language or the first language (for example, Kannada in the state of Karnataka). In this type of program, while the second-language classes in English form part of the language learning course, the academic subjects such as math and science are content-oriented rather than grammar-based. While the language classes in the students' first and third languages improve students' comprehension of languages, reading and writing and expressive skills in the other languages generally remain at the base, for the mother-tongue/regional language is often the choice for communication in school. Therefore, the term "triple-language program" appears to be more apt in the context of India.

Although a few principles of each of the above models apply at different phases in the course of bilingual education in India, there most often appears to be a successive use of languages at different stages of education, which Annamalai (1990) refers to as the "successive model of bilingual education." This model is also in conformance with the Three Language Formula (TLF). Although the objectives of the TLF are uniform across the states of India, the curriculum, the quality and the quantity of the language being taught, the grade from which the languages are taught, and the standards for language teaching differ in various states of the country.

Medium of Instruction

While empirical evidence for bilingual education is available in the Western literature to document its effectiveness (cf. the introduction to this volume), in India, there are very few studies to evaluate the process of bilingual education. The Central Institute of Indian Languages at Mysore, Karnataka, India, initiated a few projects in this direction. First, the question of whether learning more languages adds to the cognitive load of learning has been thoroughly examined from the perspectives of parents, students, and teachers. The findings show that learning additional languages as well as learning in second and/or third languages does not increase the cognitive load on a child. Rather, it helps to expand the child's cognitive skills and facilitates better learning. Second, the issue of media of instruction and the impact on educational achievement has been extensively examined. As a consequence of the positive reports from the above two studies, a transfer model of bilingual education to meet the diverse demands of language use as well as to cope with the use of minority languages by switching the medium from one language to another has been proposed (Srivastava & Ramaswamy, 1986).

Bilingual education programs in different countries emphasize the use of the mother tongue as the medium of instruction at least in the initial school years. In the 1970s and 1980s, Indian bilingual education was defined as the use of two languages, one as medium and the other as a subject. Therefore, the role of bilingual education involving the mother tongue as the medium of instruction has been subject to investigation. The studies addressed the question whether mother tongue or English is a better medium of instruction, the results of which indicated that the medium of instruction, per se, did not contribute to the effect of bilingual education, but that variables like academic achievement, intelligence, cognitive abilities, creativity, and personality are also crucial determiners of the effect of bilingual education.

Most of the studies were conducted in the 1970s (Kamakshi, 1965; Srivastava & Khatoon, 1980; and others). These studies reveal contradictory results; hence, there is no common consensus on the medium of instruction:

a) Students from English-language schools showed significantly higher scores in science subjects, as measured by achievement tests, than students taught in their mother tongue.
b) Students who were taught in their mother tongue showed significantly higher scores on achievement tests in all academic subjects than students in English-language schools.
c) There is no significant difference in academic achievement between mother-tongue and other-language students.

A number of studies have reported that education through a medium other than a person's own mother tongue has beneficial effect on the cognition of the child. Anand (1971) compared Kannada and English-medium students (with Kannada as their mother tongue) and found the former to be significantly superior in verbal intelligence and achievement and the latter to be significantly superior in nonverbal intelligence. However, a pilot study conducted by Srivastava & Khatoon (1980) in the schools of Mysore city with eighth-grade students showed that the English-medium students (with Kannada as their mother-tongue) scored significantly better than those taught in Kannada when it came to measures of nonverbal intelligence in addition to three other dimensions of verbal creativity: fluency, flexibility, and originality. However, when school-related measures were controlled, there was hardly any difference between the two streams. The study pointed out the importance of controlling school-related variables in studying the effects of the medium of instruction.

In the light of these findings, Srivastava & Ramaswamy (1986) conducted a large-scale study to examine the influence of bilingual education in which a language other than one's mother tongue is the medium of instruction. The study also examined the effect of socioeconomic status (SES) and gender on personality development, academic achievement, nonverbal intelligence, and verbal creativity. The sample consisted of 19 12-, 13-, and 14-year-old students selected from 11 trilingual Tamil-, Malayalam-, and English-language schools of the Kanyakumari district in the state of Kerala. They studied the effect of medium of instruction under three conditions: same mother-tongue and medium of instruction (Tamil–Tamil), different but cognate mother tongue and medium of instruction (Tamil–Malayalam), and different but noncognate mother-tongue and medium of instruction (Tamil/Malayalam–English). The results suggested that different factors are responsible for better achievement, one of them being English as the medium of instruction. The effect of medium on different academic subjects was, however, not uniform. English as a subject improved in the English-medium students, but in science subjects and creativity the students taught in their mother tongues had an edge over the English-medium students. There was no difference between English and mother-tongue students in social sciences. The results of the study show that higher achievement scores of noncognate (English-medium) students go contrary to the general expectations that mother tongue is the best medium of instruction. This implies that the English-medium students have abundant opportunity to develop as a result of their exposure to second-language English as a subject as well as a medium for other subjects.

Similarly, in a study comparing thinking styles among Hindi-medium students in Bhopal and English-medium students in Australia, it is reported that although there are no overall differences between the two groups, they develop preferential thinking styles (Lynch, Chipman & Pachaury, 1985). In other words, Hindi-medium students are predisposed to divergent thinking, whereas convergent thinking is used by the English-medium students. The above findings suggest that the bilingual educational research should also incorporate other variables that affect success in a specific medium of instruction and should not consider the medium of instruction as the sole variable.

The results of the documented reports do not show consensus on the impact of mother-tongue of instruction vis-à-vis use of English or a non–mother tongue language as the medium of instruction. Having the mother tongue as the medium of instruction would certainly be appealing to those who belong to the lower socioeconomic levels, because enriched contexts in the use of the English language are not easily available to them. However, it need not necessarily be so for the elite population. Yet bilingual education is currently being viewed in India as the continued use of mother tongue and the use of L2 as the medium of instruction, thus emphasizing the pivotal status of the mother tongue in education. However, the issues relating to the medium of instruction cannot be fully answered without taking the overall factors into consideration. Given the changing social and demographic factors, one can predict that the debate about the medium of instruction is bound to be more intensive over the coming years in India. In view of this, large-scale studies on the impact of bilingual education and its types, as well as the medium of instruction as applicable to Indian population, are highly warranted.

EMPIRICAL STUDIES ON BILINGUALISM AND LITERACY IN INDIA

At this juncture, large-scale empirical studies on bilingual children in classrooms in the Indian context appear very crucial. Such studies would be helpful in our understanding of the difficulties encountered by the Indian children in learning different languages with differences in linguistic structures and script features. To the best of the knowledge of the authors, no such large-scale studies have been conducted. In the absence of much-needed classroom-based research on bilingual education and its practice, the authors, who are speech language pathologists by profession, have conducted a few small-scale studies in order to examine certain factors, such as linguistic and orthographic structures, that influence acquisition of literacy in monolingual and bilingual children.

Given the fact that the majority of Indian children are, by virtue of their linguistic and cultural diversity, bilingual or multilingual before their entry into school, a spate of research on acquisition of literacy in a few Indian languages and scripts was reported in the 1990s (Karanth, 1992; Karanth & Prakash, 1996; Prema, 1998; Prema, 2006; and others). Since Indian children are forced to learn two or three languages with differing scripts in schools, it is very interesting to examine the differential skills that either facilitate or interfere in the acquisition of biliteracy.

Katz and Feldman (1983) state that the orthographic depth, or the transparency of the letter–phonology correspondence, plays a major role in deciphering the script. Therefore, children who learn literacy in shallow as well as deep orthography are likely to use differential processing strategies in learning to read in addition to exercising differential cognitive skills in order to be a good reader. For example, Indian children who learn two different types of scripts (alphabetic for English; syllabic/semisyllabic for Indian languages) are required to exercise differential cognitive skills while learning literacy in two or three languages). Finally, it can be said that the researchers find it interesting to study the phenomenon of learning two or three languages and scripts by an Indian child, whereas teachers find it equally challenging to teach literacy to an Indian child.

Phonological Awareness and Literacy

Studies carried out in the early 1990s in Indian languages focused on phonological awareness skills as related to literacy. Gokani (1992) studied phonological awareness in relation to orthographic factors in reading in children from both an English medium and a Gujarati medium. She reported a significant difference in phoneme deletion task between English- and Gujarati-medium children, in favor of English-medium children, but no difference in either the rhyme recognition or syllable segmentation abilities of children exposed to alphabetic or semisyllabic scripts. Prema (1998) conducted a study on 120 children studying in middle grades. She examined the performance of certain linguistic operations that make use of information about the speech sound structure of a given language in Kannada-speaking children studying in a Kannada language medium with English as a second language. Prema (1998)[6] examined, in particular, the role of metalinguistic skill in the acquisition of literacy in Kannada (with a semisyllabic script). She reported that metalinguistic awareness was found to be crucial for acquisition of literacy, whereas phonological awareness appeared to emerge with exposure to alphabetic script in the later grades of upper primary level.

A series of studies were conducted by Prema (1998) (Kannada), Akhila and Prema (2000) (Tamil), and Swaroopa and Prema (2001) and Seetha and Prema (2002) (Malayalam) to examine the influence of script specific features of alphabetic languages such as those of English on Kannada, Tamil, and Malayalam—the three South Indian Dravidian languages having semisyllabic script. Akhila and Prema (2000) reported that the development of rhyming skills in Tamil was not found to parallel syllable deletion as seen in Kannada language (Prema, 1998). On the other hand, Swaroopa and Prema (2001) and Seetha and Prema (2002) found that rhyming and alliteration were potential indicators for adequate reading skills in Malayalam language. The results of the three studies conducted in series indicate that

---

[6]For more details, refer to Prema, K. S. & Karanth, P. (2003). Assessment of learning disability: Language based tests. In Karanth & Rozario (Eds.), *Learning disabilities in India: Willing the mind to learn* (pp. 138-150). New Delhi: Sage Pub.

the literacy-related factors are influenced by the underlying script system. On the basis of the three studies, Prema (2006) proposed that the subclassification of languages should take into consideration not only the linguistic features but also the script-specific features. Besides the above, children undertaking bilingual education, particularly in languages with widely differing features, are likely to exercise differential skills depending on the linguistic and script features. Hence, it is extremely important to sensitize language teachers to the possibility of differential underlying skills as well as the need to focus on training/enhancing the cognitive resources that are necessary for children learning two or three languages/scripts.

The above studies reported that the phonemic awareness is a consequence of learning alphabetic script (say, English) and not a necessary skill for literacy acquisition in semisyllabic script. Alternatively stated, literacy in a semisyllabic system is insufficient for the development of phonemic awareness. Given these differences in the underlying skills necessary for literacy acquisition, an Indian child acquiring literacy in two or three different languages and scripts would have to exercise differential skills depending on the demand necessitated by the language and script employed in the school instruction. Although exposure to languages does facilitate phonological awareness skills, a beginning reader would find it difficult to acquire biliteracy in languages that differ widely from each other unless the teacher becomes sensitive and adapts suitable strategies for teaching languages and script. This, however, calls for intensive efforts to empower teachers to meet the needs of bilingual children.

Cross-Language Transfer of Literacy Skills

The linkage between phonological skills and developing literacy skills is now accepted as relatively uncontroversial even though it is not yet fully understood. This linkage has been studied in monolingual children developing literacy in one language, such as English. In recent years, there has been a considerable amount of research done on bilingual children developing biliteracy skills that suggests cross-language transfer of some of the phonological skills in bilingual children (Cossu, Shankweiler, Liberman, Katz, & Tola, 1988 [Hispanic–English]; Stuart-Smith & Martin, 1999 [Punjabi–English]; Geva & Wang, 2001 [Turkish–English]) as well as positive transfer of literacy skills across languages (e.g., Bialystok, Luk, & Kwan, 2005; Geva & Siegel, 2000; Geva, Wade-Woolley, & Shany, 1997; Oller & Eilers, 2002). The studies, however, emphasized that the subtle phonological skills do vary in children learning literacy in languages with non-alphabetic script from those of children learning alphabetic languages such as English.

Investigations of bilingual–biliterate children examining the issue of cross-language transfer of literacy skills in India with wide linguistic and cultural diversity are, however, very sparse. Shanbal and Prema conducted a series of studies (2006a; 2006b; 2006c) in which they investigated cross-language transfer of phonological skills in bilingual–biliterate children in three South Indian languages. One group of children whose mother tongue was other than Kannada but who were studying in a Kannada medium—Tamil–Kannada (Ta–K)—as well as Telugu–Kannada (Te–K) and Malayalam–Kannada (M–K) children were studied along with another group whose mother tongue and medium of instruction were both Kannada: Kannada–Kannada (K–K). The children were assessed for phonological awareness skills on tests developed by Prema (1998). The results revealed a significant difference in the performance of children between the M–K group and K–K group at 0.05 level of significance. However, there was no significant difference between the Ta–K and K–K group or the Te–K and K–K group. Drawing support from earlier studies, it was speculated that the differential performance among the groups could be attributed to the subtle differences in the linguistic structures of the languages (Prema, 2006). The study offers good potential for planning the medium of instruction and for evolving policies for languages of instruction and teaching strategies to train bilingual–biliterate children in the Indian context.

In their subsequent study on phonological awareness in bilingual–biliterate children (Shanbal & Prema, 2007b), the relationship between phonological awareness and word reading in children learning to be literate in Kannada (semisyllabic) and English (alphabetic) was investigated. Shanbal and Prema assessed 90 children, 30 each from grades 5, 6, and 7, having Kannada as their mother-tongue (L1) and English as their medium of instruction, on measures of phonological awareness, word reading, and nonword reading in both languages. The results revealed that there was cross-language facilitation with phonological awareness in Kannada (L1) contributing to word reading in English (L2). But there was also cross-language facilitation from phonological awareness in English to word and nonword reading in Kannada. This suggests that there is a reciprocal relationship for cross-language facilitation of phonological awareness in L1 to reading in L2 and phonological awareness in L2 to reading in L1 even though L2 is only the language for literacy function.

In the majority of the languages with different script structures, it is reported that the word length (defined as the number of syllables in a word) and the complexity of a word are crucial for reading development in children (Baddeley, Thomson, & Buchanan, 1975; Ziegler, Perry, Jacobs, & Braun, 2001; Perry & Ziegler, 2002; Balota, Cortese, Marshall, Spieler, & Yap, 2004). However, the influence of a nonalphabetic script over an alphabetic script or vice versa in word reading tasks in the course of literacy acquisition is not clearly understood. For this reason, Shanbal and Prema (2006b) investigated the effect of word length and lexicality in bilingual–biliterate children by employing DMDX.[7] A group of 10 bilingual–biliterate children with Kannada as their first-language (L1) learning to read and write English (L2) and a second group of 10 monolingual children with Kannada as their first-language (L1) learning to read and write in Kannada were selected for the study. The results revealed that the performance of children as measured in reaction time (RT) in the Kannada–English (K–E, with English as the medium of instruction) group on the lexical decision task was poorer than in the Kannada–Kannada group (with Kannada as the medium of instruction). In general, the word length vs. lexicality effect was significantly larger in the K–E group than in the K–K group.

Studies have demonstrated the existence of two mental lexicons for the two languages, particularly in late bilinguals (similar to the subjects in the present study). This probably explains the longer reaction time taken for lexical processing by the bilingual children as owing to the inhibitory effect (De Groot, 1992) which slows down the processing speed. Children who become bilinguals after their entry into school (late bilinguals) are more likely to show lexicality effects that might interfere in the process of literacy acquisition, at least in the beginning years. This factor has to be given due attention by teachers in language instructions for bilingual children.

While cross-language transfer of phonological skills and literacy skills are well documented (Altenberg & Cairns, 1983; Beauvillain & Grainger, 1987; Dijkstra & Van Heuven, 1998; Dijkstra, Grainger, & Van Heuven, 1999; Dijkstra, Timmermans, & Schriefers, 2000; Jared & Kroll, 2001), studies that examine the transfer of semantic skills across cognate words in two different languages are scanty. Shanbal and Prema (2006c) further investigated the effect of cross-language transfer on two groups of school-going children (Kannada monolingual and Telugu–Kannada bilingual). Twenty imaginable cognate words with the same phonological structure but differing in meaning in Kannada and Telugu were embedded in twenty meaningful sentences and programmed on DMDX for presentation. The children were required to read the sentence and select the picture on a morpho-syntactic task. The reaction time was measured using DMDX. The results revealed that while both the groups showed similar performance in accuracy on the morphosyntactic task, the bilingual group was found to take a longer time than the monolingual group in learning to read their non-native language, suggesting the likelihood of the process of cross-language transfer from the native language to the nonnative language, leading to

---

[7]DMDX was developed by Kenneth I. Forster and Jonathan C. Forster at Monash University and at the University of Arizona. DMDX is a Win 32-based display system used to measure reaction times to visual and auditory stimuli. Detailed information regarding this software is available at http://www.u.arizona.edu/~kforster/dmdx/dmdx.htm.

delay in response latency. The study gives insights for planning the teaching of bilingual children learning cognate languages.

The results of the series of studies in a few Indian languages indicate that both facilitation and interference effects are evident in bilingual children learning two different languages. Despite the dissimilarity of script features, transfer of skills by way of the facilitation effect seen at the phonological level is, no doubt, an advantage to bilingual children in India. However, in cognate languages, an interference effect is found when deciphering the meaning of words, thus slowing down the processing speed. Large-scale studies of this kind in pairs of school languages of India would be quite helpful for language planners and educational policy makers. Teaching practice with bilingual children can be more effective if the subtle characteristics of languages and scripts are taken into consideration by the language teachers.

Phonological Processing in Bilingual Children

The studies reviewed in the previous section suggested that the acquisition of literacy depends on the processing abilities of children, which are bound to be different in monolingual children than in bilingual children. Studies of the acquisition of literacy in children learning Indian languages with nonalphabetic scripts emphasize the need to consider the script-specific features in teaching languages. Further substantiation of these two premises may be found in a few Indian studies that focused on the phonological processing abilities of bilingual children.

Savithri, Prema, and Shilpashree (2004) investigated monolingual (Kannada) and bilingual (Kannada–English, with the native language being Kannada) children's ability to identify time-warped phonemes/syllables. Twelve pairs of tokens in Kannada were recorded using the external module of CSL 4300B and were warped for double the duration and half the duration using CSL 50. The original and warped token pairs were audio-recorded by either deletion of a phoneme or a syllable in each and then presented to the children for identification and naming of the phoneme/syllable deleted in each token pair. The results indicated significant difference between Kannada–English bilingual children studying in an English medium and monolingual children from a Kannada medium, with the former fairing better than the latter in the identification of both the deleted phonemes and syllables. These results suggest the subtle differences in processing abilities of children not exposed (monolingual) and exposed (bilingual) to English (alphabetic script). The teaching, evaluation, and assessment procedures and instructional practice for monolingual and bilingual children should be designed to take into consideration their differential processing abilities of the features of languages and script.

The studies reviewed so far emphasized the relation among language, script, and acquisition of literacy. It is widely known that bilingual children generally have less proficiency in the nonnative language and therefore encounter difficulties in cognitive subjects such as mathematics and science. In order to plan and evolve adequate methods for educational practice with bilingual children, it is necessary to understand the underlying linguistic components in cognitive subjects. In recent years, cross-language studies and investigations on bilingual/multilingual children have suggested that efficiency in processing digits and number words differ from language to language. The variations are accounted for the structural aspects of given languages. Literature reveals that number word processing in L1 is better than in L2 in bilinguals, attributed to differences in cognitive functions involved in learning L1 and L2.

Studies of digits and number word processing indicate that the differences in processing are not only at the feature level but also at the higher levels of language. For example, the majority of the studies have reported differences in cognitive linguistic phenomena for processing digits and number words (Ellis & Hennelly, 1980; Stigler, Lee, & Stevenson, 1986; Brysbaert & Dhondt, 1991; Neath, 1998; Bernado, 2001). These studies suggest that there are differences in processing at the semantic level between monolingual and bilingual children. Such differences do affect the learning of cognitive subjects such as science and mathematics. A few small-scale studies employing digits and number words examined the reaction time (Dheepa, Sreedevi, & Prema, 2005), digit span (Anjali, Savitha, & Prema, 2006; Anitha, Anjali, Savitha, & Prema, 2007), and semantic aspects in statement problems (Sumitha, Shwetha, & Prema, 2005) involved in processing by Kannada–English bilingual children.

In the above studies, the Kannada–English bilingual children showed better span for digits compared to number words, but a longer reaction time. However, there was a significant difference in the reaction time for processing digits and number words in each of the languages, with the performance of bilingual children being better for number words in English than in Kannada. Although the bilinguals are second-language learners of English, they performed better on L2 tasks, such as English number words. This may be attributed to the linguistic complexity of the Kannada language. Since some of the Kannada number words have longer syllable length than English (9 in English is the monosyllabic word "nine" but the trisyllabic word "ombattu" in Kannada), the processing of number words by way of a language-dependent route takes a few milliseconds more than the processing of digits by way of a direct route (Campbell, 1994; Dheepa, Sreedevi, & Prema, 2005; Frenck-Mestre & Vaid, 1993; Marsh & Maki, 1976; McClain & Huang, 1982). The Kannada number words appear to have imposed a greater load on working memory (Baddeley & Hitch, 1974; Baddeley, 2000; Anjali, Savitha, & Prema, 2006). Bilingual children who use more than one verbal code for number processing are likely to have a differential load on their working memory. While the numerical notation is translinguistic and is independent of language, the number words seem to be language-dependent. The fact that bilinguals who are second-language learners of English performed better on L2 tasks—i.e., on English number words—suggests that the nature of processing should be taken into consideration while teaching bilingual children cognitive subjects such as mathematics.

The differential skills of monolingual and bilingual children in number word processing also have their impact on higher-level mathematical problem-solving such as that of statement problems (word problems). Sumitha, Shwetha, and Prema (2005) examined comprehension of statement problems in bilingual children (with the mother tongue being one of the Indian languages) from grades 4 and 5 studying in an English medium. Statement problems were prepared using homophonous words and non-homophonous words, keeping as reference the curriculum of language and mathematics of grades 4 and 5. The selected words were incorporated in the statement problems—for example, "some"/"sum"; "tense"/"tens." The bilingual children faired poorly on the homophonous words when compared to the nonhomophonous words. The bilingual children found it difficult to extract the right sense of the homophonous words, suggesting a high possibility of interaction between language and mathematics, an important factor to be considered by both language teachers and teachers of cognitive subjects.

The studies on the phonological awareness and phonological processing, cross-language transfer of phonological and semantic skills, and processing of numbers and digits by monolingual and bilingual–biliterate children, in general, suggests that it is necessary to give due consideration to the structural differences of the languages of instruction as well as the proficiency of children in L2 when designing teaching strategies for classroom practice with bilingual children. More such studies with other Indian languages would enlighten the educators, helping them reframe their teaching practices.

CHALLENGES FOR EFFECTIVE BILINGUAL EDUCATION IN THE INDIAN CONTEXT

As stated earlier, India is a land of diverse cultures and multiple languages. The Indian subcontinent consists of innumerable linguistic communities, each of which might share a common culture. The people of India speak many languages and dialects. It is reported that schools across India teach in 58 different languages as suitable for each community's needs. Review of literacy development in India suggests clear goals for improving literacy with proposals for national educational policies. But strategies for enhancing literacy skills in bilingual children or a bilingual curriculum to enhance teacher sensitivity and skills to teach bilingual children in classroom are not clearly spelled out in national educational policies.

One of the major challenges appears to be inadequacies in teacher empowerment programs to meet the needs of bilingual children. In 1987–1988, District Institutes of Education and Training (DIETs) were set up in each district through which preservice and in-service training for secondary teachers were provided. Again, there was not much emphasis on teacher orientation to the needs of bilingual children in classrooms, whether in the preservice or in the in-service teacher training curriculum. As a consequence of the introduction of the Three Language Formula (TLF), there has been an intense effort by the NCTE and NCERT to frame curriculum for teachers that includes classroom teaching methods as well as language teacher orientation on the methodology in language teaching. Despite these efforts at the national level, there appears to be a large gap between what is prescribed or suggested and what is practiced.

Another major challenge has to do with the language of instruction. Traditionally, language instruction through the mother tongue has been repeatedly emphasized as the most appropriate way of working with preschool children. However, consequent to an increase in the socially and economically upward mobile families, there is a legitimate desire on the part of parents to send their children to English-medium schools and thus in majority of the semiurban and urban schools, the medium of instruction is invariably English. A small-scale survey was conducted of parents with the objective of knowing the native language, the language used for communication at home, and the language used in school by children taught in an English medium (Shanbal & Prema, 2007a). The results of the survey revealed that majority of children (90.6 percent) use their native language in the school for communication. Although they are enrolled in an English-medium school, English is used only for literacy-related activities. Only 9.4 percent of children used English for communication in school. All parents (100 percent) reported that English was the language used in school to teach literacy skills; 98.1 percent of the parents (all but the 1.9 percent made up of Hindi-speaking parents) used English at home only to teach literacy skills. The survey suggests that when the native language is not the language of instruction, the use of the nonnative language gets restricted to the school environment, with the native/local language predominant for other communicative purposes. In school, language teaching practices are so designed that the students learn languages through subjects rather than learning subjects through languages. Consequently, students fare poorly both in subjects as well as languages.

With regard to the preparation of language textbooks, it is observed that the principles followed in the preparation of subject textbooks are not applied satisfactorily to the production of language textbooks. "It must be remembered that English, as a supplement to mother tongue education is strength; as a substitute is debilitation" (Pattanayak, n.d.). Therefore, it is suggested that necessary minimum competence level in languages should be ensured as a precondition to the study of subjects, and that the preparation of language textbooks receive top priority by the educational authorities. Language teaching is not looked upon as a unified concept to understand and practice, but rather teaching each language is considered an autonomous activity. There are no similarities or commonalities in the methods used to teach or to improve language education.

Recognizing the immense need for teacher empowerment, in order to facilitate/empower language teachers, two national institutes of India—the Central Institute for English and Foreign Languages (CIEFL) and the Central Institute of Indian Languages (CIIL)—conduct programs for teachers to enable them to learn Indian and foreign languages as second/additional languages. While CIEFL focuses on training teachers in English and other foreign languages, the Central Institute of Indian Languages (CIIL) located at Mysore, Karnataka, has the objective of training teachers, in addition to other categories of professionals, in Indian languages other than the trainees' native languages. CIIL has imparted Indian languages as second/additional languages to 10,885 teachers to date (personal e-mail communication, dated August 9, 2008). The two institutions together facilitate teachers' handling of bilingual children in classrooms by imparting knowledge of Indian and foreign languages in teachers. Considering the enormity of bilingual children in schools and the number of schools and teachers in the country, intensive efforts are called for at the national level to impart similar training to all preservice and in-service teachers.

Another crucial issue for India is the recruitment of teachers to meet the needs of bilingual/multilingual children. There is no mandate to ensure language proficiency of teachers who teach children in bilingual medium. This leads to problems in teacher–student communication. Although the majority of teachers in the higher secondary schools have postgraduate qualifications and teaching experience ranging from 10–15 years and more, they reported that shifting to English as a medium of instruction has posed problems in classrooms. The State Council of Educational Research and Training (SCERT) of Kerala organized training of higher secondary teachers at the state level. Communicative English was dealt with in the training program. Similar training programs are also being held to empower teachers to teach other languages like Hindi and Tamil. The training programs also covered aspects such as the impact of bilingualism on achievement in the mother tongue, educating bilingual children, providing opportunities for expressing in the mother tongue in bilingual situations, and use of colloquial language for education (SCERT, Kerala, Annual Report, 1999–2000). Similar programs at the national level are highly warranted.

Teacher education in India, by and large, is conventional in its nature and purpose. The integration of theory and practice and consequent curricular response to the requirements of the school system has remained inadequate. Teachers are prepared in competencies and skills that do not necessarily equip them for becoming professionally effective with bilingual children. Their familiarity with latest developments in research remains insufficient. Several of the skills acquired and methodologies learned are seldom practiced in the actual school system. This highlights the need to bring realism and dynamism into curriculum. As a result, curriculum reconstruction has been focused at addressing some perceptible gaps in teacher education. Yet the revised curriculum does not also have components to prepare teachers to handle bilingual children in classrooms, and neither is there any move toward equipping teachers to evaluate bilingual children's classroom performance. The time is now ripe for concerned authorities to take a serious look at this issue in order to strengthen educational practice as regards the challenging bilingual population in India.

Major factors prevailing in the Indian context that pose challenges for promotion of literacy activities arise both from within the community as well as from the administrative systems. Since the community is so diverse in its cultures, languages, and literacy levels, one can hardly envision strategies that fit multiple groups of people and communities. The educational system and the government also pose additional challenges at many levels. The National Policy in Education, the dearth of resources (be it financial, knowledge-based, or attitudinal) for teacher training, inadequate emphasis on early childhood education, and low levels of awareness about the significance of early childhood education are some of the important factors that need to be addressed if India is to meet its mission—"Education for All"—successfully by 2015 (Prema, 2008).

SUMMARY

The issue of bilingualism and biliteracy has received much attention in the recent decades all over the world. Many monolingual countries invest a great deal in order to develop into "bilingual" nations (Reed, 2003). India is fortunate enough to inherit language diversity in its population and thus sincere efforts should be made to nurture bilingualism. In this unique situation in which many languages and dialects exist, bilingualism and biliteracy in school get further enriched in an additive manner[8] by virtue of national

---

[8] The term additive bilingualism refers to the form of bilingualism that results when students add a second language to their intellectual tool-kit while continuing to develop conceptually and academically in their first language (Cummins, 2000).

education policies such as the Three Language Formula (TLF) for school education. Therefore, instead of the term "biliteracy," it seems appropriate to embrace the term "multiple literacies" to address most of the questions and concerns raised in this chapter with reference to complexity of languages, distinctness of script features, media of instruction, and national policies for education. Nurturing bilingualism and biliteracy requires a comprehensive analysis of the educational system, national policies, and existing educational practices as regard bilingual/multilingual children in India.

The general notion among educationists and researchers is that children will not learn academic subject material if they fail to understand the language of instruction. But language acquisition studies have repeatedly emphasized the cognitive advantage that is available for bilingual/multilingual children. Since cognition, language, and literacy go hand-in-hand, there are bound to be advantages that bilingual/multilingual children have over monolingual children in the development of cognition and literacy. While the monolingual countries try to build up bilingual community by way of literacy activities through programs such as immersion in L2, the Indian children are immersed in two or more languages right from their early childhood by virtue of their country's cultural and linguistic diversity. Therefore, such notions may not entirely apply in the Indian context.

Khurana and Prema (2008) conducted a survey in Mysore city to evaluate the emergent literacy experiences of 140 preschool children in their home environment. The subjects for this survey were parents of native Kannada-speaking children studying in preschools having English as the medium of instruction. They found that 69.1 percent of parents provided adequate emergent literacy experiences to their children through storytelling, storybook reading, print awareness, and oral language activities. The parents preferred Kannada for oral activities like daily conversation and storytelling and English for reading storybooks and other reading and writing activities. Shanbal and Prema (2007a) also reported similar findings in schoolgoing children, supporting the premise that immersion in L2 is unwritten law embraced in India's social structure.

The proficiency in languages in which literacy skills are acquired is also highly debated from the theoretical point of view. Studies carried out on predominantly monolingual children from the West state that a child must attain a certain level of proficiency in both the native and second-language in order to accrue the beneficial aspects of bilingualism. On the contrary, those carried out in countries with bilingual children state a positive association between additive bilingualism and students' linguistic, cognitive, and academic growth—for example, in French–English, Irish–English, and Ukrainian–English bilinguals (Cummins, 1979). Some of the studies reported of Indian children also substantiate that bilingualism and multilingualism offer linguistic, academic, and cognitive growth. The educational implication of these findings is that the development of literacy in two or more languages entails linguistic and academic benefits.

Comparative study at the All India Institute of Speech and Hearing, Mysore, India, of children exposed predominantly to one language (monolinguals) in comparison with those exposed to multiple languages (multilinguals) has revealed that multilingual children fare significantly better in their cognitive skills and comprehension of language than monolingual children do (Prema & Geetha, 2005). The differences in linguistic structures and features of speech sounds of Indian languages and English (the language learned in school) invariably turn out to be advantageous to the children, who exercise different types of metalinguistic and metaphonological skills while learning two or more languages. Exposing children to English right from their preschool years or even before should therefore be viewed as a positive influence on success in literacy (Prema, 2006).

Per the 1991 census, India has around 150 million children below the age of six years, constituting 17.5 percent of India's population. The parents have a right to choose the medium of instruction.[9] Being a multilingual country, there are many languages to choose for the medium of instruction. Despite knowledge of the advantages of exposure to two or more languages in Early Child Education (ECE), policymaking to this end at the national level seems to be inadequate. Without a policy of compulsory preschool education, policies and practices for preschool children from bilingual environment appears to be a remote possibility in the near future. The discrepancy in the demand vs. supply of quality education in bilingual medium is an important issue to be pursued if India has to meet the vision and mission of "Education for All."

The National Curriculum Framework for School Education: A Discussion Document, released on January 1, 2000, states that "[i]n a number of states/organizations/boards, however, the spirit of the formula has not been followed"[10] and the mother tongue of the people has been denied the status of the first language because of the changed socioeconomic scenario, causing the difference between the second and third languages to dwindle. Thus for all intents there may be two second languages. Some states follow only a two-language formula, whereas in some others, classical languages like Sanskrit and Arabic are being studied in lieu of a modern Indian language. Some boards/institutions permit even European languages like French and German in place of Hindi. In this scenario, the Three Language

---

[9] The right to education is a fundamental right that includes the right to choose the medium of instruction can be exercised by the parents on behalf of their children (April 20, 2000: Madras High Court).

[10] Tamil Nadu (state) and Pondicherry (UT) are following the two-language formula of teaching Tamil and English.

Formula exists only in curriculum documents and other policy statements. Although the Three Language Formula is the strategy and goal of Indian multilingual situation, it is necessary to subject the policy to microexamination in view of the empirical studies reviewed earlier in this chapter.

In our small-scale studies cited in this chapter, significant findings were observed in the performance of bilingual/multilingual children as regards constructs such as phonological processing, phonological awareness, digits and number word processing, cross-language transfer of literacy related skills, and processing of cognate languages. These constructs influence literacy learning in the preschool and school years and thus should be given much weight in this time of evolving national policies for education as well as framing national curriculum for children. Furthermore, it is very crucial to sensitize all preservice and in-service teachers to the subtleties and nuances of literacy-related constructs so that optimal education can be imparted to bilingual/multilingual children.

The challenges of bilingual education can be successfully met if we take suitable measures to reduce the dropout rates of school children. In spite of significant attempts to reduce the numbers of school dropouts, around 40 percent of children drop out before completing grade 5, and 70 percent drop out before completing high school. If the dropout rate is to be reduced, the system of education in India should gear up to meet the requirements of bilingual and multilingual children—among many other factors.

The quantitative expansion of the educational system that happened in the post-independent period should be followed by a concerted effort to experiment with new approaches to education, particularly for bilingual and multilingual children. The need of the hour is to restructure the education system to meet the challenges of the 21st century. Among the several approaches to achieve this objective, it is important to equip prospective school children and preschool children with prerequisite skills for learning—i.e., imparting emergent and early literacy skills and choosing language in consultation with researchers, forerunners in the education system, and the public. Moreover, it is equally important to reframe the curricular structure for teacher training programs to meet the above objectives. In a nutshell, it can be said that the situation in India is very complex and thus extremely challenging to language planners.

National language policies have a significant impact on language development and literacy acquisition in school children. While there is little research that has examined the relationship between language policies and literacy acquisition in typically developing children in schools, understanding of the acquisition of language and literacy in bilingual–biliterate children and children with special needs from bilingual/multilingual backgrounds (for example, children with hearing impairment) who form linguistic minority groups is much more limited. Therefore, it is also essential to take into consideration the special population of children whose needs are different from those of mainstream children while framing national policies for education.

Bilingual instructional programs should be integrated with language instruction so that students acquire the academic content of science, math, social studies, art, and other related courses and do it in the target language. Language proficiency should be fostered by developing critical awareness for language by encouraging students to compare and contrast their languages (e.g., phonics conventions, grammar, cognates), providing students with extensive opportunities to carry out projects investigating their own and their community's language use, practices, and assumptions. In summary, it can be said that instructions in a bilingual/multilingual program should be geared to provide adequate input on the content and the language in question as well as providing opportunities to use all the languages offered in the school environment for both communication and literacy.

Thus, there is an immense need to emphasize the importance of high-quality training to India's teachers of young children—training that will focus on curricular and intervention strategies to promote literacy and strategies to teach, monitor, and assess monolingual and bilingual children's academic outcomes. Empowerment of in-service teachers by offering additional requisite skills with specially designed courses through a correspondence model (whether by conventional distance education and learning or through virtual classrooms) appears to be the best option. The availability of technology for this mode of skill delivery facilitates a large number of teachers, thus speeding up the entire process. Reorienting education to improve quality outcomes requires an education system geared to meet the challenges posed by the special population of India.

In light of the peculiarities of the situation, is it possible to promote literacy and biliteracy in India? In addition to the issue of bilingualism and multilingualism, what other challenges should be met by India in order to promote biliteracy/multiliteracy? Is it feasible to draw uniform principles and strategies to promote biliteracy/multiliteracy skills in a country where there is no standard language, culture, or system? High-quality education facilitating knowledge and cognitive skills within a safe, learner-friendly environment is a significant challenge even in highly resourced countries, but it is high time that India plan and propose ideas and activities for public education, teacher education, and education programs for policymakers. There is also an urgent need to incorporate curricular changes in teacher education and devise courses to train teachers for designing and implementing literacy activities in the classroom, particularly with bilingual/multilingual children.

An overview of linguistic diversity, the system of education, a few limitations in the implementation of the national policies for education, lack of consensus among the apex bodies involved in the educational administration, and existing programs for teacher education and empowerment have provided a brief background to India and its education system, along with the challenges posed by the culturally and linguistically diverse population of India. At this juncture, it is essential for India to review, to revise, and to adopt fresh approaches for early childhood education as well as for teacher empowerment. Such an approach can facilitate literacy in all children, bilingual children included, thereby achieving the goal of Education for All (EFA) by 2015.

REFERENCES

Aggarwal, J. C. (1992). *History and philosophy of pre-primary and nursery education.* New Delhi: Doaba House.

Akhila, P. & Prema, K. S. (2000). Phonological awareness and orthographic skills in Tamil speaking children. Unpublished master's dissertation submitted to the University of Mysore, Mysore.

Altenberg, E. P. & Cairns, H. S. (1983). The effects of phonotactic constraints on lexical processing in bilingual and monolingual participants. *Journal of Verbal Learning and Verbal Behavior, 22,* 174–188.

Anand, V. S. (1971). In D. P Pattanayak. *Research in language education: A trend report.* Retrieved June 3, 2008, from http://education.nic.in/cd50years/g/Z/9I/0Z9I0E01.htm.

Anjali, G., Savitha, S., & Prema, K. S. (2006). Digit span: Does language play a role? Paper presented at the National Conference organized by the Indian Speech and Hearing Association (ISHA 38), February 3–5, Ahmedabad, India.

Anitha, T , Anjali, G., Savitha, S., & Prema, K. S. (2007). Visual number processing in bilingual children with dyslexia. Paper presented at the 40th National Conference of the Indian Speech and Hearing Association, India.

Annamalai, E. (1986). The sociolinguistic scene in India. *Sociolinguistics, 16*(1), 2–8.

Annamalai, E. (1990). Dimensions of bilingual education in India. *New Language Planning Newsletter, 4*(4), 1–3.

Baddeley, A. D. (2000). Working memory and language processing. In B. E. Dimitrova & K. Hyltenstam (Eds.). *Language processing and simultaneous interpreting: Interdisciplinary perspectives* (pp. 1–16). Amsterdam: Benjamins Translation Library.

Baddeley, A., & Hitch, G. (1974). Working memory. In G. Bower (Ed.). *The Psychology of Learning and Motivation* (pp. 47–89). London: Elsevier Academic Press.

Baddeley, A. D., Thomson, N., & Buchanan, M. (1975). Word length and the structure of short-term memory. *Journal of Verbal Learning and Verbal Behavior, 14,* 575–589.

Balota, D. A., & Cortese, M., Sergent-Marshall, S. D., Spieler, D., & Yap, M. (2004). Visual word recognition of single syllable words. *Journal of Experimental Psychology: General, 133,* 283–316.

Beauvillain, C. & Grainger, J. (1987). Accessing interlexical homographs: Some limitations of a language selective access. *Journal of Memory and Language, 26,* 658–627.

Bernado, A. B. (2001). Asymmetric activation of number codes in bilinguals: Further evidence for the encoding complex model of number processing, *Memory and Cognition* (7), 968–978.

Bialystok, E. & Hakuta, K. (1994). *In other words: The psychology of science of second language acquisition.* New York: Basic Books.

Bialystok, E., Luk, G., & Kwan, E. (2005). Bilingualism, biliteracy, and learning to read: Interactions among languages and writing systems. *Scientific Studies of Reading, 9*(1), 43–61.

Brysbaert, M. & Dhondt, A. (1991). The syllable-length effect in number processing is task dependent. *Percept Psychophysiology, 50*(5), 449–458.

Campbell, R. N. (1994). *Korean/English Bilingual Immersion Project: Title VII developmental bilingual education evaluation report year two, 1993–1994.* Federal Grant #T003C20062-93.

Census India. (2001). Retrieved June 4, 2008, from http://www.censusindia.net.

Cossu, G., Shankweiler, D., Liberman, I. S., Katz, L., & Tola, G. (1988). Awareness of phonological segments and reading ability in Italian children. *Applied Psycholinguistics, 9*(1), 1–16.

Cummins, J. (1979). Linguistic interdependence and the educational development of bilingual children. *Review of Educational Research, 49,* 222–251.

De Groot, A. M. B. (1992). Bilingual lexical representation: A closer look at conceptual representations. In R. Frost & L. Katz (Eds.), *Orthography, phonology, morphology, and meaning* (pp. 389–412). Amsterdam: Elsevier.

Dheepa, D., Sreedevi, M., & Prema, K. S. (2005). Digit vs. number word processing in bilinguals. Paper presented at the International Conference of South Asian Languages, Tamil Nadu, India.

Dijkstra, A. & Van Heuven, W. J. B. (1998). The BIA model and bilingual word recognition. In J. Grainger & A. Jacobs (Eds.), *Localist connectionist approaches to human cognition* (pp. 189–225). Hillsdale, NJ: Erlbaum.

Dijkstra, T., Grainger, J., & Van Heuven, W. J. B. (1999). Recognition of cognates and interlingual homographs: The neglected role of phonology. *Journal of Memory and Language, 41,* 496–518.

Dijkstra, T., Timmermans, M., & Schriefers, H. (2000). On being blinded by your other language: Effects of task demands on interlingual homograph recognition. *Journal of Memory and Language, 42,* 445–464.

DISE (2005–2006). Retrieved June 6, 2008, from http://www.ncte-in.org.

Ellis, N. C. & Hennelly, R. A. (1980). A bilingual word-length effect: Implications for intelligence testing and the relative ease of mental calculations in Welsh and English. *British Journal of Psychology, 71,* 43–52.

Frenck-Mestre, C. & Vaid, J. (1993). Activation of number facts in bilinguals. *Memory and Cognition, 21,* 809–818.

Geva, E., Wade-Woolley, L., & Shany, M. (1997). Development of reading efficiency in first and second language. *Scientific Studies of Reading, 1,* 119–144.

Geva, E. & Siegel, L. (2000). Orthographic and cognitive factors in the concurrent development of basic reading skills in two languages. *Reading and Writing, 12,* 1–30.

Geva, E. & Wang, M. (2001). The development of basic reading skills in children: A cross language perspective. *Annual Review of Applied Linguistics, 21,* 182–204.

Gokani, V. P. (1992). The orthographic factor in phonological awareness with relation to reading. In M. Jayaram & S. R. Savithri (Eds.), research at AIISH, dissertation abstracts: Volume 3, D 236, (pp. 47–48), AIISH, Mysore, India.

Jared, D. & Kroll, J. (2001). Do bilinguals activate phonological representations in one or both of their languages when naming words? *Journal of Memory and Language, 44*, 2–31.

Kamakshi (1965). In D. P. Pattanayak, *Research in language education: A trend report.* Retrieved June 3, 2008, from http://education.nic.in/cd50years/g/Z/9I/0Z9I0E01.htm.

Karanth, P. (1992). Developmental dyslexia in bilingual-biliterates. *Reading and Writing: An Interdisciplinary Journal, 4*, 297–306.

Karanth, P. & Prakash, P. (1996). A developmental investigation of onset, progress and stages in the acquisition of literacy. Project funded by NCERT, India.

Katz, L. & Feldman, L. B. (1983). Relation between pronunciation and recognition of printed words in deep and shallow orthographies. *Journal of Experimental Psychology: Learning, Memory and Cognition, 9*, 157–166.

Kaur, B. (2004). "Keeping the infants of coolies out of harm's way": Raj, Church, and infant education in India, 1830–51. *Contemporary Issues in Early Childhood, 5*(2), 221–235.

Khurana, S. & Prema, K. S. (2008). Emergent literacy experiences at home: A sample survey in Mysore city. *Language in India, 8,* .

Koul, O. N. (2006). A survey of language preferences in education in India, *Language in India, 6*(3). Retrieved July 3, 2008, from http://www.languageinindia.com.

Kothari, B. & Joshi, A. (2002). Benchmarking early literacy skills: Developing a tool. *Economic and Political Weekly, 37*(34), 3497–3499.

Lynch, P. P., Chipman, H. H., & Pachaury, A. C. (1985). In D. P. Pattanayak (Ed.), *Research in language education: A trend report* (pp.). Retrieved June 3, 2008, from http://education.nic.in/cd50years/g/Z/9I/0Z9I0E01.htm.

Mallikarjun, B. (2001a). Languages of India According to the 1991 Census. *Language in India*, 1(7).

Mallikarjun, B. (2001b). Language(s) in the school curriculum: Challenges of the new millennium. *Language in India, 1*(4). Retrieved June 3, 2008, from http://www.languageinindia.com.

Mallikarjun, B. (2004). Indian multilingualism, language policy and the digital divide. *Language in India, 4*(4). Retrieved June 3, 2008, from http://www.languageinindia.com.

Marsh, L. & Maki, R. (1976) Efficiency of arithmetic operations in bilinguals as a function of language. *Memory and Cognition, 4*, 459–464.

McClain, L. & Huang, J. (1982). Speed of simple arithmetic in bilinguals. *Memory and Cognition, 10*, 591–596.

Mohanty, A. K. (1994). Bilingualism in a multilingual society: Implications for cultural integration and education. Keynote address in the XXIII International Congress of Applied Psychology, Madrid, Spain.

National Council of Educational Research and Training (2005). *National Curriculum Framework for School Education* Retrieved from http://www.ncert.nic.in/html/schoolcurriculum.htm.

National Policy on Education (University Grants Commission, 1968, 1986). Retrieved June 6, 2008, from http://www.ugc .ac.in/policy/npe86.html.

Neath, I. (1998). *Human memory: An introduction to research, data and theory.* Pacific Grove, CA: Brooks/Cole.

Obler, L. (1984) Dyslexia in bilinguals. In R. Malatesha & H. A. Whitaker (Eds.), *Dyslexia: A global issue* (pp. 339–356). The Hague: Martinus Nijhoff Publishers.

Oller, D. K. & Eilers, R. E. (Eds.). (2002). *Language and literacy in bilingual children.* Clevedon: Multilingual Matters.

Pandit, P. B. (1972). *India as a sociolinguistic area.* Pune: University of Pune.

Pang, E. & Kamil, M. (2004). Second language issues in early literacy and instruction in early childhood education. In O. Saracho & B. Spodek (Eds.), *Contemporary perspectives on language policy and literacy instruction in early childhood education* (pp. 29–56). Greenwich, CT: Information Age Publishing.

Pattanayak, D. P. (n.d.). *Research in language education: A trend report.* Retrieved June 3, 2008, from http://education.nic.in/cd50years/g/Z/9I/0Z9I0E01.htm.

Perry, C. & Ziegler, J. C. (2002). On the nature of phonological assembly: Evidence from backward masking. *Language and Cognitive Processes, 17*(1), 31–59.

Prema, K. S. (1998). Reading acquisition profile in Kannada. Unpublished doctoral thesis submitted to University of Mysore, India.

Prema, K. S. & Geetha, Y. V. (2005). Language acquisition in multilingual children: Project report. Project funded by AIISH Research Fund, All India Institute of Speech and Hearing, Mysore, India.

Prema, K. S. (2006). Reading acquisition in Dravidian languages. *International Journal of Dravidian Linguistics, 35*(1), 111–126.

Prema, K. S. (2008). What concrete challenges have countries faced in implementing policies and programmes to tackle exclusion? EFA Global Monitoring Report. Retrieved from UNESCO.org/EFA-GMR.htm. http://www.unesco.org/education/GMR/2007/Draft-for-EFAGMR-2008.doc

Reed, T. (2003). The literacy acquisition of Black and Asian "English as additional language" (EAL) learners: Anti-racist assessment and intervention challenges. In L. Peer & G. Reid (Eds.), *Multilingualism, literacy and dyslexia: A challenge for educators* (pp. 111–119). London: David Fulton Publishers.

Savithri, S. R., Prema, K. S., & Shilpashre, H. N. (2004). Performance of learning disabled children on time-warped words in phoneme/syllable stripped condition. Frontiers of Research on Speech and Music (FRSM), ITC Sangeet Research Academy, Kolkata and Center for Advanced Study in Linguistics (CASL), Annamalai University, Tamil Nadu.

Seetha, L. & Prema, K. S. (2002). Reading acquisition in Malayalam: A profile of secondary graders. Unpublished master's dissertation submitted to the University of Mysore, Mysore.

Shanbal, J. C. & Prema, K. S. (2006a). Phonological skills in bilingual-biliterate children: Cross-language transfer within Dravidian languages of India. *Language Forum, 32,* 1–2, 125–145.

Shanbal, J. C. & Prema, K. S. (2006b). Word length and orthographic complexity in bilingual-biliterate children: An investigation in reading Kannada Presented at 34th All India Conference for Dravidian Linguists, Trivandrum, India.

Shanbal, J. C. & Prema, K. S. (2006c). Cross-language transfer in bilingual children—effect on literacy in a second-language? Presented at 2006 Second Language Research Forum Conference, University of Washington, Seattle, USA.

Shanbal, J. C. & Prema, K. S. (2007a). Languages of school-going children: A sample survey in Mysore. *Language in India, 7.*

Shanbal, J. C. & Prema, K. S. (2007b). Phonological awareness and reading in bilingual-biliterate children. Presented at the 35th All India Conference for Dravidian Linguists, Mysore, India.

Sharma, J. C. (2001a). Multilingualism in India, *Language in India, 1,* 8. Retrieved June 3, 2008, from http://www.languageinindia.com.

Sharma, J. C. (2001b). Indian multilingualism: A historical perspective. *Language in India, 1.* Retrieved June 2, 2008, from http://www.languageinindia.com.

Srivastava, A. K. & Khatoon, R. (1980). Effect of difference between mother tongue and other tongue as medium of instruction on achievement, mental ability, and creativity of VIII Standard children. In E. Annamalai (Ed.), *Bilingualism and achievement in school* (pp. 1–2). Mysore, India: Central Institute of Indian Languages.

Srivastava, A. K. & Ramaswamy, K. (1986). In M. S. Padma, *Research in correlates of achievement: A trend report.* Retrieved June 3, 2008, from http://education.nic .in/cd50years/g/Z/9I/0Z9I0J01.htm.

State Council of Educational Research & Training (1999). *Annual report.* Retrieved from http://www.scert.kerala.gov.in/archives.htm.

Stigler, J. W., Lees, S-Y., & Stevenson, H. W. (1990). *Mathematical knowledge: Mathematical knowledge of Japanese, Chinese, and American elementary school children.* Reston, VA: National Council of Teachers of Mathematics.

Stuart-Smith, J. & Martin, D. (1999). Developing assessment procedures for phonological awareness for use with Punjabi-English bilingual children. *The International Journal of Bilingualism, 3,* 1, 55–80.

Sumitha, M. M., Shwetha, P., & Prema, K. S. (2005). Language of mathematics or mathematics of language? Paper presented at the National Conference of Indian Speech and Hearing Association, India.

Swaroopa, K. P. & Prema, K. S. (2001). Checklist for screening language based reading disabilities (Che-SLR). Unpublished master's dissertation submitted to the University of Mysore, Mysore.

Tzeng, O. J. L. & Hung, D. L. (1981). Linguistic determinism: A written language perspective. In O. J. L. Tzeng & H. Singer (Eds.), *Perception of print: Reading research in experimental psychology* (pp. 237–255). Hillsdale, NJ: Erlbaum.

University Grants Commission (1968). *National Policy on Education.* Retrieved June 6, 2008, from http://www.ugc.ac.in/policy/npe86.html.

Wong-Fillmore, L. & Valadez, C. (1986). Teaching bilingual learners. In M. Wittrock (Ed.), *Handbook on research on teaching* (pp. 648–685). Washington, D.C.: American Educational Research Association.

Ziegler, J. C., Perry, C., Jacobs, A. M., & Braun, M. (2001). Identical words are read differently in different languages. *Psychological Science, 12,* 379–384.

CHAPTER 6

MAKING CHOICES FOR SUSTAINABLE SOCIAL PLURILINGUALISM: SOME REFLECTIONS FROM THE CATALAN LANGUAGE AREA[1]

F. Xavier Vila i Moreno
Universitat de Barcelona/Institut d'Estudis Catalans, Spain

A COMPLEX HISTORY OF LANGUAGE-IN-EDUCATION POLICIES

Catalan is a Romance language—i.e., closely related to Occitan, French, Italian, and Spanish. It is the autochthonous language of a geographical area divided among Spain, France, Andorra, and Italy. In Spain, the

[1] This paper has been made possible by the support of the Spanish Ministery of Education and Science for the research project RESOL: Resocialization and Languages: The Linguistic Effects of the Passage from Primary to Secondary Education (HUM2006-05860) and the support of the Catalan Ministry for the Consolidated research Group on Language Variation; (2009 SGR 521).

International Perspectives on Bilingual Education: Policy, Practice, and Controversy, pages 131–152
131

historical Catalan language area covers the autonomous communities[2] of Catalonia; most of Valencia (also called the Valencian Country or Valencian Community); the Balearic Islands; a stretch of land in Aragon on the border with Catalonia, known as La Franja; and a handful of hamlets in Murcia Region known as *Carxe/Carche*. In France, Catalan is the historical language of the Department of Eastern Pyrenees (Catalunya Nord in Catalan), also known as Rosselló/Roussillon. Catalan is the historical and sole official language of Andorra, the small independent state in the Pyrenees. Finally, Catalan has also been the traditional language of the Sardinian city of Alghero (l'Alguer in Catalan), in Italy, since the fourteenth century.

Catalan derives from the Latin imported two thousand years ago by Roman settlers to what is now Catalonia, Andorra, and Northern Catalonia.[3] In the thirteenth century, Catalan spread to Valencia and Balearic Islands after they were conquered and annexed to the dual crown formed by Catalonia and Aragon. The language became standardized and flourished between the thirteenth and fifteenth centuries. But by the turn of the fifteenth century, Catalan passed from being the language of the Crown of Aragon, a Mediterranean economic and military power, to occupying a peripheral position within the Habsburg's multinational empire. Soon the imperial authorities became associated with the kingdom of Castile and with Castilian,[4] a country that was beginning its Golden Century. The *Decadència* (decay) of Catalan literature and cultural life had started.

---

[2] According to the current Spanish constitution, Spain is divided into several *autonomous communities*, territories that have their own parliaments and varying degrees of political autonomy.

[3] For a a short introduction to the social history of Catalan, see Hall (2001), in English; de Melchor, Vicent and Albert Branchadell (2002), in Castilian; and Ferrando and Nicolás (1993), in Catalan.

[4] *Castilian*-also known as *Spanish*-is the historical name for the language born and developed in the Kingdom of Castile, which eventually spread to the rest of the Hispanic Empire, much in the same way as English, the language of England, spread across the British Empire. In fact, the term *castellano* is very widely used both among L1 and L2 speakers, so much so that the current Spanish Constitution (Article 3) says that "Castilian is the official Spanish language of the State . . . The other Spanish languages shall also be official in their respective Autonomous Communities." In the Spanish context, the use of *español* ("Spanish") to refer to *Castilian* has more often than not been associated with nonpluralistic, non-egalitarian positions that try to grant Castilian a hegemonic role all over Spain as *the* language of Spain. This view is not shared by the author, thus the use of *Castilian* instead of *Spanish* in this article.

The institutional position of Castilian in the Catalan language area was greatly reinforced after the Spanish War of Succession (1700–1714).[5] Successive administrations showed increasing zeal in pursuing the linguistic homogenization of Spain by spreading the knowledge and use of Castilian (Ferrer i Gironès, 1985). The military dictatorships of Miguel Primo de Rivera (1923–1929) and, especially, Francisco Franco (1936/1939–1975) were particularly severe in their anti-Catalan practices, but even in the most liberal parliamentary regimes, many efforts were deployed by the central power to grant and preserve a hegemonic place for Castilian in the Catalan-speaking area (Vila i Moreno, 2008).

The educational system was a key agent in promoting a language shift from Catalan to the official languages (Pueyo, 1996). In France, schools to teach French language and culture were established in Northern Catalonia already in the late seventeenth century, a short time after the annexation (Ferrer i Gironès, 1985). In Spain, the Spanish King Charles III imposed that primary education should be in Castilian in 1768. Once education was declared universal and compulsory by the mid-nineteenth century, the schools' capacity to promote the state language increased exponentially (Pueyo, 1996).

In this context, the Catalan-speaking population learned the state language little by little and tended to internalize its hegemonic position vis-à-vis Catalan. Both processes were accelerated by the massive immigration of native speakers of the official languages during the twentieth century, as well as by the increasing presence of mass media. Thus, between 1900 and 1950, monolingual Catalan speakers gradually disappeared, replaced by bilingual and, in some areas, monolingual speakers of the official languages. By the 1970s, in many respects, it could be said that policies leading to the extinction of Catalan had almost succeeded. The nation-state languages (Castilian, French, and Italian) had become prevalent in the Catalan language areas as never before in history, not only in legal but also in sociodemographic terms. The trends leading towards total language shift were so well established that the disappearance of Catalan appeared to be just a matter of a few generations.

CURRENT LANGUAGE-IN-EDUCATION POLICIES: THE MODELS

Despite this bleak state of affairs for Catalan, things evolved in a different direction. The last decades of the twentieth century witnessed a remarkable change in language policies regarding Catalan. In Spain, changes were

---

[5] In 1659, and as a result of the Treaty of the Pyrenees, the Catalan counties of Roussillon and Cerdagne were annexed by France and became subject to France's language policies.

deeply connected with the evolution from Franco's dictatorship to a constitutional, parliamentary monarchy with a semi-federal structure known as the "State of Autonomies." This structure allowed national minorities to make their voices heard and even implement partly autonomous language policies. As a consequence, the three largest Catalan-speaking societies—Catalonia, Valencia, and Balearic Islands—started to develop their own language-in-education policies. These new policies put considerable emphasis on raising the status of Catalan from an outcast language to that of a normalized one. In almost all territories, Catalan became a compulsory subject for all students, and soon the language became a medium of instruction in many schools. But the extent to which Catalan was to be recovered varied enormously from one place to another.

It should be borne in mind that these policies were, and still are, only partially autonomous. Indeed, both the Spanish general framework and the local demolinguistic situations imposed severe restrictions on the degree of autonomy when designing language-in-education policies. To give just two examples, Article 3 of the current Spanish constitution requires that all citizens be competent in Castilian and makes this language official throughout Spain. In other words, the language-in-education models developed in each Catalan-speaking territory must guarantee that every student becomes highly proficient in the state language, irrespective of his or her first language. On a different level, following current education policy, 55 percent of the subject matter taught at schools in Spain's Catalan language territories is designed by the central Ministry of Education—in other words, the power of the Catalonian, Valencian, and Balearic authorities is limited in some ways in setting educational policies.

This is not the place for a detailed analysis of the language-in-education policies and models that are currently in vigor in the different territories of the Catalan language area (for recent analysis in English, see Vila i Moreno, 2008; Vila i Moreno, in press *a*; Vila i Moreno, in press *b*). Nevertheless, an overview of these policies allows classifying the current language-in-education systems in the Catalan language areas according to four crucial questions:

1. Is Catalan optional or compulsory subject matter for the school population?
2. Is the educational system based on the principle of conjunction or disjunction?
3. To what extent are two languages used as media of instruction within the same programs?
4. Does the system aspire to making all children bilingual and biliterate?

The first question allows us to distinguish those educational systems in which Catalan is merely optional—even extracurricular—subject matter from those in which where this language is, at least theoretically, expected to be learned by all pupils. The educational systems of French Catalonia, the Italian city of l'Alguer/Alghero, and la Franja, in Aragon, Spain, which have French, Italian, and Castilian, respectively, as their media of education, belong to the first group, since they offer some optional tuition in Catalan. In the other historically Catalan-speaking regions, Catalan is a compulsory subject for all students. Furthermore, some bilingual or even trilingual programs aimed at fostering language maintenance have been launched both in the French Department of Eastern Pyrenees and in l'Alguer/Alghero (for an overview of these programs in English see Vila i Moreno, 2008).

The second question—whether the educational system is based on the principle of conjunction or disjunction—is quite relevant to understanding the architecture of language-in-education policies in the Catalan language area. Most of the educational systems reviewed here are based on the *principle of conjunction*: the system does not foresee that children from different language backgrounds may be separated to receive education in their first language (L1).[6] Only in Valencia and Andorra is the *principle of disjunction*— according to which children may be separated on the basis of some criteria such as first language, ethnic background, gender, etc.—widely applied, although choice only applies to Catalan and Castilian and not to allochton languages. In Valencia, parents are in theory allowed to opt for a program with Castilian as the medium of instruction, or a program with Catalan as the medium of instruction.[7] In Andorra, the choice is made not among different programs, but rather among different educational systems: parents can opt to take their children to Andorran, French, Spanish and even international schools, each one with its own curriculum, agendas and, of course, language policies.[8]

It has to be pointed out that the conjunction/disjunction principles do not coincide entirely with choice of language of education. The conjunction principle forbids that different groups of students be organized on the basis of different languages of instruction, but it does not prevent the use of more than one language within the same classroom. In other words, both monolingual and bilingual education models may fall under this principle.

---

[6] The term *mother tongue* is widely perceived as inaccurate and sexist in the Catalan language area and will not be used in this paper.

[7] In practical terms, however, Catalan language programs are often unavailable, especially in secondary education.

[8] It should be taken into account that Andorra used to be a poor, weakly populated independent state between two giant states, France and Spain. Andorra did not develop its own national educational system until the last decades of the twentieth century. Before that time, children went either to parochial schools or to schools promoted by the French and Spanish States.

In Catalonia, for instance, educative legislation does offer the possibility for children to receive their first years of primary education in Castilian, if their parents ask for it, but always within a mainstream Catalan classroom. Indeed, a handful of families do apply for this option every year, and in those cases tuition in Castilian is provided by an assistant teacher.

The third question should be answered in mere demographic terms: to what extent are two languages used as media of instruction? This appears to be a rather simple question, but it is in fact quite difficult to answer, for at least two reasons. First, almost no authority involved furnishes up-to-date data on this issue. Second, even the figures available should be taken *cum grano salis* (with a grain of salt), to say the least. It should be taken into account that in practically all the territories involved here, language-in-education policies are a politically highly sensitive area that is customarily the object of heated debates on the media. Furthermore, actual classroom practices may be very different from declared data. For instance, it is quite common for Catalan to be recorded as the medium of instruction when, in actual terms, classroom activities include numerous codeswitching practices and abundant use of Castilian-language resources in the form of books, press, audiovisual materials, Internet resources, and so forth.

Unsurprisingly, data on the language of instruction is clearer for the three territories where Catalan has a marginal position: Northern Catalonia, l'Alguer/Alghero, and la Franja. In these regions, the medium of instruction is almost, by definition, the corresponding state language (French, Italian, and Castilian, respectively). Bilingual experiences and practices in the classroom are very limited. As far as the rest of the territories are concerned, data are much more confused. On the basis of the available data (see Vila i Moreno, in press *a*), and taking into account the whole process of preprimary, primary, and secondary education, it can be said that in Catalonia, Catalan is the predominant medium of instruction. Use of Castilian is weak in primary education but more significant in secondary education.

In the Balearic Islands, Catalan is the predominant medium of instruction, but Castilian is also widely used in both primary and secondary education. In Valencia,[9] the majority of children are educated in Castilian-medium programs that make scarce use of Catalan. Ironically, Castilian-medium programs are called "Programs of progressive incorporation [of Valencian[10] as a means of instruction]," for they are supposed to progressively include tuition in Catalan. No data are available on this particular, but anecdotal evidence from many Valencian teachers suggests that this progressive incorporation is at best symbolic. Only a numerical minority of students follow

[9]These comments do not apply to some historically Castilian-speaking areas in Western Valencia, where Catalan is merely an optional subject at school.

[10]"Valencian" is the name usually given to Catalan in Valencia.

the educational program in Valencian or the Valencian Immersion Program in which Castilian is weakly used as a medium of instruction (cf. the yearly reports on language policy by the Teachers Trade Union STEPV).[11]

In Andorra, language-in-education models depend on the educational system: the Andorran School Model is explicitly plurilingual, making partial use of French and Castilian as media of instruction in addition to Catalan, the predominant language of instruction. The rest of educational systems tend to be monolingual as far as language of instruction is concerned.

Finally, the fourth question is crucial here: to what extent does each system aspire to produce fully bilingual and biliterate students? For the purpose of this chapter, bilingualism and biliteracy are here implied to mean Catalan plus the state language (Castilian, French, or Italian)—foreign and or immigrant languages are not taken into account here. Again, the educational systems in which Catalan is simply an optional subject matter remain aside from the rest, for they do not aspire to producing bilingual and biliterate students. It is only those students who take the optional courses on Catalan language that may aspire to acquiring some level of bilingualism and biliteracy. For the rest of educational systems here analyzed, highly developed bilingualism and biliteracy stand as goals. In Catalonia, Valencia, and Balearic Islands, all children should finish their education highly competent in both Catalan and Castilian. Again, the complex educational landscape of Andorra is an exception. In some systems, children are explicitly expected to become at least trilingual and triliterate (pupils in the Andorran Schools learn Catalan/French/Castilian). In other systems, such as the French and Spanish public systems, the goal of bilingualism and biliteracy are more vague.

The criteria suggested allow for a classification of the systems involved here (see Table 1). Through this classification, a difference becomes apparent between those systems in which Catalan has a peripheral position (Northern Catalonia, La Franja, and l'Alguer/Alghero) and the rest of systems. In the first three territories, the educational system does not aspire to bilingualism and biliteracy, uses only the state language, and tends to include Catalan just as an option for schools and students who express an interest in it. The position of Catalan in these territories is clearly connected to its official and demolinguistic status (cf. Querol [coord.] , 2007). In France and Italy, there has been severe language shift from Catalan, and it is clearly a minority language. In la Franja, Catalan is a vibrant language spoken by the vast majority of the population as their L1, but this territory has no administrative autonomy, and language policies are dictated by the Aragon government—Aragon being an autonomous community in which 95 percent of the population is Castilian monolingual and generally highly suspicious of recognizing the presence of Catalan in what they consider to

---

[11] Available at http://www.intersindical.org/stepv/polival/inforval08.pdf.

**TABLE 1. A CLASSIFICATION OF THE EDUCATIONAL SYSTEMS ACCORD-
ING TO THEIR PREVALENT LANGUAGE-IN-EDUCATION MODELS
IN PREPRIMARY, PRIMARY, AND SECONDARY LEVELS IN THE
CATALAN LANGUAGE AREA**

	1. What is the status of Catalan as a subject matter?	2. Are the two languages used as means of instruction?	3. The educational system is based on the principle of . . .	4. Are bilingualism and biliteracy goals?
North Catalonia	*An optional subject matter*	*No*	*Conjunction*	*No*
La Franja	*An optional subject matter*	*No*	*Conjunction*	*No*
L'Alguer/Alghero	*An optional subject matter*	*No*	*Conjunction*	*No*
Valencia (Catalan-speaking territory)	*A compulsory subject matter*	*Weakly*	*Disjunction*	*Yes*
Balearic Islands	*A compulsory subject matter*	*Weakly*	*Conjunction*	*Yes*
Catalonia	*A compulsory subject matter*	*Weakly*	*Conjunction*	*Yes*
Andorra	*A compulsory subject matter*	*Dep. on system*	*Disjunction*	*Dep. on system*

In this table, the other educational systems are comparable in that they theoretically aspire to producing bilingual and biliterate students and make some use of two languages as means of instruction. The major difference among them is the extent to which they allow for organizing different language-in-education school models In this respect, the Valencian and Andorran systems do offer more choice than the Balearic and Catalonian systems. But does freedom of choice benefit societal bilingualism?

be solely their territory. In these three regions, Catalan is reduced to the status of a regional minority language with scarce official presence; language policies and the school systems reflect this position.

RESULTS AND EXPLANATIONS

In order to speak about the reality of bilingual education in the Catalan language areas, two results are especially relevant: competence in Catalan and competence in Castilian. Competence in Catalan is probably the best indicator of language-in-education policies in the Catalan language area. After centuries of persecution and minoritization, Catalan has become the weakest language in its own historical area. Official data about knowledge of Catalan are clear enough to show the actual impact of the reviewed language-in-education policies on language competence (see Figure 1). On

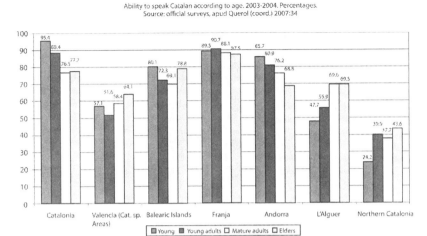

Ability to speak Catalan according to age. 2003-2004. Percentages.
Source: official surveys, apud Querol (coord.) 2007:34

Figure 1. Ability to Speak Catalan by Age, 2003–2004

the one hand, in Catalonia, Balearic Islands, and Andorra, the youngest generations have a command of spoken Catalan that is significantly higher than that of the preceding generations. In other words, the language-in-education policies implemented over the past 20 to 30 years have had a visible, positive impact on competence.

On the other hand, the ability to speak Catalan is not significantly raised by the language-in-education policies deployed not only in Franja, l'Alguer/Alghero, and Northern Catalonia, but also in Valencia. In all of these territories, the ability to speak the minority language is closely related to having inherited it from parents or picked it up in heavily Catalan-speaking environments. In truth, the high results for competence in Catalan in la Franja simply reflect the fact that few immigrants are attracted to this rural area. And what about Valencia? The demolinguistic data from Valencia make clear that the Castilian-language programs in which Catalan is only minimally used are simply unable to bilingualize their Castilian-speaking clientele. In other words, (quasi)monolingual programs in the hegemonic language produce (quasi)monolingual pupils.

Such results are hardly surprising. But what about the other way round? What about competence in Castilian in the territories where it has become less used as a means of instruction? In comparative terms, less research has been done to analyze the competence of Castilian in the Catalan language areas. But still, a significant corpus of research has been amassed over the last decades. After reviewing a number of studies realized by several independent organizations—including the Spanish Institute for Educational Quality, and the OECD Pisa Report—Arnau (2004)concluded that "Competence in Castilian among school children in Catalonia is not lower than that of school children in the rest of Spain [and] [in] Catalonia there are

TABLE 2. PERCENTAGE OF SECONDARY STUDENTS DECLARING MAXIMAL COMPETENCE IN CATALAN, CASTILIAN, AND ENGLISH (10 ON A 0–10 SCALE)

	Catalan $n = 1420$	Castilian $n = 1422$	English $n = 1344$
Understanding	84.5 percent	87.4 percent	5.5 percent
Speaking	63.4 percent	73.6 percent	2.5 percent
Reading	73.9 percent	79.7 percent	8.5 percent
Writing	42.1 percent	47.3 percent	4.5 percent

Source: Enquesta sociodemogràfica i lingüística, Consell Superior d'Avaluació de Catalunya

more factors that limit [school children's] competence in Catalan than factors limiting competence in Castilian" (p. 6, author's translation).

In fact, even self-declared perceptions about language competence support the idea that Catalonian students perceive their competence in Castilian to be slightly higher than their competence in Catalan. In another recent example, Table 2 shows data on self-declared competence in Catalan and Castilian from a sample of students of secondary education tested by Catalonia's Highest Council of Evaluation of the Educational System. The sample coincided with the students analyzed for the OECD's PISA-2006 report[12] in Catalonia and aspired at being representative of Catalonia's students of that level. The table shows the percentage of students declaring to have maximal competence of Catalan, Castilian, and English. Their competence was measured by the students themselves on a 0–10 scale, similar to that used for school marks and thus an instrument quite familiar to the students. In the table, the percentage of students declaring maximal competence in Castilian is somewhat higher than those claiming maximal competence in Catalan.

In other words, both the tests analyzed by Arnau (2004) and the self-declared data suggest that, in general terms, Catalan students in Catalonia achieve higher competence in their second language (L2), despite the fact that Catalan is the main language of instruction. Again, interactions on the ground may have much to do with these results. Such interactions were exactly the object of analysis in the Llengua i ús (Language and Usage) project (see Vila i Moreno, Vial i Rius, and Galindo 2005; Galindo, 2006). This project observed and analyzed the language choices of a sample of sixth-grade students from Catalonia in leisure time within the schools—on the playgrounds, corridors, excursions, and so on. Among many other results,

---

[12] See http://www.pisa.oecd.org/pages/0,2987,en_32252351_32235731_1_1_1_1 _1,00 .html.

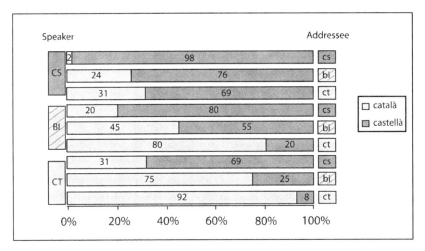

Figure 2. Language Used by 6th Grade Pupils in Their Interactions with Classmates in Peer-Conversation (per speech turn) According to Speakers' and Addresses' Family Language

Source: Vila, Vial, and Galindo, 2005

the project confirmed that children tended to reproduce the language choice etiquette that has been predominant among adults at least since Franco's dictatorship (cf. Woolard, 1989; Boix 1993). Indeed, as Figure 2 shows, speakers tended to choose language on the basis of their own family language and that of their interlocutor. Thus Castilian speakers tended to speak Castilian with other Castilian speakers (98 percent of speech turns), while Catalan speakers tended to speak Catalan with other Catalan L1 speakers (92 percent of speech turns). In other words, in-group communication functioned mostly in the in-group language. The major differences were to be found in out-group contacts. In these contacts, while Castilian speakers only used Catalan in a minority of opportunities (24 percent of turns with bilinguals and 31 percent with Catalan L1), Catalan L1 children tended to speak Castilian with Castilian L1 children (69 percent).

In other words, peer-to-peer, spontaneous interaction, the ideal arena for actual second-language acquisition, favours the bilingualization of Catalan speakers. If one adds to this the predominance of Castilian in mass media[13] and pop culture and its weight as a state language, it is not difficult to understand why Catalan speakers reach higher levels of bilingualism than their Castilian L1 peers, even in Catalonia.

---

[13] The main TV stations in Catalonia broadcast from Madrid and hardly include any Catalan among their programs, not even as music.

NEW REALITIES, NEW CHALLENGES, NEW PRACTICES

The language-in-education policies in the Catalan language area were designed to cope with the process of recovering an autochthonous language that had undergone minoritization for centuries, which explains their emphasis on conjunction and their aim of making the totality of the population bilingual and biliterate. Indeed, it can be said that language policies in the principal territories point at a *Gesellschaft* strategy of making the historical language available to everyone irrespective of his or her origin.

But during the last 10–15 years, the Catalan language territories have received an unprecedented number of foreign immigrants attracted by the growing labor market (see Table 3). A percentage of these immigrants come from Spanish-speaking countries, but a majority (60–70 percent) of the newcomers are alloglot—i.e., they speak neither Catalan nor Castilian.

Newcomers or *new* immigrants, as they are often referred to, do pose a number of challenges to established language policies, especially to language-in-education policies. Teachers in the Catalan language area were used to being competent in the languages of their pupils; this is no longer the case. Diversity within the classrooms has increased exponentially, as has the risk for racism, xenophobia, school failure, social fractures, and all the educational problems that are well known in countries with long histories of multilingual immigration.

Faced with these new challenges, the educational systems in the Catalan language area are coping in different ways (see, for instance, the conclusions of the Advisory Council for the Language at School at Consell assessor, 2006). In fact, even some of their basic principles are being reviewed, even if in a discrete form. Thus, for instance, in Catalonia, newcomer children are being separated from their mainstream classes during some hours per day in order to give them language lessons in what are called *aules d'acollida*

TABLE 3. EVOLUTION OF FOREIGN RESIDENTS IN CATALONIA, VALENCIA, AND BALEARIC ISLANDS, 1994–2007.

	1994		2003		2007	
	Number of foreigners	Percent of total population	Number of foreigners	Percent of total population	Number of foreigners	Percent of total population
Catalonia	83,296	1.3	623,947	9.3	966,004	13.4
Valencia	56,163	1.4	488,080	10.9	727,080	14.9
Balearic Isl.	25,895	3.3	146,046	15.4	189,437	18.4

Adapted from Padrones 1994, 2003, and estimated for January 1, 2007. Website Instituto Nacional de Estadística, http://www. ine.es.

or "welcoming classes," and since 2008, children newly arrived attend basic language courses at separated centers called *Espais de benvinguda,* or "welcoming spaces," for one month. Not without conflict, some separation is being introduced in Catalonia to deal with newcomers. At the same time, in Valencia concern is growing over the fact that immigrant children tend to concentrate in Castilian-language programs. In some areas in Valencia, thus, the choice between Castilian/Catalan-medium reinforces, rather than reduces, the social distance between immigrant and local children. A complete synthesis of the beneficial instructional practices currently being employed is impossible in the limited space of a book chapter. A number of these practices may be found on the Web site of Linguamón, House of Languages[11] (in English) or at the Web site LIC (Llengua, interculturalitat i Cohesió Social [Language, Interculturality and Social Cohesion]) of the Department of Education of the Catalan Government (in Catalan).[15] In the following pages I simply comment on a number of innovations that may be of interest to the non-Catalan reader, basically dealing with the treatment of newcomer children.

TEACHING THE LANGUAGE TO NEWCOMER CHILDREN

Newcomer children are tested on a number of dimensions.[16] In primary education, for instance, children complete a short evaluation of social integration and another one on linguistic abilities.[17] The first evaluation is a short questionnaire designed to understand the children's process of integration to the school environment. The second evaluation focuses on the child's abilities in understanding, speaking, reading, and writing Catalan. Secondary education pupils are tested on roughly the same dimensions, although with a higher degree of complexity.[18] These data are entered into an electronic database maintained by the Department of Education.

The language curriculum for newcomer children is detailed in Department d'Educació (n.d.). Evaluation of the children is supposed to be based on the Common European framework of reference for languages: learning, teaching, and assessment. So far, however, only the initial levels have been adequately developed (Rancé, 2005).

In the complex sociolinguistic situation of the Catalan language area, the teacher plays a crucial role in the process of language socialization. In the

---

[11] See http://www10.gencat.net/casa_llengues/AppJava/en/index.jsp.

[15] See http://www.xtec.cat/lic/index.htm.

[16] See http://www.xtec.cat/lic/nouvingut/professorat/prof_ori_estrategies1.htm.

[17] See http://www.xtec.cat/lic/nouvingut/professorat/prof_ori_avaluacio1.htm.

[18] See http://www.xtec.cat/lic/nouvingut/professorat/prof_ori_avaluacio2.htm.

Catalan-language societies, due to the social position of Castilian, Catalan may be difficult to pick up in informal interaction, and the wide offering of Castilian mass media makes it easy to cut oneself off from Catalan input. Teachers become the most important linguistic model and must promote the acquisition and use of the language, becoming interlocutors and subtly correcting mistakes. To achieve these goals, teachers are encouraged to apply a number of strategies to help their pupils.[19] Dealing specifically with correction, for example, teachers are encouraged to actively intervene during the process of language learning in order to correct the learners. These corrections, however, are expected to be subtle and implicit.

It should be underlined that corrections should be implicit—i.e., never saying explicitly, "This is wrong," or "This should not be said that way," but, rather, building right utterance. The most important goal is for communication to go smoothly and for the speaker to feel like communicating. Correction should be selective and adapted to the level of language being acquired by the learner.[20] Additionally, corrections are not to be metalinguistic; rather, they should be connected to the speech act. A number of strategies are provided to teachers in order to achieve these goals of subtle correction.

Teachers are also expected to adapt their speech to the competence of their pupils "without deforming or impoverishing it".[21] A number of strategies are used: speaking slowly; using nonverbal language (taking into account that visual contact between teacher and pupil should be maintained, even if it is not easy to fulfill in some cases given that in some cultures respect toward adults is shown by avoiding eye contact); repeating the message when needed; pausing more frequently so that nonnative speakers have the time to process the message; using standard, clearly articulated language, avoiding informal formulae and contractions; emphasizing suprasegmental features (intonation) to make clear the pragmatic intention of each utterance; simplifying vocabulary; simplifying grammar; and avoiding both telegraphic messages and long sentences, especially those having subordinate clauses. In early stages, compound verbal forms may be avoided, but not to the extent of deforming the language. Discourse should be modified so that it becomes easier to understand, as when, for instance, the teacher provides examples of answers to his or her own questions:

> On és la llibreta? . . . On és la llibreta? . . . La llibreta és dins del calaix . . .
>
> (Where is the notebook? . . . Where is the notebook? . . . The notebook is in the drawer . . .)

---

[19] See http://www.xtec.cat/lic/nouvingut/professorat/prof_ori_estrategies.htm.

[20] See http://www.xtec.cat/lic/nouvingut/professorat/prof_ori_estrategies4.htm.

[21] http://www.xtec.cat/lic/nouvingut/professorat/prof_ori_estrategies1.htm.

Teachers might also add linguistic elements to the ones the pupil already knows so that understanding is made possible:

> *Tanca la porta. (dirigint-se a l'alumne nouvingut i ajudant-se del gest)*
> *Sisplau, tanca la porta. (a l'alumne nouvingut)*
> *Sisplau, pots tancar la porta. (a l'alumne nouvingut)*
> *Algú pot tancar la porta? (dirigint-se al grup classe)*
> *Podeu tancar la porta quan sortiu.*

English:
> *Close the door. (speaking to the alloglot pupil, using gesture)*
> *Please, close the door. (to the alloglot pupil)*
> *Could you please close the door. (to the alloglot pupil)*
> *Could someone close the door? (to the class)*
> *Could you close the door when you get off.*

ACTIVITIES TO PROMOTE THE POSITION OF IMMIGRANT LANGUAGES IN CATALONIA: TAMAZIGHT AS AN EXAMPLE

During the last decades, the educational systems have evolved toward assuming bilingualism as an asset and have developed techniques and discourse in favor of the local languages. However, the arrival of new languages poses a conceptual problem to the language-in-education policies in the Catalan language area. Furthermore, globalization favors the teaching of English as a lingua franca. All of these practices can be easily subsumed in a conceptual framework based on conjunction, and even disjunction as it has been practiced so far. Regardless of program model, all students should end up learning the same subject area content.

But newcomer languages constitute a different reality. Early on, these languages represented a barrier that had to be overcome. Efforts were thus directed at reorienting the educational systems so that newcomer pupils could be integrated into the pre-existing system. But the more these new languages are becoming part and parcel of the daily reality of Catalonian, Valencian, and Balearic schools, the more they are being taken into consideration as a resource to be promoted. However, efforts to face this challenge have only just begun. In Catalonia, under the program *Llengües d'origen*—languages of origin—the Department of Education is timidly supporting the teaching and learning of some of these languages, namely Arabic, Chinese, Dutch, Tamazight, and Portuguese.[22] To date, these languages are only being taught as separate subjects in a handful of schools and institutes on a

---

[22] See http://blocs.xtec.cat/llenguadorigen/.

TABLE 4. NUMBER OF PUPILS FOLLOWING EXTRACUR-
RICULAR LANGUAGE COURSES SUPPORTED
BY THE DEPARTMENT OF EDUCATION

Language of the extraschool classes	Number of pupils
Arabic	1.338
Romanian	179
Dutch	131
Chinese	129
Tamazight	68
Portuguese	57

* Data for 2007–2008.
Source: Generalitat de Catalunya

voluntary basis, and participation, as indicated in Table 4, is low. So far, no bilingual school experience has been recorded.

One of the most widely spoken allochton languages in Catalonia is Berber, or Tamazight. Although there are no official figures, its speakers probably number more than 100,000.[23] A main activity of Tamazight in Catalonia is the Amazigh Spring[24] (Primavera Amaziga in Catalan).[25] Each year, the organizers arrange one or two days for cultural manifestations (concerts, photographic exhibitions, poetry recitals, etc.) and lectures from experts on different aspects of Amazigh life (Tamazight and its status, the Amazigh culture, the political situation, etc.). Amazigh Spring is essentially a showcase for a number of permanent projects. The event raises awareness of the work carried out all year round by the various organizations involved in the promotion of Tamazight in Catalonia. This work includes producing educational materials, giving Tamazight courses in primary and secondary schools and universities, raising the profile of Tamazight through the Catalan media, and conducting projects involving cooperation with the countries of origin. The Spring is organized by a number of public and private institutions, including the University of Barcelona and the Autonomous University of Barcelona, as well as different Catalan–Amazigh Associations. In 2008, the Observatori Català de la Llengua Amaziga (Catalan Observatory of the Tamazight Language)[26] was presented during the Spring.

---

[23] In July 2006, 197,918 people of Moroccan origin and 8,096 from Algeria were registered in Catalonia (Institut Nacional d'Estadística de Catalunya,).

[24] The term Amazigh Spring can be traced back to 1980, when people looking to stage cultural acts in Kabylie (Algeria) were repressed by the Algerian authorities.

[25] See the program for 2008 at http://isuraf.jeeran.com/SAID/archive/2008/5/559028.html.

[26] See http://www10.gencat.cat/casa_llengues/AppJava/ca/multilinguisme/ocla/quisom .jsp.

In recent years, the level of awareness of the presence of Amazighs in Catalonia has risen significantly in primary and secondary education, universities, governmental institutions, the media, and society in general. This might not have been possible without the annual Amazigh Spring events held since 2002. This increased recognition is being translated into a number of solid initiatives. On the one hand, Tamazight courses at different levels are being organized (see, for instance, the program for two courses in Figueres, Alt Empordà, in Autumn–Winter 2008).[27] Indeed, Tamazight has started to be taught at some schools as an extracurricular subject on a voluntary basis.[28] On the other hand, the production of educational materials is in its infancy. So far, the most important development is the publication of a bilingual Catalan–Tamazight, conversation guide both on paper and online.[29]

RAISING AWARENESS OF LINGUISTIC DIVERSITY: THE "GIMCANA DE LES LLENGÜES"

The case of Tamazight highlights some specifics on new language programming in schools. However, recent immigration has also given rise to strategies to raise awareness of and educate around language issues more generally. A good example here is the "Languages Gymkhana."

The Languages Gymkhana[30] is a game designed by the Grup d'Estudis de les Llengües Amenaçades—GELA (Universitat de Barcelona; see Junyent i Figueras, 2002).[31] Its goal is promoting awareness of the value and importance of linguistic diversity, and it is especially connected with the languages of new immigrants who have arrived in Catalonia over the last decade.

The game, which is designed to be held within a town, aims to involve a number of different organizations (the municipal library, schools, the media, etc.) and various target audiences (students, schoolchildren, members of organizations and associations, townspeople in general, etc.). Participants are divided into six different categories or age groups: (1) students aged 5–8, (2) students aged 8–12, (3) students aged 12–18, (4) university students, (5) community members, and (6) representatives of myriad organizations. Schools are especially encouraged to take part in the gymkhana.

---

[27] See http://amazic-catala.blogspot.com/2008/12/curs-damazic-per-nens-i-nenes-figueres.html.

[28] See http://blocs.xtec.cat/llenguadorigen/files/2008/10/amazic103.pdf.

[29] See http://www.ub.edu/guiaconversa/amazic/.

[30] See http://www10.gencat.net/pres_casa_llengues/AppJava/frontend/llengues_bp.jsp?id =61&idioma=5.

[31] See http://www.gela.cat/doku.php?id=.

This Language Gymkhana involves a series of tests relating to the world's linguistic diversity in a way that is made relevant and fun to the local population. Questions may be related, for instance, to the etymology of the locality's name ("Do you know from what language comes the name of this city, and what its name means?") or of everyday words ("Do you know the linguistic origin of the names of each one of your pieces of clothing [e.g., pyjamas, tuxedo]?") or to the number of languages spoken in the same area, and so forth. It is structured into three 10-week phases. Each week, there are six different tests, adding up to a total of 180. The tests are organized by subject, target audience, the way information has to be searched for, and so on. The competition has been designed to be adaptable in terms of time and space. Most of the tests have a range of possible solutions to encourage people to search for information and to stimulate debate with respect to the subjects addressed. There are specific tests for each target group. The tests for the week ahead and the answers for the previous week are distributed each Monday. They are distributed by the local radio and TV stations and in letterboxes, public places (e.g., libraries, town council offices), schools, local organizations, shops, workplaces, and so on. People can get hold of the tests and entry forms in any of these places. A team of volunteers and town council workers collect the completed forms each week and enter the answers into a database. There are prizes for participants each week. Usually, these are books provided by a publisher.

The Gymkhana took place initially in the city of Masquefa (Anoia, near Barcelona) under the banner of the European Year of Languages 2001. The significant growth in the town's population, with people from different origins, and the isolation of many new arrivals in different areas did not enhance communication between the townspeople, nor did it allow them to take part in creating new meeting points or forums to help bring the community together. The competition took place thanks to collaboration from different collectives, including the town council, which was very willing to organize events for the European Year of Languages; several civic institutions that organized the Competition; the GELA; the townspeople who responded to the initiative; and several teams of volunteers.

Since 2001, the initiative has been repeated in many other towns and *comarques* (counties), such as L'Hospitalet de Llobregat, Tortosa,[32] Osona,[33] Girona,[34] Sabadell,[35] and Olot,[36] among others. The organizers of the

---

[32] See http://webfacil.tinet.cat/gimcana/.

[33] See http://gimcanaosona.cpnl.cat/.

[34] See http://www.gimcanagirona.cat/.

[35] See http://www.cal.cat/Default.aspx?tabid=307.

[36] See http://gimcanallenguesolot.blogspot.com.

competition believe that the main purposes were met. It seems clear that there is a greater level of understanding about linguistic diversity thanks to participation in the competition, something that has led, in one way or another, to the alteration of certain preconceived notions or even prejudices about languages.

SUMMARY AND CONCLUSIONS

The Catalan language area has a history of language-in-education policies that goes back several centuries. In the past, these policies were designed to annihilate linguistic diversity and linguistically homogenize the different nation-states. During the last three decades, however, a number of policies have been developed to promote the position of historical languages in a framework of societal plurilingualism. A number of conclusions may be derived from the Catalan experience. Probably one of the most important has to do with identifying the real locus of language learning for school-aged children.In fact, bilingual and multilingual societies constitute huge language-learning environments. Learning languages in a bilingual or multilingual environment is a complex task in which schools play an important, although secondary, role. The example of Catalonia shows clearly that schools on their own cannot modify patterns of language use that are prevalent outside the school.

A second lesson from the Catalan case has to do with the very definition of bilingual education. One may legitimately wonder whether the hegemonic definition of bilingual education as one using two or more languages as media of instruction retains all the sense it is supposed to have. In the Catalan-language area, programs extensively using both official languages have tended to reproduce the unbalanced linguistic situation that exists out of school. It is only by making (very) extensive use of Catalan—in fact, as the predominant means of communication within schools—that schools manage to bilingualize all the student population. Bilingual competence is a prerequisite for bilingual practices: it is only bilingualized students that will eventually engage in bilingual interactions. In other words, in defining bilingual education, it might be wise to move the emphasis from a procedural perspective to one more concerned with actual outcomes: from bilingual education to education for bilingualism, or rather for plurilingualism.

A third conclusion of interest raised by the Catalan experience is that it makes clear the difficulty of making choices in complex, plurilingual sociolinguistic situations. In the Catalan language area, as in many other plurilingual societies such as Quebec, Brussels, Finland, and so on, a conflict exists between freedom of choice and aspirations of bilingualism. In this case, the conflict is posed as a crude alternative: in educational systems such as the one in Valencia, parents can choose the language of education, but only the minority who attend Catalan-medium schools really become bilingual. On the contrary, in Catalonia and Balearic Islands, general bilingualism and biliteracy is obtained, but only at the cost of a reduced capacity to select the medium of education. In other words, language planners and educationalists should be aware that the alternative between conjunctive/disjunctive language policies can only be analyzed adequately in terms of their eventual consequences. But both conjunctive and disjunctive policies may have undesired consequences, and no automatic formulae are available for all societies. Again, extra-school conditions cannot be overstated: the Spanish general language policy framework imposes the duty to learn Castilian on every citizen. There is no choice to remain monolingual if one so desires. It is precisely against this general context that language-in-education policies should be analyzed, and not only in a narrow, exclusively pedagogic framework.

Another issue here is whether language-in-education policies should aim at education for potential bilingualism or rather at education for actual bilingualism. To the extent that schools are substantially modifying the linguistic repertoire of their pupils and providing models for behavior, those in charge of designing a language-in-education policy cannot escape the crucial question of what sort of bilingual community they are preparing their children for and, in the long run, what sort of community they are shaping. Are they content with simply distributing some generous doses of language competence in L1/L2? Or, rather, do they expect their pupils to actively use some of the languages at their disposal? If so, what models, discourses, and rationales are they transmitting?

This is a challenge that is posed in different terms for schools. Schools or even some education systems with a more convenient societal context may dispense with some of this reflection. For instance, international and foreign language schools that mostly serve the purpose of developing competence in a foreign language with wide support—most especially English—may be satisfied with providing access to valuable linguistic capital and opening doors to resources waiting beyond the school gates. But in many situations, this behavior is simply not enough. In minority situations, schools do want to encourage the actual use of the minority language; in other words, these schools do want to promote changes in hegemonic language practices that help reinvigorating the weakest languages. For many communities which have limited access to many powerful language domains such as the Internet, the mass media, or the leisure industry, schools constitute a crucial social environment to reproduce the language and endow it with the indispensable prestige needed for language reproduction.

The challenge remains, of course: how can minority language promotion be combined with respect for pluralism? Raising a significant challenge to this ideal is the increased presence of speakers of languages other than Catalan and Castilian in Catalonia. Their arrival during the last decade stretches a system which so far has been based on the principles of conjunction and widespread bilingualism and biliteracy, with a strong emphasis on the national language. These speakers challenge all of the language-in-education models reviewed here in at least two directions: on the one hand, it cannot be assumed that they will learn Catalan (and Castilian) as soon as their Catalonian counterparts; therefore, new strategies have to be designed to integrate newcomer alloglots. Welcoming classes, welcoming spaces, and innovation in language didactics are the tentative solutions for this challenge. It is still too early to gauge their results, but it is worth pointing out that the experience of conjoint schools in Catalonia has so far managed to reduce the separation between Catalan and Castilian speakers. It remains to be seen whether these experiences will have the same result in encouraging the social integration of newcomer children.

On the other hand, Catalan schools are still striving to find the proper place for all these newcomer languages. So far, initiatives have combined traditional extracurricular language courses with general activities designed to raise awareness and respect for foreign languages. Real bilingual schooling experiences involving newcomer languages are still not in practice, and one can imagine that this sort of experience will be difficult to implement in the near future, given the sociodemographic composition of the schools. Nevertheless, schools should be encouraged to reconsider some of their practices so that multilingualism stops being simply celebrated and becomes a real asset for the Catalan-language societies. We have seen that a first step in this direction is now being timidly taken with the development of a handful of extracurricular newcomer language courses. A next step might be that of introducing these options in the regular curriculum so that children attending these courses can see their efforts rewarded by mainstream educational institutions. That might be a crucial step in normalizing the status of these languages in the eyes of the rest of the community.

REFERENCES

Arnau, J. (2004). "Sobre les competències en català i castellà dels escolars de Catalunya: una resposta a la polèmica sobre el decret d'hores de castellà." *LSC: Llengua Societat i Comunicació, 1,* 1–7. Retrieved from http://www.ub.edu/cusc/LSC_set.htm.

Boix, E. (1993). *Triar no és trair. Identitat i llengua en els joves de Barcelona.* Barcelona: Ed. 62.

Consell assessor de la llengua a l'escola. (2006). *Conclusions.* Barcelona: Departament d'Educació i Universitats, Generalitat de Catalunya. Retrieved from http://www.gencat.net/educacio/depart/pdf/llengua_escola/llengua_escola.pdf.

de Melchor, V. & Branchadell, A. (2002). *El catalán. Una lengua de Europa para compartir.* Bellaterra: Servei de Publicacions de la Universitat Autònoma de Barcelona.

Departament d'Educació. n.d. *Programació de llenga catalana per a l'alumnat nouvingut.* Barcelona: Generalitat de Catalunya, Departament d'Educació. Retrieved December 28, 2008, from http://www.xtec.cat/lic/nouvingut/professorat/documenta/prog_lcatalana.pdf.

Ferrando, A. & Nicolás, M. (1993). *Panorama d'història de la llengua.* València: Tàndem.

Ferrer i Gironès, F. (1985). *La persecució política de la llengua catalana.* Història de les mesures preses contra el seu ús des de la Nova Planta fins avui. Barcelona: Ed. 62.

Galindo, M. (2006). "Les llengües a l'hora del pati. Usos lingüístics en les converses dels infants de primària a Catalunya." Doctoral thesis. Barcelona: Departament de Filologia Catalana, Universitat de Barcelona.

Hall, J. (2001). Convivència in Catalonia: Languages living together. Barcelona: Fundació Jaume Bofill.

Junyent i Figueras, C. (2002). *La gimancana de les llengües.* Barcelona: Octaedro.

Pueyo, M. (1996). *Tres escoles per als catalans.* Lleida: Pagès editors.

Querol Puig, E. (coord.), Chessa, E., Sorolla, N., Torres i Pla, J., with the collaboration of Sanjuán, X. & Solís, M. (2007). *Llengua i societat als territoris de parla catalana a l'inici del segle XXI. L'Alguer, Andorra, Catalunya, Catalunya Nord; la Franja, Illes Balears i Comunitat Valenciana.* Barcelona: Generalitat de Catalunya, Departament de Vicepresidència, Secretaria de Política Lingüística.

Rancé Jordana, L. (2005). *Nivell inicial de català A1-Usuari bàsic.* Barcelona: Generalitat de Catalunya, Departament d'Educació. Retrieved December 28, 2008, from http://www.xtec.cat/lic/nouvingut/professorat/documenta/nivell_inicial.pdf.

Vila i Moreno, F. X., Vial i Rius, S., & Galindo, M. (2005). "Language practices in bilingual schools: Some observed, quantitative data from Catalonia." In X. P. Rodríguez-Yáñez, A. M. Lorenzo Suárez, & F. Ramallo (Eds.), *Bilingualism and education: From the family to the school* (pp. 263–273). Muenchen: Lincom.

Vila i Moreno, F. X. (2008). Catalan in Spain. In G. Extra & D. Gorter (Eds.), *Multilingual Europe: Facts and Policies.* Berlin: Mouton de Gruyter.

Vila i Moreno, F. X. In press *a.* Language-in-education policies. In E. Boix-Fuster & M. Strubell i Trueta (Eds.), *Language policies in the Catalan language area* (pp. 157–183). Berlin: Springer.

Vila i Moreno, F. X. In press *b.* Language-in-education policies in the Catalan language area: Models, results and challenges. *AILA Review 21.*

Woolard, K. A. (1989). *Double talk: Bilingualism and the policy of ethnicity in Catalonia.* Palo Alto, CA: Stanford University Press.

SECTION III

CONTROVERSY

CHAPTER 7

REORIENTING LANGUAGE-AS-RESOURCE[1]

Richard Ruiz
University of Arizona, USA

ANTICIPATIONS AND ADUMBRATIONS OF LANGUAGE-AS-RESOURCE[2]

The idea that language is a societal resource has been part of the language-planning literature for at least several decades (see, e.g., Das Gupta & Ferguson, 1977; Fishman, 1991a; Jernudd, 1977; Jernudd & Das Gupta, 1971; John & Horner, 1971). In fact, one could say that the notion was an

---

[1] I want to acknowledge helpful critiques of the ideas included here from faculty and student colleagues in the department of Language, Reading and Culture at the University of Arizona, as well as students in the Language Planning seminars. Especially helpful have been commentaries by Karen Spear-Ellinwood, Emilio Reyes Arenas, Janelle Johnson, and Kevin Carroll. I have also profited immensely from conversations with Joseph Lo Bianco (Australia) and Neville Alexander and Kathleen Heugh (South Africa).

[2] These terms are taken from Robert Merton's (1968) commentary on Kuhn's writings on paradigms (an interesting reference since I confess in my original 1981

(continued)

International Perspectives on Bilingual Education: Policy, Practice, and Controversy, pages 155–172

organizing concept in the development of the field itself. Bjorn Jernudd's early conceptual work suggests that it is a starting point for language planning: "The logic of language planning is dictated by the recognition of language as a societal resource. The importance of this resource is due to the communicational and identific values attached by the community to one or more languages" (1971, p. 196). Ofelia Garcia (2009) credits Joshua Fishman's work on language maintenance in the United States (Fishman, 1966) as an early indication of the importance of the idea of language as a resource in language-planning projects. In spite of this relatively long history of use, however, there has been relatively little elaboration of the concept. What kind of "resource" is it? What is the nature of the value that attaches to it? What is the "market" in which it acts as currency? Who profits more or less from its acquisition and use? Who is responsible for its development, cultivation, and management as a resource? To whom does it "belong"? These questions are of the sort asked about other things routinely characterized as resources—oil, water, gas, woodlands, air, coal, gemstones, and more. It is fair to ask for a response to them from those of us who have tried to elaborate the notion of language-as-resource. This response should go some way, as well, toward answering some of the critiques of such a view of language. I will attempt a response for some of these; the others will be part of a later elaboration.

Recent critiques of the conceptualization of the language-planning orientation I call "language-as-resource" (LAR) have developed into a controversy among friends. Many of us who assert the theoretical justification and pedagogical need for strong bilingual education at the same time disagree about how these arguments are to be advanced. For example, Petrovic (2005) characterizes language-as-resource as a corollary of the neoconservative agenda whereby the value of social goods is determined by its demonstrable economic and military utility; he criticizes that aspect of the model as "a strategic mistake" that works "to preserve the inequitable

---

(continued from previous page)

paper [cf. also Ruiz 1984, note 1] that my conceptualization of "orientation" was influenced by Kuhn's work). "Anticipations" are terms or incomplete formulations of ideas that may overlap or merely point to later, more fully developed ones. Adumbrations are even more inchoate assertions that "foreshadow" later ones, "[having] only dimly and vaguely approximated the subsequent ideas, with practically none of their specific implications having been drawn and followed up" (1968, p. 13). This is all merely to say that "language-as-resource" is an elaboration of an old idea. It is a fair criticism that my elaboration perhaps has not gone far enough, but then again "far enough" is not far enough as long as reasonable people keep the discussion going.

linguistic status quo." Other advocates of bilingual education and language rights (e.g., Kontra, Phillipson, Skutnabb-Kangas, & Várady, 1999; Ricento, 2005) come to their criticisms from slightly different angles. Petrovic's critique is reasonable in a fundamental way: language-as-resource (as a normative orientation) is easily linked conceptually to language-as-tool (as a descriptive orientation). In other words, and in spite of what I might have meant initially, it appears to be essentially and primarily an instrumental orientation to language. That orientation leads without too much effort to the idea that language must have some sort of extrinsic utility for it to have any value. That is, if the language is not seen as one that will facilitate one's access to social or material goods (social or economic capital, after Bourdieu, 1977), then it has little if any value. To be sure, language has been linked to the economic marketplace in various contexts, sometimes even encoded in policy statements. See, for example, the way Spanish has been conceptualized as an economic resource in South Florida (Fradd & Boswell, 1996), as well as the way the former National Policy on Languages in Australia (Lo Bianco, 1987) and the ensuing National Languages and Literatures Institute created many projects of economic development that had at its center proficiency in foreign and indigenous languages as well as English (e.g., Australian Advisory Council on Languages and Multicultural Education, 1991). Perhaps even more direct is Coulmas's (1992) analysis of the economic vitality of societies depending on the number and status of the languages they comprise.

In this chapter I will try to address some of these concerns about the concept of language-as-resource and how it has been used, not so much as a defense of an entrenched position but as a way to understand how intellectual colleagues can frame arguments that will have positive influences on policies we can support. Critical discussions and arguments of the sort outlined here help us to conceptualize more clearly what we all want to promote—more socially just policies and practices for members of minority communities.

As a preamble to our discussion, I need to emphasize that I have posited language-as-resource as an orientation, a set or configuration of dispositions or predispositions that can be disembedded from policy statements. Considered from this conceptualization, it is similar to "paradigm" (Kuhn) or "frame" (Goffman) in the sense that it evokes a variety of discourses that can be distinguished from those that emerge in the other normative orientations (problem-identification or rights-affirmation). Just as in Kuhn's paradigms, orientations give order to phenomena; the "same" things in different orientations are in different universes of discourse that give them their distinct meaning. Two people using the "same" expression ("language-as-resource," for example) could be meaning radically different things. Perhaps this can help to explain some of the conflicts identified here.

CRITIQUES OF LAR

Criticisms of language-as-resource are of various sorts; I will focus on three, all of which appear in Ricento (2005) but are also found in other writings, with slight variations. I will list them here and then attempt to respond.

1. Language-as-resource has been used by those who want to promote the development, promotion, and use of heritage languages primarily as an economic and military construct.
2. Language-as-resource, construed in this instrumentalist way, detaches language from its cultural and ethnic foundations, thus advancing the sense that language has value only to the extent that it can be useful to those wielding power over others; language-as-resource thus serves the interests of capitalistic power brokers rather than those of the communities in which the languages reside.
3. Language-as-resource discourse inhibits, if not precludes, the promotion of language rights.

LANGUAGE-AS-RESOURCE AS AN ECONOMIC CONSTRUCT

Both Ricento and Petrovic criticize LAR because in their view it creates a violent push toward economic rationalism, or what Petrovic calls neoliberalism. Petrovic puts it this way: "The language-as-resource orientation is, in large part, an economic defense of minority language maintenance" (Petrovic, 2005, p. 397). He continues:

> The language-as-resource orientation, as Ruiz argues it, provides a win–win outcome. The language and the languages of minority groups benefit not only the capitalistic trade and global expansion missions of the dominant group but also the maintenance of the primary languages and cultural identities of minority groups. Indeed, it has been argued that the latter requires the former. As Magnet . . . has argued, "languages can be maintained only to the extent that they are endowed with an economic value." . . . While more extremely stated, Magnet's position is a language-as-resource one . . . . (Petrovic, 2005, p. 399)

Ricento makes a similar argument, although his focus is more specifically on the effects of this discourse on the promotion of heritage languages in the United States: "The main point of this article is to indicate how some professional academic discourses are more concerned with advancing the particular military and economic interests of powerful (including state) interests than with the promotion of linguistic diversity" (p. 350). Asserting that LAR is the controlling metaphor in the arguments for maintaining heritage languages, he further says that LAR "may be complicit with unstated agendas of maintaining current social arrangements that favor policies not particularly favorable to linguistic diversity as intrinsically good or as a national resource, where 'national' tends to exclude non-English languages and cultures" (p. 364).

I appreciate the criticism. I take it as a call for vigilance and further elaboration by those of us who see LAR as way to affirm heritage and other minoritized languages, rather than as an invitation to abandon the discourse completely. In fact, neither Ricento nor Petrovic recommend doing away with LAR as a discursive strategy; what remains then is to see how it can be improved. Responses to these concerns need not be constructed *ab ovo;* a number of writers more thoughtful than I am have already taken up the charge. Michael Clyne discussed and debated these questions with respect to Australia with a panel of colleagues at a seminar sponsored by the journal *Current Issues in Language and Society* in the late 1990s. The resulting monograph, with the unfortunate title of *Managing Language Diversity* (Wright & Kelly-Holmes, 1998) is a record of their remarks. Clyne takes it for granted that "Australia's language resources are of value to the nation as well as to the individual, in the interests of social justice and cohesion, cultural enrichment, and economic assets" (p. 4). His interest is in developing "a strategy for not only maintaining but also developing our language resources" (p. 5). Much of the debate focuses on one of the main topics of his paper: "What happens to a socially motivated language policy intended to further cultural democracy . . . when rampant economic rationalism sets in and takes over education and all other public domains?" (p. 4). "Economic rationalism" is essentially the same concept that Ricento and Petrovic criticize.

The strongest comments on economic rationalism are by Stephen May: "The argument for the economic value of multilingualism rests on the assumption that the minority languages present in the community have some instrumental value and/or economic collateral elsewhere. . . . It seems to me that economic arguments for language maintenance have tended to work against minority languages far more than for them. This is particularly evident with regard to the hegemonic influence of English, for example, and its role in minority language shift" (Wright & Kelly-Holmes, 1998, p. 33).

Clyne and others respond by first rejecting the premise that minority languages, even the smallest, cannot be seen as advantageous at least for limited functions; they can gain a place in the "linguistic marketplace" whether in local or more expanded contexts. See, for example, Saravanan's comments on the role of Tamil and Malay in Singapore (Wright & Kelly-Holmes, 1998, pp. 63ff). Similarly, Mkhulisi (2000) refers to Article 6 of the new South African constitution: "The value of the African languages—not only their intrinsic value, but also their potential as economic resources, giving access to jobs in the language and language-related industries, their importance as media of instruction and as subjects of academic study and fields of research—has been grossly underestimated and neglected" (p. 124). Some have even included those languages that are in the process of revitalization as ones that could have such potential value. Pedersen (1996) argues that Gaelic can be developed as a resource for economic development through a process of "linguistic and cultural normalization" to "enable the language and culture within given communities to achieve a standing such that they can in due course sustain themselves and grow naturally" (p. 82).

So, to summarize, the first response to the argument that LAR is primarily an economic defense of minority languages (Magnet, Petrovic, Ricento, and others), and that such a position places these languages at a distinct disadvantage (May), is to reject its premise—that minority languages have no extrinsic value, at least no value that can serve as currency in the linguistic marketplace. Clyne asserts that quite the opposite is true for Australia, and others make the case for such value in a variety of other contexts.

The second response is to argue that a purely economic argument is too narrow as a basis for language planning for cultural democracy. This is echoed for Australia by others such as Djité (1994), who is concerned that the prevailing language policy (Dawkins, 1991) presents an exceedingly narrow view of "resource." The same sentiment is voiced for other global contexts. Labrie (1998) bemoans the increasing commodification in Canada of various social goods after the passage of the North American Free Trade Agreement: "The supremacy of economics over politics in the very creation of NAFTA and of its institutions, where politics is concealed but implicitly present, could, moreover, favor the establishment of market rules in linguistic matters" (p. 360). Bamgbose (2000) affirms the need to see language as a resource in African societies, suggesting that it is a "valuable asset" and "a stock that can be drawn on," yet he rejects the purely economic model as too narrow for adequate public policy. He expresses his wish for the future of African languages: "Multilingualism will cease to be looked at as a problem rather than an enrichment of the sociocultural life of a community, and acquiring more than one language becomes something to be envied and sought after rather than a necessary evil" (p. 32). For his part, Clyne is also hopeful that a comprehensive policy of the sort outlined in the National Policy on Languages can be part of Australia's future. But it cannot *start* with the economic argument. Instead, it must be based on the intrinsic value of multilingualism; this in turn will be the framework in which economic value is defined: "[I]t is only within the context of a truly multicultural society that economic advantage will be derived from our language resources" (p. 27).

We should be clear on this point. There is hardly a large, multicultural society that has developed a national language policy that did not have economic interests as one of its major dimensions. Clyne's Australia is not an exception, even in the case of the few years at the end of the 1980s when the National Policy on Languages (Lo Bianco, 1987) was in play. In the NPL, aboriginal and immigrant languages were included for promotion, but the economically vital Asian languages were also a centerpiece of the policy. A series of monographs touting the business and commercial benefits of multilingualism were produced by the government and its various institutes. The following statement from a discussion paper characterizes the prevalent mood:

> The "economic" dimension of multiculturalism means that Australia should be able to make effective use of all the nation's human resources. . . . Multicultural policy embraces such issues as . . . maintaining and developing the language resources of our nation in order to advance Australia's trade and tourism interests. Such concerns go to the heart of contemporary economic priorities. They recognize that the cultural diversity of Australia is not a problem. Rather it gives us resources, provides us with assets, that can help to secure our future in an increasingly competitive world. (Australian Council on Multicultural Affairs, 1988, p. 6; cf. Australian Advisory Council on Languages and Multicultural Education, 1991)

While the National Policy on Languages included these economic considerations as one part of a more comprehensive plan, the shift away from the NPL with the new government in the early 1990s brought the economic argument front and center, thus verifying the tendency that is the focal criticism of Ricento and Petrovic. The new policy, codified in the white paper called *Australia's Language* (Dawkins, 1991), "mandated and funded prioritization of language learning in each state according to each language's projected economic benefit for the nation . . ." (Papademetre & Routoulas, 2001, p. 137). This has resulted in a hierarchy based on perceived economic utility, with "Australian English" obviously the most important, followed by a variety of foreign, especially Asian, languages.

There are other examples of attempts at or proposals for comprehensive language policy development that includes but does not privilege economics. See, to name a few, Labrie, Bélanger, Lozon, and Roy (2000) for Canada, Craith (1996) for the European Union, Salinas and Nuñez (2000) for Bolivia, and McKay and Wong (2000) for the United States. I will discuss briefly another case—that of South Africa, where the post-apartheid language policy rests on two bases: "Acknowledgement that multilingualism is a fact of life in that country, then accepting multilingualism as a resource, underpin the 11 official languages policy in South Africa" (Roy-Campbell, 2001, p. 186). The new constitution and the subsequent language policy are central parts of the reconciliation program spearheaded by Mandela and his reorganized African National Congress party. It was seen as a corrective to the brutal policies under apartheid in which "Black languages had been devalued" and "multilingualism was experienced as a 'problem,' best solved by the institution of one or more lingua francas—and these, of course, would be the colonial languages" (deKadt, 1997, p. 152). The designation of 11 official languages that are the focus of the policy reflects the new attitude toward the indigenous languages (Mkhulisi (2000). But here again, the view of languages as resources is comprehensive—cultural, social, political, academic, and economic.

One of the most comprehensive approaches to LAR in the literature is that by Lo Bianco, the author of the original National Policy on Languages for Australia. In his monograph on language policy in Scotland (2001), he uses LAR as the principal orienting framework for his analysis of the status of languages in that country:

> "Language" in its widest sense can be productively thought of as a social and personal resource and asset. By this logic a society can cultivate and develop its language resource enhancing its social communication, and unity, by ensuring that the many "voices" of its community can be heard. (2001, p. 4)

He then describes six important dimensions in which language can be conceptualized in this way: as an intellectual, cultural, economic, social, citizenship, and rights resource. It is noteworthy that an important aspect of his work is the revitalization of heritage language in Scotland; such a concern applies to all of his six dimensions. It is useful as a direct response to Ricento's concern about arguments promoting heritage languages in the United States. Beyond that, the fact that Lo Bianco's conception of LAR was developed independently is indicative of the generative power of the idea.

The ultimate lesson in all these cases is that it is a virtual certainty that any large society that formulates a policy based on LAR will wrestle with the economic argument. Those who criticize any inclusion of economics in discussions of language policy will butt up against this reality. The issue is how we can accommodate it without having it define the entire effort. While I am inclined to agree with those who reject the idea that minority languages can have no instrumental usefulness and accrue economic value over time, I concede that such value is largely a potential that inheres in these languages, a potential that will need long and sustained efforts to be realized; there is little evidence that economic elites will be inclined to collaborate in any such efforts, and some of these languages have little time for such developments. I am more at ease with those who argue that those who place LAR in the orbit of economic rationalism are thinking too narrowly. Value is multifaceted; many of these languages have lived for many generations without the esteem of outside communities in large part because their speakers give them value that others may not appreciate in even their own languages. LAR is a call to create opportunities for the rest of us to gain some of that appreciation.

LANGUAGE-AS-INSTRUMENT

The original papers (Ruiz, 1981, 1984) in which the orientations model was presented included some sketchy remarks about language as a tool (see, for example, my discussion of Tauli in Ruiz 1984, p. 16). Since then, I have elaborated these ideas and expanded the notion of orientations by suggesting that they are of two sorts—normative (or evaluative) and descriptive orientations (Ruiz, 2004). Descriptive orientations have as their basis a particular view of language itself—that it is a means of expression, that it is a conveyer of cultural identity, that it is a tool to obtain social goods, and so on. While these can be closely linked to normative orientations, and in many cases are, the latter sort is qualitatively different: language-as-problem, -right, and -resource directs us to particular sorts of affects and ideologies toward language that are then expressed in policy.

Language Planning Orientations

It is worth reflecting on the strength of the instrumentalist, language-as-tool, orientation. First, there is little argument that language is at least a tool. It is also extremely difficult to engage in maintenance, reversing language shift, or revitalization activities without acknowledging that some measure of instrumentalization is required. Joshua Fishman has said that "a language dies when it loses its place" (1998); by "place" he means "function." His program for reversing language shift (RLS) (Fishman 1991a, 1991b) is based on the

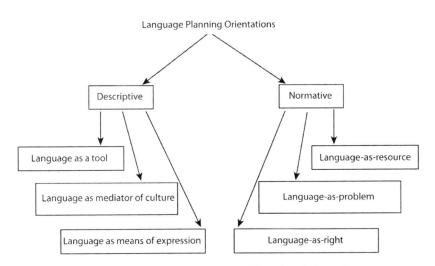

Figure 1. Descriptive and Normative Language Planning Orientations

use of endangered languages in various social contexts. Michael Krauss's language vitality scale (Krauss, 1992) characterizes the status of the health of languages based on how much and who *uses* them. The growing literature on language endangerment (e.g., Bradley & Bradley, 2002; Grenoble & Whaley, 1998) and language death (Hill, 2001) has the question of use and contexts of use at their center.

Second, one cannot deny that the descriptive instrumental orientation is easily, perhaps naturally, linked to language-as-resource, thus reinforcing the Ricento–Petrovic argument that one essentially entails the other. Other links across categories of orientations (language-as-cultural mediator with language-as-right, for example) are less easily made, perhaps. My only response is that LAR includes but is not limited to instrumentalism. Indigenous communities engaged in RLS activities are not constrained from making cultural continuity and intergenerational communication priorities over economic ones. If they are, RSL is not possible.

Third, I have also suggested (Ruiz, 2004) that the instrumental orientation is one that characterizes English more than others. This does not mean that English-speakers are not sensitive to the need for cultural integration or emotional attachments. What I do mean is that the orientation that predominates in English speakers (whether they speak it as a first or an additional language) is instrumental. That is no doubt influenced by the economic, technological, and political power that English and predominantly English-speaking countries are perceived to have. There are more people who speak English as an additional language than speak it as a first. What this reflects is not that the world wants to become culturally American or Australian or British; it does mean that people want to gain access to some of the advantages that have accrued to these societies. For speakers of English as a first language, the instrumentalist orientation may also explain why there seems to be relative indifference, at best, to the loss of minority, local, indigenous languages. Since these bring little if any advantage to their communities, the argument goes, much better to replace their languages with something better, a better tool. What is ignored in this dynamic is that these communities have a different orientation toward their language: it is part of their identity, their world, embodied in the title of Norma Gonzalez's book *I Am My Language* (2003). This orientational difference explains much of the misunderstanding and dissension with respect to language loss and revitalization.

The argument that a language-as-resource discourse promotes an instrumentalist orientation is difficult to refute; the connection may be unavoidable both conceptually and practically. Our interest should therefore be to explain how a call for instrumentalization may include, but goes beyond, economics, while at the same time we give guidance on how to promote the use of minority languages in school curricula, media, commerce, and other domains of everyday life. The tendency to use policy and other language-use practices to exclude marginalized communities by privileging a colonialist mentality needs to be fought on several fronts. I am still convinced that educating people about the intrinsic value of languages by promoting and elaborating a resource-discourse is the best starting point for that fight.

LANGUAGE-AS-RESOURCE AND LANGUAGE RIGHT

Petrovic asserts that I dismiss the rights-affirmation argument prematurely (2005, p. 409). Ricento is more direct with respect to the relation of LAR to language rights:

> [W]hile the contemporary metaphor of language-as-resource does not ascribe lower status to heritage languages, it does little in terms of recognition of intrinsic non-quantifiable resources associated with languages, including psychological, cultural, affiliational, aesthetic, and historical aspects, among others. And, of course, it is silent with regard to the rights claims of language minority communities to receive official and financial support and recognition which is reserved for the dominant language, English. (2005, p. 362)

Here, their criticisms are consistent with those of Skutnabb-Kangas, Phillipson and colleagues (Kontra, Phillipson, Skutnabb-Kangas, & Várady, 1999), who argue for an integration of right and resource as a corrective to my model; their view is that LAR is deficient in its subordination of language rights. What I have said is that a rights orientation is part of the legal universe of discourse where the ethos of advocacy leads inevitably to confrontation (Ruiz, 1984). I will concede that my early writing seemed to create an antagonism between right and resource, but whatever the shortcomings of my initial conceptualization, it is not fair to suggest that LAR has nothing to say about rights affirmation. I am now prepared to be clearer about the relation between rights and resources: the latter is conceptually prior to the former. This does not subordinate rights; it merely asserts that one cannot reasonably talk about rights, much less affirm them, without a prior understanding of how rights are resources.

One might even posit an internal relationship between language-as-resource and language-as-right; more, one might see language-as-resource as a precondition for language-as-right. Let me say it more forcefully: unless one sees a language as a good thing in itself, it is impossible to affirm anyone's right to it. To say that one has a right to (be educated in) one's mother tongue—to say that access to one's mother tongue is a linguistic human right—is to say, first, that the mother tongue is a good thing in itself. The distinction between language rights and linguistic human rights rests on that entailment: rights are only rights if they are resources (goods in themselves) first. The obverse of that argument is made time and time again by those who argue for the rights of indigenous and minority communities to their languages: viewing the language as a problem (not a resource) is to see it as something that should be eliminated—from the community, from the school curriculum, from the child. See, for example, the papers in the many books that are being written on the maintenance of indigenous languages in different parts of the world. Kamwangamalu (2003) says that when multilingualism is seen "as a problem" in Africa, it is logical to assume that language policies will be developed "within the language-as-problem paradigm . . . aimed at eliminating the source of the problem" (p. 176). The logic is unimpeachable. Why would one want to perpetuate a malignancy, much less affirm anyone's human right to it? Why would Zubeida Desai (2003), in trying to make the case for mother-tongue education for speakers of indigenous African languages, as the same is a "given" for speakers of English or Afrikaans, have to ask why this *right* is "so *wrong* for the majority of learners in African countries such as South Africa?" (p. 46). The answer in all of these texts, whether explicitly stated or not, is that for these children we have made routine the notion in policy or practice that "the language of their parents is not good enough to be used in school" (Meerkotter, 2003, p. 41). And in many cases the conclusion is far beyond that: Eva Yerendé (2005) describes how schools in Guinea build into the structure of their classrooms the image of the inferiority of the child's home language. She notes how other writers have traced the use of symbols such as the horn to symbolize the stupidity of the African language speaker. While in the past the horn was placed around the neck of children to humiliate them into using the colonial language, the horn hanging on the classroom wall "is used as powerful reminder of what could happen to the students if they refuse or forget to speak French" (p. 207).

Still, I must acknowledge that the original expression "language-as-resource" was simply and naively conceptualized as a way to counter the pervasive discourse of the time, perhaps of this time as well, that assumed that minority languages and their communities were problems that created disadvantages for not only their speakers, but the society as well. My preoccupation with promoting a sharp alternative to the problem orientation excluded the important notion that language planning also needed to consider how it would deal with language rights. I give credit to my students at Madison, especially Dianne Bowcock, Maria Dalupan, Nancy Hornberger, Julia Richards, and Joan Strouse, for bringing language rights into our conversation on language planning. The cases they examined in their doctoral programs—Gambia, Philippines, Peru, Guatemala, and the Hmong in the United States—made it obvious that the original model was incomplete.

SUMMARY AND CONCLUSION

In the preceding pages I have tried to answer some of the major challenges to the language-as-resource orientation (LAR) and the discursive arguments that have proceeded from it. Ricento's three criticisms reflect the concerns of a number of other researchers: (1) that LAR is too easily construed in economic terms, so that (2) the value of minority languages is seen as negligible or nonexistent in relation to more powerful languages, and (3) that LAR discourses diminish if not preclude a consideration of language rights. My assumption in responding is that these criticisms are hard but friendly; that is, they are derived from a concern that the intent of the resource model is noble but flawed, so we all have a common interest in correcting the distortions that subvert the primary intent of the model—promotion of cultural democracy and social justice.

I have made use of the work of a number of others in addressing these criticisms. As to the framing of LAR in economic terms, I agree that this has often happened and will continue to happen; it is also true that many of the arguments for it construe the value of minority languages much more broadly, including Lo Bianco's (2001) six dimensions mentioned previously. Although it will take much time and effort to realize the potential of some of these languages in formalized contexts such as classrooms and scientific laboratories from which they have been historically excluded, their curricular value as media of instruction and their more general value as vehicles for social and cultural integration should not be minimized. Finally, while I concede that early formulations of LAR may have given little attention to language rights, they have not been excluded from the analysis (it is, after all, one of the three prongs of the model). The conceptual point to be made is that strong rights affirmation is not possible without acknowledging that rights are resources—that they are good in themselves. Without accepting that premise, there are no grounds for asserting rights.

The hope of academics in applied fields such as education is that our work will be both useful and used. The fact that, as academics, we argue among ourselves about our ideas, undoubtedly a healthy thing, also sometimes gives those who make decisions on policy and practice grounds for ignoring them. Although Ricento makes the case that LAR has been the conception of language underpinning the promotion of heritage languages by academics, it is clear that it has not been the controlling metaphor in the development of policy in areas such as bilingual education and the inclusion of home languages in programs for English learners. That is a situation I lament. But I also take some encouragement from developments in the early 1990s when, through collaborative teams such as Kenji Hakuta's Stanford Working Group (Hakuta, 1993), people with a common purpose but divergent ideas of how to achieve it formulated strong statements about what bilingual education should look like. That report begins with the premise that "bilingualism enhances cognitive and social growth" (p. 1) and prods federal policy makers to create programs that "maintain a focus on bilingualism as a national and local resource" (p. 2). What resulted was the eventual appointment of a director for the Office of Bilingual Education and Minority Languages Affairs who helped to promote the idea that language diversity was a good thing and that bilingual education could be a vehicle to enhance this strength that had been devalued in both policy and practice for decades. The sense of commitment to a common paradigm for the education of language minority communities created the energy to refashion the 1994 version of the Bilingual Education Act, one that emphasized the notion of language as a national resource. It is no accident that the 1990s saw significant expansion of developmental bilingual programs in the United States. One can note a similar development in post-apartheid South Africa, where the reconciliation movement advanced the need for inclusion of Black African communities and their languages in public policy and programs. A major contributor to the new South Africa was the Language Plan Task Force (Language Planning Task Group, 1996) whose report asserted from the outset that "language is a resource, not a problem" (p. 12). Perhaps now is a propitious time for those who see a need to take back LAR from those who have used it narrowly to the detriment of minority communities to caucus on how the concept should be refashioned for good.

As a conclusion, let me return to the first criticism, one that seems the most central to the concerns raised by Ricento, Petrovic, Skutnabb Kangas, and others. To reiterate, their aim is not to point out structural deficiencies in the model itself, but to assert that the orientation that I have tried to promote, language-as-resource, may itself be misguided, perhaps even dangerous, in large part because of the ease with which it can be interpreted in purely instrumental–economic–military terms. Petrovic (2005) puts this most forcefully:

> For I believe that the resource orientation is doomed to negative reappropriation by capitalist forces. This is because power has not been factored into the relationship. As we continue to capitalize language, meaning the process by which proficiency in more than one language becomes a marketable skill leading to pecuniary rewards that otherwise would not be gained, the control of the means to develop language(s) as such an asset will be in the hands of those in power (language diversity taken hostage). (p. 410)

Academic work is by nature public. We write papers and books, give presentations, deliver lectures, and in many other ways create opportunities for others to comment, question, challenge, criticize, and perhaps appropriate and adapt our work. In fact, this is as it should be. To be sure, we need to understand that people of different persuasions will use our work in ways we did not intend and of which we do not approve. The "reappropriation" that

Petrovic speaks of is an artifact of the academic community—an unavoidable result of the public nature of scholarly discourse: the more we publish in the academic marketplace, the more likely our ideas are to be pushed, pulled, bent, and sometimes totally mangled. But we need not be passive about it when we think these interpretations are wrong. It is both an academic and a moral failing to cede the intellectual ground to those who use our work to reproduce or reinforce the interests of the powerful and thus impede the advance of social justice. In the case of LAR, to abandon it to those interests would be foolish and politically reckless. Too much good has come from the application of even the simple version of this metaphor to reorient societies toward cultural democracy. All we can do with undesirable applications is to argue against them. At the same time, we can work toward refining our discourse to make it more likely that good rather than evil will come of it. Discussions such as these can help realize this end.

REFERENCES

Australian Advisory Council on Languages and Multicultural Education. (1991). *Language is good business: The role of language in Australia's economic future.* Melbourne: The National Languages and Literacy Institute of Australia.

Australian Council on Multicultural Affairs. (1988). *Towards a national agenda for a multicultural Australia: A discussion paper.* Canberra: AGPS.

Bamgbose, A. (2000). *Language and exclusion: The consequences of language policies in Africa.* Hamburg: Lit Verlag.

Bourdieu, P. (1977). The economics of linguistic exchanges. *Social Science Information/ Information Sur Les Sciences Sociales, 16*(6), 645–668.

Bradley, D. & Bradley, M. (Eds.). (2002). *Language endangerment and language maintenance.* London & New York: Routledge Curzon.

Coulmas, F. (1992). *Language and economy.* Oxford: Blackwell Publishers.

Craith, M. N. (Ed.). (1996). *Watching one's tongue: Issues in language planning.* Liverpool: University of Liverpool Press.

Das Gupta, J. & Ferguson, C. A. (1977). Problems of language planning. In J. Rubin, B. H. Jernudd, J. Das Gupta, J. A. Fishman, & C. A. Ferguson (Eds.), *Language planning processes* (pp. 3–7). The Hague: Mouton.

Dawkins, J. (1991). *Australia's language: The Australian language and literacy policy.* Canberra: Australian Government Publishing Service.

deKadt, E. (1997). McWorld versus local cultures: English in South Africa at the turn of the millennium. In L. E. Smith & M. L. Forman (Eds.), *World Englishes 2000* (pp. 146–168). Honolulu: University of Hawaii Press.

Desai, Z. (2003). A case for mother tongue education? In B. Brock-Utne, Z. Desai, & M. Qorro (Eds.), *Language of instruction in Tanzania and South Africa (LOITASA)* (pp. 45–68). Dar-es-Salaam, Tanzania: E&D Limited.

Djite, P. G. (1994). *From language policy to language planning: An overview of languages other than English in Australian education.* Deakin: Australian National Languages and Literacy Institute.

Fishman, J. A. (1966). *Language loyalty in the United States: The maintenance and perpetuation of non-English mother tongues by American ethnic and religious groups.* The Hague: Mouton.

Fishman, J. A. (1991a). An inter-polity perspective on the relationship between linguistic heterogeneity, civil strife and per capita gross national product. *International Journal of Applied Linguistics, 1*(1), 5–18.

Fishman, J. A. (1991b). *Reversing language shift.* Clevedon, UK: Multilingual Matters.

Fishman, J. A. (1998, June). *Family, playmates, neighbors, and ethnic community school: Case studies of successful urban language maintenance.* Paper presented at the 19th annual American Indian Language Development Institute, University of Arizona, Tucson, Arizona.

Fradd, S. & Boswell, T. (1996). Spanish as an economic resource in metropolitan Miami. *Bilingual Research Journal, 20*(2), 283–337.

Garcia, O. (2009). *Bilingual education in the 21st century: A global perspective.* Malden, MA: Wiley-Blackwell.

Gonzalez, N. (2003). *I am my language: Discourses of women and children in the borderlands.* Tucson: University of Arizona Press.

Grenoble, L. & Whaley, L. J. (Eds.). (1998). *Endangered languages: Current issues and future prospects.* Cambridge, UK: Cambridge University Press.

Hakuta, K. (1993). *Federal education programs for limited-English-proficient students: A blueprint for the second generation.* Stanford, CA: Author.

Hill, J. H. (2001). Dimensions of attrition in language death. In L. Maffi (Ed.), *On biocultural diversity: Linking language, knowledge and the environment* (pp. 175–189). Washington & London: Smithsonian Institution Press.

Jernudd, B. H. (1977). Prerequisites for a model of language treatment. In J. Rubin, B. H. Jernudd, J. Das Gupta, J. A. Fishman, & C. A. Ferguson (Eds.), *Language planning processes* (pp. 41–54). The Hague: Mouton.

Jernudd, B. H. & Das Gupta, J. (1971). Towards a theory of language planning. In J. Rubin & B. H. Jernudd (Eds.), *Can language be planned? Sociolinguistic theory and practice for developing nations* (pp. 195–215). Honolulu: University of Hawaii Press.

John, V. P. & Horner, V. M. (1971). *Early childhood bilingual education.* New York: Modern Language Association.

Kamwangamalu, N. M. (2003). Language and education in Africa: Emancipation or alienation? In P. Culvelier, T. Du Plessis, & L. Teck (Eds.), *Multilingualism, education and social integration: Belgium, Europe, South Africa, Southern Africa* (pp. 175–184). Pretoria, South Africa: Van Schaik Publishers.

Kontra, M., Phillipson, R., Skutnabb-Kangas, T., & Várady (Eds.). (1999). *Language: A right and a resource: Approaching linguistic human rights.* Budapest: Central European University Press.

Krauss, M. (1992). The world's languages in crisis. *Language, 68*(1), 4–10.

Labrie, N. (1998). The role of the French language in maintaining linguistic diversity in North America: Some glottopolitical considerations. In D. A. Kibbee (Ed.), *Language legislation and linguistic rights.* Selected proceedings of the Language Legislation and Linguistic Rights Conference, The University of Illinois at Urbana-Champaign, March 1996 (pp. 351–362). Amsterdam: Benjamins.

Labrie, N., Bélanger, N., Lozon, R., & Roy, S. (2000). Mondalisation et exploitation de resources linguistiques: Les défis des communautés francophones de l'Ontario. [Globalization and exploitation of linguistic resources: Challenges for the francophone communities of Ontario]. *The Canadian Modern Language Review, 57*(1), 88–117.

Language Planning Task Group. (1996). *Towards a national language plan for South Africa: Final report of the Language Plan Task Group (LANGTAG)*. Pretoria, South Africa: State Language Services.

Lo Bianco, J. (1987). *National policy on languages*. Canberra: Australian Government Publishing Service.

Lo Bianco, J. (2001). *Language and literacy policy in Scotland*. Stirling, Scotland: University of Stirling, Scottish Centre for Information on Language Teaching and Research.

McKay, S. & Wong, S. L. (Eds.). (2000). *New immigrants in the United States: Readings for second language educators*. New York: Cambridge University Press.

Meerkotter, D. (2003). Markets, language in education and socio-economic stratification. In B. Brock-Utne, Z. Desai, & M. Qorro (Eds.), *Language of instruction in Tanzania and South Africa (LOITASA)* (pp. 35–44). Dar-es-Salaam, Tanzania: E&D Limited.

Merton, R. K. (1968). *Social theory and social structure*. New York: The Free Press.

Mkhulisi, N. (2000). The National Language Service and the new language policy. In K. Deprez & T. du Plessis (Eds.), *Multilingualism and government: Belgium, Luxembourg, Switzerland, Former Yougoslavia, South Africa* (pp. 121–129). Pretoria, South Africa: Van Schaik Publishers.

Papademetre, L., & Routoulas, S. (2001). Social, political, educational, linguistic and cultural (dis-)incentives for languages education in Australia. *Journal of Muiltilingual and Multicultural Development, 22*(2), 134–151.

Pedersen, R. (1996). Scots Gaelic: An economic force. In M. N. Craith (Ed.), *Watching one's tongue: Issues in language planning* (pp. 81–102). Liverpool: University of Liverpool Press.

Petrovic, J. E. (2005) The conservative restoration and neoliberal defenses of bilingual education. *Language Policy, 4*, 395–416.

Ricento, T. (2005). Problems with the "language as resource" discourse in the promotion of heritage languages in the USA. *Journal of Sociolinguistics, 9*(3), 348–368.

Roy-Campbell, Z. M. (2001). *Empowerment through language: The African experience: Tanzania and beyond*. Trenton, NJ/Asmara, Eritrea: Africa World Press.

Ruiz, R. (1981, December). *Orientations in language planning: An essay on the politics of language*. Paper presented at the International Conference in Language Problems and Public Policy, Cancun.

Ruiz, R. (1984). Orientations in language planning. *NABE Journal, 8*(2), 15–34.

Ruiz, R. (2004, July). *Language rights and language interests*. Keynote address to the meeting of the Southern Africa Applied Linguistics Society, Pietersberg, South Africa.

Salinas, S. C. & Nuñez, J. M. J. (2000). Education, culture and indigenous rights: The case of educational reform in Bolivia. *Prospects, 30* (1), 105–124.

Wright, S. & Kelly-Holmes, H. (Eds.). (1998). *Managing language diversity.* Clevedon, UK: Multilingual Matters.

Yerendé, E. (2005). Ideologies of language and schooling in Guinea-Conakry. In B. Brock-Utne & R. K. Hopson (Eds.), *Languages of instruction for African emancipation: Focus on postcolonial contexts and considerations* (pp. 199–230). Dar-es-Salaam, Tanzania: Mkuki na Nyota Publishers.

CHAPTER 8

THE ROLE OF LANGUAGE IN THEORIES OF ACADEMIC FAILURE FOR LINGUISTIC MINORITIES

Jeff MacSwan and Kellie Rolstad
Arizona State University

INTRODUCTION

Why do English-language learners (ELLs) struggle in school? Since concern for educational equity reached public awareness some time in the middle of the last century, numerous educational researchers have addressed this important question. Language has often been posited as a causal factor, often in ways characterizing the language that immigrant children bring to the school setting as the principal culprit. We review the history of this literature in the specific context of language minority students and argue that it adopts a traditional prescriptivist perspective on language inconsistent with linguistic research. We conclude with a description of an alternative perspective.

International Perspectives on Bilingual Education: Policy, Practice, and Controversy, pages 173–194
Copyright © 2010 by Information Age Publishing
All rights of reproduction in any form reserved.

LANGUAGE AS A THEORETICAL CONSTRUCT

Language has played a central role in theories of academic achievement differences but is rarely explicitly defined as a psychological construct. In order to evaluate or measure language in any group, we must first clearly understand what it is. In the context of language minority education, the matter is especially important, as attitudes and prejudices about language differences have often served as a proxy for less socially and politically acceptable kinds of prejudice.

Research on language acquisition has found cross-culturally that all normal children acquire the language of their respective speech communities and do so effortlessly and without formal instruction (Slobin & Bowerman, 1985; Pinker, 1994). During the most active acquisition period in the preschool years, children learn approximately 10–12 new words per day, often on one exposure and in highly ambiguous circumstances (Gleitman & Landau, 1994), and they acquire knowledge of elementary aspects of sentence structure for which they have no evidence at all (Lightfoot, 1982). Moreover, as Tager-Flusberg (1997, p. 188) has pointed out in a review of the literature, "by the time children begin school, they have acquired most of the morphological and syntactic rules of their language," and possess a grammar essentially indistinguishable from adults. These facts and others have led many researchers to believe that language acquisition is inwardly directed by innate principles of Universal Grammar (Chomsky, 1981), or an internal "bioprogram," as Bickerton (1981) has termed it.

Universal Grammar (UG) is presumed to be a biological endowment common to the human species, and unique in essential respects. It defines a narrowly delineated hypothesis space for the language learner who uses primary linguistic data from the speech community to set options permitted by UG. Thus, UG begins in an initial state, S_0, which successively approximates the language of the speech community through a series of intermediate states, $S_1 \ldots S_n$, until it reaches a steady state, S_s, after which it appears to undergo only peripheral changes (acquisition of new vocabulary, development of new speech styles, and so on) (Lightfoot, 1982; Pinker, 1994; Chomsky, 1986; Ritchie & Bhatia, 1999).

Of course, languages differ across communities of speakers and across individuals as well (Fillmore, Kempler & Wang, 1979). Thus, when we identify a speech community as "speakers of English" or "speakers of Tyrolian German" we engage in an idealization, assuming homogeneity for the purpose of discussion, much in the way that natural scientists assume homogeneity of body organs and other objects of study. We might usefully think of "speakers of a language L" as those speakers whose languages are each sufficiently alike as to permit intelligible intercommunication in L. In doing so, however, we recognize that, in actual fact, speech communities have considerable internal variation, even to the level of individual speakers (idiolects), and that speakers may be members of multiple speech communities.

Thus, a particular language—such as English, German, or Swahili—is a set of expressions defined by a grammar, a psychological mechanism that maps sound to meaning and that is represented in the mind/brain of a speaker–hearer, and a vocabulary. The grammar of a particular language is a set of values over the range of variation permitted by UG once it has entered the steady (or "mature") state (Chomsky, 1995). In the context of first language (L1) acquisition, then, we take "language proficiency" to be a state of linguistic maturity in which a learner has acquired a grammar that is compatible with the language of the community of origin.

Although children's acquisition of their native language is essentially complete by the time they reach school, school-aged second-language learners (SLLs) may exhibit linguistic errors of a sort that typically developing school-age children do not exhibit in their native language. Unlike school-aged native speakers, SLLs have developed only partial knowledge of the structure of their target language and exhibit substantial errors associated with tense, case, grammatical agreement, word order, pronunciation, and other aspects of language structure. In addition, while all normal human beings acquire a language effortlessly and without instruction, second-language (L2) acquisition often meets with only partial success, at times depends upon considerable effort, and may be facilitated by purposely structured input (Bley-Vroman, 1989; Coppieters, 1987). Thus, in the case of school-aged SLLs of English, we expect "English proficiency" to reflect growing mastery of the structure and vocabulary of English over some range of time.

Literacy and other school subjects will no doubt make use of a child's language ability, but these seem substantially different in character. Humans acquire language by instinct, upon exposure, the way birds acquire birdsong; but the learning of school subjects, such as literacy, physics, and mathematics, do not follow a biologically endowed program (Chomsky, 1986; Gee, 2001; MacSwan, 2000; MacSwan & Rolstad, 2003). Academic achievement denotes a domain of knowledge that is specific to a particular human context—namely, the world of schooling. While all (typically developing) children develop a vocabulary and a grammatical system, not all children will come to know specific facts about geography, history, or physics. Nonetheless, when features of literary discourse (peculiar vocabulary, impersonal author, distant setting, special order of events, so on) are familiar to children and are present even in their oral language, as has been found among very young middle-class children, then achievement in school literacy becomes a much easier task, since a considerable portion of it has been accomplished before students enter school. This "middle-class advantage" relates to the special alignment of children's particular home experiences and speech styles with those encountered at school (Heath, 1983; Wiley, 1996).

In addition, a child's tacit understanding of the rules that govern language use are also sensitive to social and situational contexts, and the interpretation of particular linguistic expressions is tied to a language user's appreciation of relevance, coherence, and context (Sperber & Wilson, 1986; Kehler, 2002). As Gee (1999) has pointed out, language use has the effect of establishing a *who* and a *what*, a socially situated person engaged in a particular kind of craft or activity—a teacher, doctor, a member of a club or street gang, a regular at a local bar, or a student at school. These roles enter into a speaker–hearer's perspective and are part of what Gee calls "Discourses"—ways of acting, interacting, thinking, and valuing within a particular community of speakers. Gee (1999) uses the term "social language" to denote the role of language in discourse, the set of conventions that result in an expression of personal and social identity, and of relationships among interlocutors and participants. Thus, as we each make meaning out of language, we do far more than compute an interpretation deriving from the interaction of syntax and word meaning. We make use of a wealth of knowledge and theories about the world and of a particular set of cultural models, practices, and beliefs.

We might usefully regard these components of our mental life as part of the domain of *language use,* classically termed linguistic performance, and take *knowledge of language,* or linguistic competence, to refer more narrowly to the speaker–hearer's knowledge of language structure (Chomsky, 1965; Kasher, 1991). While knowledge of language and knowledge of school subjects are certainly different psychological constructs, the language of an academically successful student will be affected in concrete ways by school experience, introducing (or reinforcing) new vocabulary, speech styles, and "social languages," in Gee's (1999) sense.

To sum up, we define knowledge of language as a linguistic construct, reflecting a grammatical system that consists of the rules and principles that govern syntax (word order), morphology (word formation), and phonology (pronunciation) and that interface with principles of discourse, pragmatics, and semantic interpretation. Speakers and communities differ with regard to the particular form these principles might take, resulting in the formation of distinctive varieties and conventions of language use, but each community nevertheless has a language every bit as rich and complex as the next (Crystal, 1986; Newmeyer, 1986; Milroy & Milroy, 1999). With regard to L2 acquisition among school-aged children, we naturally expect to see a maturational process that proceeds on an independent timetable, with ongoing evidence of development in core linguistic systems.

Central to these points about the nature of linguistic knowledge is the observation that languages vary within and across communities, as previously noted. Some varieties have higher social prestige than others, but the prestige associated with a linguistic variety results from social and political forces that are altogether independent of the linguistic system itself. Prescriptivists make the error of assuming that language varieties each reflect certain cognitive advantages underlying the relative social and political success of the groups represented, an assumption that made its way into educational theories about the academic achievement of minorities in U.S. schools. We turn to this topic in greater detail directly.

LANGUAGE VARIATION AND DEFICIT THEORIES: A BRIEF HISTORY

Prescriptivism is the view that one or another language or variety of language has an inherently higher value than others, and that it ought to be imposed on the whole of the speech community to maintain standards of communication; prescriptivists have often characterized minority languages (or dialects) as "inexpressive," "primitive," or lacking complexity in comparison to their own language (Crystal, 1986; Pinker, 1994). Language academies employed with the task of "purifying" the regional linguistic descendants of Latin were set up as early as 1582 in Italy, 1635 in France, and 1713 in Spain. Proposals for a language academy in England were also popular in the seventeenth century, but the suggestion lost support as it became evident that the continental academies could not halt the tide of language change. (See Crystal, 1986, and Pinker, 1994, for further discussion.)

The prohibitions regarding English usage, which are most familiar from U.S. school curricula, typically turned to Latinate analyses advanced in the late nineteenth and early twentieth centuries that were used to validate varieties of speech associated with the educated classes in England and the United States (Baugh and Cable, 1978; Nunberg, 1983). In contrast to work in the prescriptivist tradition, the structuralist linguists in the United States had undertaken an empirical project, following Bloomfield's (1933) lead, in which all languages were analyzed using the same taxonomy, leading to the conclusion that all languages, even "primitive languages," were equally complex. This research agenda ultimately had serious consequences that threatened sacred distinctions that kept privilege and social prestige in the hands of the educated classes. As Newmeyer (1986) has put it:

> As long as American structuralists confined their campaign to the languages of remote tribes, they did little to upset their colleagues in departments of modern and classical languages—in which almost all linguists were situated in the interwar years. But such was certainly not the case when they began crusading for the linguistic equality of *all* dialects of English and other literary languages, no matter how "substandard" they were regarded. This egalitarian view came in direct conflict with the long-seated tradition in the humanities that values a language variety in direct proportion to its literary output. (p. 42)

While much of seventeenth-century Europe was preoccupied with the "special languages" of elites, the *Port Royale Grammar* of 1660 advanced a very different view of language and of the human condition. Written in French, the *Port Royale Grammar* formed part of the movement to displace Latin as an outdated mode of academic discourse. However, what marked the *Port Royale Grammar* as deeply distinct from contemporaneous approaches was its devotion to philosophical and universal properties of human language in descriptive terms (Robins, 1967; Chomsky, 1968; Newmeyer, 1988). As in modern approaches in linguistic science, the Port Royale grammarians worked on the Cartesian assumption that normal human intelligence is capable of acquiring knowledge through its own internal resources, making use of the data of experience but moving on to construct a cognitive system in terms of concepts and principles that are developed on independent grounds.

The fear that languages might "decay" in the process of change, or the notion that groups from different cultural backgrounds speak "diminished" or "simplified" languages when compared to Europeans, is incompatible with these assumptions since languages are held to "grow" in virtue of common human resources (today, UG). Indeed, in the early twentieth century, Franz Boas (1911) and others painstakingly showed that non-Western languages were every bit as linguistically sophisticated and rich as their European counterparts represented in the universities.

In contrast, early work in the sociology of language followed in the tradition that viewed culturally distinct languages as related hierarchically, with the languages of the dominant social classes at the top of the "intellectual" scale. According to Dittmar (1976), Schatzmann and Strauss (1955) were the first to formulate what he terms "the Deficit Hypothesis"—the view that the linguistic abilities of particular social groups are deficient or restricted in some way. Schatzmann and Strauss (1955) interviewed members of the lower class and middle class about their impressions and experiences after the occurrence of a disaster and found that the former used a significant amount of emotional language that reputedly gave rise to "elliptical syntax." Accordingly, Schatzmann and Strauss (1955) concluded that the lower classes only conveyed their meaning "implicitly," while the educated classes conveyed their meaning "explicitly."

This and other work led Basil Bernstein (1971) to formulate a distinction between "public language" and "formal language," later termed "restricted" and "elaborated" code. Bernstein studied speakers of a stigmatized dialect in London and characterized their speech as accessing restricted code, but not elaborated code. According to Bernstein (1971), restricted language is characterized by "fragmentation and logical simplicity." By contrast, elaborated code may be used to express "universal meaning," which was ill defined in Bernstein's work. For Bernstein, the restricted code expresses meanings which form a proper subset of the range of meanings expressed in the elaborated code. The appropriate remediation, then, ". . . would seem to be to preserve *public* language usage but also to create for the individual the possibility of utilizing a *formal* language" (1971, p. 54).

Numerous commentators have portrayed Bernstein as positioned squarely within the camp of the "deficit" theorists, as we do here (Trudgill, 1974; Dittmar, 1976; Boocock, 1980; Bennett & LeCompte, 1990), while others have come to his defense (Halliday, 1995; Danzig, 1995; other papers in Sadovnik, 1995, and Atkinson, Davies, & Delamont, 1995). However, as Dittmar (1976) points out, what makes Bernstein's view a species of the Deficit Hypothesis is his perspective that the speech of the educated classes is in some way *greater* (more expressive, less elliptical, and so on) than working-class speech; that is, the characteristics of "better speech" are taken to be precisely those characteristics that socially less prestigious groups lack.

About the same time, Bereiter and colleagues (Bereiter & Engelmann, 1966; Bereiter, Engelman, Osborn, & Reidford, 1966) posited a relationship between African American vernacular English and the poor educational achievement of African American school children. Bereiter reported that the four-year-olds he studied communicated by gestures, "single words," and "a series of badly connected words or phrases." According to Bereiter and colleagues, these children could "without exaggeration . . . make no statements of any kind," and could not ask questions. Of particular significance was Bereiter's expectation that children answer in complete sentences. In response to the question "Where is the squirrel?" Bereiter's subjects tended to answer, "In the tree"—a response Bereiter characterized as illogical and badly formed. As Labov (1970) pointed out, the response "In the tree" is the natural response in this context, and the one that anybody would use under normal circumstances—except, perhaps, in the context of an academic exercise. Labov (1970) concluded his review of Bereiter and others with a harsh rebuke 40 years ago: "That educational psychology should be strongly influenced by a theory so false to the facts of language is unfortunate; but that children should be the victims of this ignorance is intolerable" (p. 260).

Language and its relation to lower educational achievement dominated conversations about African American students amid the American civil rights movement. Language similarly moved to the forefront of conversations about achievement among other linguistic-minority students at about the same time, particularly in the wake of the Mexican American student walkouts in East Los Angeles in 1968 (Crawford, 2004). Thus, educational researchers concerned with academic underachievement among bilingual students began to address important questions about the language these children bring to school and how it may factor into our understanding of student achievement.

EXPLAINING ACHIEVEMENT DIFFERENCES AMONG ENGLISH-LANGUAGE LEARNERS

Educational researchers concerned with explaining academic achievement differences among ELLs considered at least two distinct paths. Paulston (1975), for instance, observed that "in every single study where monolingual children did as well as or better in L2 instruction than did native speakers, those children came from upper- or middle-class homes" (p. 9). Similarly, the U.S. Commission on Civil Rights (1975) noted, "Those individuals who are commonly designated 'bilingual' . . . in this country are also those who, bearing the brunt of many forms of discrimination, tend to be of a low socioeconomic status [SES] such as Mexican Americans, Native Americans, Puerto Ricans, and many immigrant groups" (p. 68).

SES has been shown to be a consistent predictor of academic success, both in the general population and among language minority children (Rosenthal, Milne, Ellman, Ginsburg, & Baker, 1983; Genesee, 1984; Berliner & Biddle, 1995). This is not a surprising finding. The language and literate practices of the middle and upper classes are valued at school in ways that put children of other cultural backgrounds at a decided disadvantage (Heath, 1983), and schools that service the poor and working-class tend to have inadequate resources (Kozol, 1991) and to be much more focused on obedience to authority, punctuality, and other forms of social control (Willis, 1981). By contrast, children from higher SES backgrounds generally have caregivers who are more educated, better prepared to assist with school work, and have the time and bureaucratic know-how to interact with the school (Berliner & Biddle, 1995). For these children, education in school literacy and academic discourse begins at home and remains in place as a continual support throughout the school years.

The wide range of cultural capital linked to SES is arguably a central difference between successful and unsuccessful school experiences for linguistic minorities as well. ELLs have two objectives that they must meet in order to achieve academic success in the United States. Like language majority children, they must master academic content; but unlike language majority children, they must also learn English at school. In programs in which all instruction is in English, language minority children of lower SES tend to fall further and further behind by the end of elementary school (Ramirez et al., 1991), showing the accumulative effects of only partially understanding the language of instruction. By contrast, children of higher SES who either immigrated to the United States with prior educational experience or who have parents who are better prepared to assist with schoolwork at home, or both, do well even in the absence of native-language instruction, because their caregivers and their own past experience provide content area assistance through a language children understand, or what Krashen (1996) has referred to as "de facto bilingual education." Indeed, years of formal schooling in L1 have been identified as an important predictor affecting school achievement for language minority children, whether the schooling takes place in the home country or the United States (Collier, 1992; Turner, Laria, Shapiro, & Perez, 1993; Krashen, 1996; Thomas & Collier, 1997). According to this perspective, language minority children benefit from native-language instruction because it allows them to keep up academically while learning English. We might refer to this perspective as the facilitation theory; it posits that bilingual education and other remedies provide ELLs with intelligible access to school content, transferring to and thereby facilitating growth in school-related knowledge (MacSwan & Rolstad, 2005).

Despite early support for the facilitation theory in language minority education, the field as a whole has been strongly dominated by the idea that the quality of children's native language is the principal culprit underlying minority children's difficulties at school. Cummins, for instance, who has played a major role in promoting what we might call the *primary-language theory*, has argued that while SES may play a role, "the linguistic competence attained by bilingual children" is nonetheless one of the "intervening variables in the causal chain whose influence needs to be specified" (Cummins, 1976, p. 19). Cummins's work, embodied in the Threshold Hypothesis and the BICS/CALP distinction, came to dominate the field of language minority education and to this day remains the dominant perspective internationally. We turn now to a critical review of each in turn.

THE THRESHOLD HYPOTHESIS AND SEMILINGUALISM

Cummins's (1976, 1979) Threshold Hypothesis embeds a specific conception of language which posits a condition known as *semilingualism*. The core idea underlying the Threshold Hypothesis was that the level of linguistic competence attained by a bilingual child in an L1 and L2 may affect cognitive growth in other domains. In his early work, Cummins believed that there were two thresholds, and that attainment beyond the lower threshold "would be sufficient to avoid retardation, but the attainment of a second, higher level of bilingual competence might be necessary to lead to accelerated cognitive growth" (1976, p. 24). For him, children with low levels of proficiency in both their L1 and L2 may suffer "negative cognitive effects." Once mastery in one language has been obtained, the child has moved beyond the first threshold and will suffer neither positive nor negative effects. Finally, "positive cognitive effects" result when a child develops high proficiency in both languages. Cummins represents these ideas graphically as in Figure 1 (Cummins (1979, p. 230).

"Semilingualism" was first introduced in a 1962 radio talk by the Swedish philologist Nils Erik Hansegård (who called it *halvspråkighet*). The term,

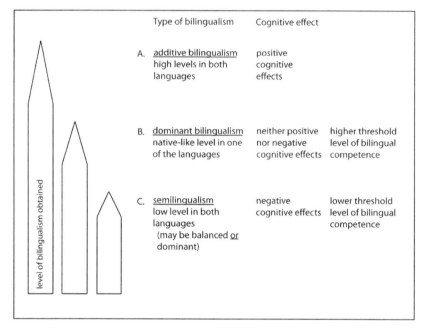

Figure 1: Threshold Hypothesis: Cognitive Effects of Different Types of Bilingualism

Reproduced from Cummins, 1979, p. 230

which denotes a lack of competence in all languages an individual knows, was introduced to scholars in the United States by Skutnabb-Kangas and Toukomaa (1976) and was adopted by Cummins as a component of his Threshold Hypothesis:

> [N]egative cognitive and academic effects are hypothesized to result from low levels of competence in both languages[,] or what Scandinavian researchers (e.g. Hanseg[å]rd, 196[8]; Skutnabb-Kangas & Toukomaa, 1976) have termed "semilingualism" or "double semilingualism" . . . . Essentially, the lower threshold level of bilingual competence proposes that bilingual children's competence in a language may be sufficiently weak as to impair the quality of their interaction with the educational environment through that language. (Cummins, 1979, p. 230)

Cummins's use of the term and concept of semilingualism was strongly criticized. Edelsky and colleagues (1983, p. 2), for example, characterized the notion as "a confused grab-bag of prescriptive and descriptive components," and Martin-Jones and Romaine (1986) called it "a half-baked theory of communicative competence" in the title of a highly critical article. Perhaps due in part to remarks such as these, Cummins soon began using the phrase "limited bilingualism" instead of "semilingualism," but the definition of the term and the role it played in Cummins's overall account of language minority children's difficulty in school, captured in the Threshold Hypothesis and related notions, remains unchanged (Cummins, 1981).

It is important to note what, in the context of the controversy, Cummins meant by "language proficiency." Language proficiency, Cummins (1981) wrote, can be conceptualized along two continua called context-embedded and context-reduced:

> In general, context-embedded communication derives from interpersonal involvement in a shared reality that reduces the need for explicit linguistic elaboration of the message. Context-reduced communication, on the other hand, derives from the fact that this shared reality cannot be assumed[,] and thus linguistic messages must be elaborated precisely and explicitly so that the risk of miscommunication is minimized. (p. 11)

The continua Cummins posited were strongly reminiscent of Bernstein's restricted and elaborated codes discussed a decade earlier.

The value of a continua-based system, in Cummins's view, was that it reflected a "developmental perspective"—a view of language as growing and developing over time. Moving beyond the acquisition of the "species minimum" (a term borrowed from Jerome Bruner to denote the acquisition of the rules of word order, word formation, pronunciation, and meaning), Cummins believed "other aspects of language proficiency continue to develop throughout the school years and beyond," principally including "literacy-related language skills such as reading comprehension, writing ability, and vocabulary/concept knowledge" (1981, p. 8).

Cummins's objective was to find a unified view of language proficiency befitting both the goals of second-language instruction in school and children's home language, one that differentiated the two in terms of developmental levels of language growth. However, the apparent implications for children's home-language proficiency were troubling: Cummins positioned the language of school as developmentally superior to the language of other contexts, recalling traditional claims by linguistic prescriptivists, the view that some language varieties are inherently superior to others (as discussed above), and ties to traditional deficit psychology. Baetens Beardsmore (1986), for instance, suggested that "the notion of semilingualism has been influenced by the deficit hypothesis put forward by Bernstein (1971) in which the social-class-determined notions of restricted and elaborated code account for different linguistic behaviour" (p. 12).

Efforts have been made to empirically evaluate the notion of semilingualism, and these have consistently found no basis for the notion.

Paulston (1983), for example, who conducted a review of empirical research on the topic, concluded her report this way: "Semilingualism does not exist, or put in a way which is non-refutable, has never been empirically demonstrated" (p. 54). Similarly, MacSwan (2000) reviewed four sources of reputed evidence for semilingualism—studies of language variation, linguistic structure, school performances, and language loss—and could find no empirical grounds for the idea.

Studies of commercially available Spanish-language tests, frequently used in school and that have been used to assess Spanish-language-background children as "non-" or limited speakers of their native language, have also been studied and found to lack validity. For instance, MacSwan and Rolstad (2006) found that while the Language Assessment Scales-Oral (LAS-O) Español and the Idea Proficiency Test I-Oral (IPT) Spanish identify 74 percent and 90 percent (respectively) of Spanish-speaking ELLs as limited speakers of their first language, a natural language measure found only 2 percent of participants to have unexpectedly high morphological error rates ($n = 145$). Children with higher error rate were conjectured to be primary speakers of English with limited exposure to their heritage language. See also MacSwan, Rolstad, and Glass (2002) and MacSwan and Mahoney (2008).

Skutnabb-Kangas (1981) has suggested that the term no longer be used. "In the scientific debate," she wrote, "the word has outlived its usefulness" (p. 248). Cummins (1994, pp. 3813–3814) remarked, "There appears to be little justification for continued use of the term 'semilingualism' in that it has no theoretical value and confuses rather than clarifies the issue." He then added,

> However, those who claim that "semilingualism does not exist," appear to be endorsing the untenable positions that (a) variation in educationally-relevant aspects of language does not exist, and that (b) there are no bilinguals whose formal language skills are developed only to a relatively limited level in both L1 and L2. (p. 3814)

However, while Cummins insisted that literacy and school-related language were aspects of language proficiency, he also conceded that the "species minimum"—involving phonological, syntactic, and semantic knowledge of language—are acquired by "most native speakers . . . . by age six" (p. 8). The core problem, as suggested by critics (Edelsky, Hudelson, Flores, Barkin, Altweger, & Jilbert, 1983; Martin-Jones & Romaine, 1986; Baetens Beardsmore, 1986; Wiley, 1996; MacSwan, 2000; Petrovic & Olmstead, 2001; MacSwan & Rolstad, 2003, 2006), has been the embedded presumption that school-based practices of language use have special properties that distinguish the language of school (that is, of the educated classes) from language used in other contexts for other purposes (say, the language of farming or skilled craftsmanship). For Cummins, these differences amount to distinctions of *ability*, not distinctions of *context and use*. In other words, language varieties of distinct communities are characterized as hierarchically and developmentally related, making the semilingualism thesis indistinguishable from classical prescriptivism and other deficit-oriented conceptions of language proficiency. As Martin-Jones and Romaine (1986) remarked,

> The type of literacy-related skills described by Cummins are, in fact, quite culture-specific: that is, they are specific to the cultural setting of the school. In this setting, only a narrow range of prescribed uses and functions of literacy is seen as legitimate. (p. 30)

THE BICS/CALP DISTINCTION

While we join Cummins in supporting bilingual education programs (see especially Rolstad, Mahoney & Glass, 2005), we believe there are undesirable conceptual consequences of the BICS/CALP distinction as it is currently formulated. Specifically, we argue that the distinction confounds language ability and academic achievement and does not take into account the crucial differences between L1 and L2 development outlined earlier; as a result, a consequence of the BICS/CALP distinction is the ascription of special linguistic status to the language of the educated classes, a view we find indistinguishable from classical prescriptivism and reminiscent of semilingualism.

We argue that Cummins's view entails that schooling has the effect of improving our language, and that the language of the educated classes is, in certain respects, intrinsically richer than—or an improved version of—the language of the unschooled or working class, a view we reject. Furthermore, we argue that because the BICS/CALP distinction is applied in the context of native-language development—not just second-language—it is conceptually indistinguishable from prescriptivism and related deficit views of working-class language.

Cummins identifies "schooling and literacy" as the agency by which this more advanced stage of development, called CALP, or "academic language," is reached:

> In monolingual contexts, the [BICS/CALP] distinction reflects the difference between the language proficiency acquired through interpersonal interaction by virtually all 6-year-old children and the proficiency developed through schooling and literacy which continues to expand throughout our lifetimes. For most children, the basic structure of their native language is in place by the age of 6 or so but their language continues to expand with respect to the range of vocabulary and grammatical constructions they can understand and use and the linguistic contexts within which they can function successfully. (Cummins, 2000a, p. 63)

Similarly:

> In short, the essential aspect of academic language proficiency is the ability to make complex meanings explicit in either oral or written modalities by means of language itself rather than by means of contextual or paralinguistic cues such as gestures and intonations (Cummins, 2000a, p. 59).

Cummins also sees BICS and CALP as different with regard to how much "knowledge of language" is involved in each:

> Considerably less knowledge of language itself is usually required to function appropriately in interpersonal communicative situations than is required in academic situations. . . . In comparison to interpersonal conversation, the language of text usually involves much more low frequency vocabulary, complex grammatical structures, and greater demands on memory, analysis, and other cognitive processes. (Cummins, 2000b, pp. 35–36)

Let us consider for a moment a few of the specific properties Cummins associates with academic language—characteristics of the linguistic system which he believes distinguish BICS from CALP, or conversational language from academic language, in the L1 context. CALP is said to involve the ability to make meanings explicit by means of language itself rather than by means of gestures and intonations. However, there is no reason to believe, and no evidence to support, the presumption that academics are better at explaining their craft than the less-schooled are at explaining theirs, or that accompanying gestures are less useful to academics than to others. Imagine a typical professor of English, for instance, trying to talk in detail about farming, boatbuilding, or auto repair. Academics would typically lack knowledge of relevant vocabulary in these contexts—words which would be "low frequency" for them but not for many others. Moreover, evidence must be presented to demonstrate that academic language involves "complex grammatical structures" in ways that nonacademic language does not, lest it appear to be little more than a traditional assertion by academics of the superior quality of their own language variety. Minimally, we would expect to see an explicit and theoretically defensible definition of linguistic complexity accompanying the claim that academic language is more complex than nonacademic language, and then we would expect empirical evidence showing that, for some distinctive trait t of academic language that meets the definition of linguistic complexity, there is no trait t of nonacademic language that is as linguistically complex as t. Historically, a number of attempts have been made to distinguish languages or language varieties in such terms, but none have succeeded (see Crystal, 1986; Milroy & Milroy, 1999, for discussion).

Although Cummins has frequently stressed that he did not intend to rank CALP above BICS (Cummins, 1979, 2000a, 2000b), it is essentially *necessary* in his framework for BICS to precede CALP developmentally in order for his basic argument to succeed. Cummins's proposal was that while BICS develops fairly rapidly in immigrant children, producing "surface fluency" early on, several more years are usually required before children develop sufficient levels of CALP to warrant placement in an all-English classroom. Cummins argued that this developmental dimension was essential to a theory of language proficiency, advocating that such a theory "must incorporate a developmental perspective so that those aspects of communicative proficiency mastered early by native speakers and L2 learners can be distinguished from those varying across individuals as development progresses . . ." (1981, p. 11).

In response to criticisms, Cummins (2000b) has written that "the greater relevance of academic language proficiency for success in school, as compared to conversational proficiency, does not mean that it is intrinsically superior in any way" (p. 75). If "academic language proficiency" were indeed understood in terms of *contextual relevance* or *situational/cultural appropriateness*, the notion would not be problematic. That would indeed be a description of language difference, relative to distinct sets of purposes of contexts, rather than the attribution of special linguistic and cognitive properties to one variety over another, as one sees in Cummins's discussions of BICS and CALP. Thus, the advantage that middle-class children have in school relates not to some presumed superior quality of the oral language of middle-class children, but to the special alignment of their particular home experiences and speech registers with those encountered at school. As Wiley (1996) has put it,

> [L]anguage proficiency is important in understanding academic success not because it is associated with universal cognitive thresholds, or common underlying language proficiencies, but because it is associated with the norms, practices, and expectations of those whose language, cultural, and class practices are embodied in the schools. Failing to appreciate this, we are left with the illusion that school practices involve universal, higher order cognitive functions and that all other uses of language are merely basic. (pp. 172–173)

Our disagreement with Cummins is over the specific way in which CALP is defined: Rather than identifying cultural and linguistic *differences* that privilege some children, Cummins describes CALP as having specific context-independent properties from which advantages related to academic achievement are derived, seeing schooling as the agency by which basic conversational skills are transformed into the linguistically complex language of the educated classes. More specifically, Cummins distinguishes CALP from BICS by asserting that the former is characterized by an expanded range of vocabulary and complex grammatical structures (Cummins, 2000a, p. 63; Cummins, 2000b, p. 35–36), by an ability to make complex meanings explicit (Cummins, 2000a, p. 59), and by greater demand on memory, analysis, and other cognitive processes (Cummins, 2000b, p. 35–36). Considerable research has shown that there simply is no human language or language variety that does not have complex grammatical structures or mechanisms to create new words as new situations arise or to make complex meanings explicit by means of language itself, as discussed earlier. The common belief that academic language has specially enriched properties results from a long tradition of prescriptivist dogma, now propagated primarily in the academy—a tradition that has had the principal effect of justifying social inequalities in terms of "objectively assessed" deficiencies located in language, culture, and behavior.

In the context of children's native language, it is important to think critically about how we characterize linguistic changes that may take place as a result of schooling. Proficiency is presumed to be quantifiable, and *levels* of language proficiency are presumed to be ordered with respect to one another. If we claim that the usual effects of schooling on native language constitute *improvements* or *gains* in native-language proficiency in ways that other typical sustained experiences do not, then we have developed a conception of language proficiency that is not easily distinguished from classical prescriptivism. In other words, if we say that schooling has a special effect on language proficiency that makes it better (higher, expanded, improved) than the likely effects of out-of-school experiences, then we imply that the language proficiency of the unschooled or working class is inferior (lower, basic) to that of the educated classes.

Cummins explicitly endorses the view that schooling improves our language. For example, he asserts that instruction in school has the effect of extending "students' basic knowledge of syntax, semantics, and phonology . . . into new functional registers or genres of language" (2000b, p. 75) and vigorously challenges the view, adopted here and elsewhere (MacSwan, 2000), that schooling plays little role in developing language proficiency in the context of native-language ability (2000b, pp. 106–108). However, while the language used at school may differ in some respects from that used in other contexts, one cannot conclude that school has the effect of improving children's language, as Cummins claims. Schooling may change our language, but what results is different, not more complex. In the same way, taking up a new line of work, moving to a new region of the country, or undergoing an apprenticeship to work as a craftsman may very well make one's language different—but not more complex. Therefore, in the absence of relevant empirical evidence that shows academic language to be a "complex" or "expanded" version of nonacademic language, we strongly reject the view that school improves our language, or that the language of the educated classes is in any sense richer or more complex than the language of the unschooled.

Cummins nowhere intended these consequences and has vigorously defended the BICS/CALP distinction against claims that it represents a deficit theory (Cummins & Swain, 1983; Cummins, 2000b). We believe that it does, but we wish to suggest here that the implications of deficiency inherent in the distinction may be largely avoided by carefully distinguishing between language ability and academic achievement, and between L1 and L2 ability in school-aged children.

CONCLUSIONS

We have argued that languages differ, at the level of both communities and individuals, but that they also possess well-studied universal properties that might be said to constitute a common linguistic core (e.g., Comrie, 1981; Chomsky, 1995). Early twentieth-century linguists refuted the prescriptivist idea that some communities are linguistically impoverished by showing that this claim is put forth in the absence of evidence, and that comparable richness and complexity in such languages may be readily exhibited. Semilingualism is a claim about individuals who reputedly do not know the language of their community, rather than a claim about a socially definable community of speakers. As such, it has the same political force as prescriptivism and may be dismissed on similar grounds: it is put forth in the absence of relevant evidence, and the richness and complexity of the language of "semilinguals" may be readily shown.

Our language continues to change in various ways as we encounter new experiences, and both schooling and school-based literacy are certainly among the common life experiences in literate societies that can influence the structure and vocabulary of our language throughout our lives. But schooling is not unique in this regard; any sustained experience can lead to new specialized vocabulary, new speech styles, and even structural changes. A skilled shipwright will know numerous vocabulary items completely foreign to non-specialists, will have expressions and a way of talking that academics find difficult to understand, and will use his language along with other cognitive resources to accomplish the goals and tasks of the trade. But as academics we would not attribute our own lack of success in boatbuilding to having an intrinsically less complex grammar and impoverished vocabulary with respect to the craft. Rather, we realize that the language difference and skill difference both relate to our limited exposure and apprenticeship in boatbuilding.

We see bilingual education in particular as beneficial to ELLs not because it lifts them to a new threshold or transforms BICS to CALP, but because it provides them with intelligible access to school content, transferring to and facilitating growth in school-related knowledge (MacSwan & Rolstad, 2005). The *primary language theory*, which seeks to explain achievement differences in terms of qualitative differences in children's native language, seems to us to be a theoretical dead end, and one closely associated with the history of deficit psychology applied to educational settings.

REFERENCES

Atkinson, P., Davies, B., & Delamont, S. (Eds). (1995). *Discourse and reproduction: Essays in honor of Basil Bernstein.* Cresskill, NJ: Hampton Press, Inc.

Baetens Beardsmore, H. (1986). *Bilingualism: Basic principles* (2nd ed.). Clevedon, UK: Multilingual Matters.

Baugh, A. C. & Cable, T. (1978). *A history of the English language* (3rd ed.) Englewood Cliffs, NY: Prentice-Hall, Inc.

Bennett, K. & LeCompte, M. (1990). *How schools work: A sociological analysis of education.* New York: Longman.

Bereiter, C. & Engelmann, S. (1966). *Teaching disadvantaged children in the pre-school.* Englewood Cliffs, NY: Prentice-Hall.

Bereiter, C., Engelman, S., Osborn, J., & Reidford, P. A. (1966). An academically oriented pre-school for culturally disadvantaged children. In F. M. Hechinger (Ed.), *Pre-school education today* (pp. 105–135). New York: Doubleday.

Berliner, D. & Biddle, B. (1995). *The manufactured crisis: Myths, fraud, and the attack on America's schools.* Reading, MA: Addison-Wesley.

Bernstein, B. (1971). *Class, codes and control: Volume 1, Theoretical studies toward a sociology of education.* London: Routledge and Kegan Paul.

Bickerton, D. (1981). *The roots of language.* Ann Arbor, MI: Karoma Press.

Bley-Vroman, R. (1989). What is the logical problem of foreign language learning? In S. M. Gass & J. Schachter (Eds.), *Linguistic perspectives on second language acquisition* (pp. 41–67). New York: Cambridge University Press.

Bloomfield, L. (1933). *Language.* New York: Holt, Rinehart and Winston.

Boocook, S. (1980). *Sociology of education: An introduction* (2nd ed.). Boston: Houghton Mifflin.

Chomsky, N. (1965). *Aspects of the theory of syntax.* Cambridge, MA: MIT Press.

Chomsky, N. (1968). *Language and mind.* New York: Harcourt.

Chomsky, N. (1981). *Lectures on government and binding.* Dordrecht: Foris Publications.

Chomsky, N. (1986). *Knowledge of language: Its nature, origin, and use.* New York: Praeger.

Chomsky, N. (1995). *The minimalist program.* Cambridge, MA: MIT Press.

Collier, V. (1992). A synthesis of studies examining long-term language minority student data on academic achievement. *Bilingual Research Journal, 26*(4), 443–472.

Comrie, B. (1981). *Language universals and linguistic typology: Syntax and morphology.* Chicago: Chicago University Press.

Coppieters, R. (1987). Competence differences between native and near-native speakers. *Language, 63,* 544–73.

Crawford, J. (2004*). Educating English Learners: Language Diversity in the Classroom* (5th ed.) Los Angeles: Bilingual Education Services.

Crystal, D. (1986). The prescriptive tradition. In D. Crystal (Ed.), *The Cambridge encyclopedia of language* (pp. 2–5). Cambridge, UK: Cambridge University Press.

Cummins, J. (1976). The influence of bilingualism on cognitive growth: A synthesis of research findings and explanatory hypotheses. *Working Papers on Bilingualism, 9,* 1–43.

Cummins, J. (1979). Linguistic interdependence and the educational development of bilingual children. *Review of Educational Research, 49*, 221–251.

Cummins, J. (1981). The role of primary language development in promoting educational success for language minority students. In C. Leyba (Ed.), *Schooling and language minority students: A theoretical framework* (pp. 3–49). Sacramento: California State Department of Education, Office of Bilingual Bicultural Education.

Cummins, J. (1994). Semilingualism. In R. R. Asher (Ed.), *Encyclopedia of language and linguistics* (2nd ed.) (pp. 3812–3814). Oxford: Elsevier Science Ltd.

Cummins, J. (2000a). Putting language proficiency in its place: Responding to critiques of conversational/academic language distinction. In J. Cenoz & U. Jessner (Eds.), *English in Europe: The acquisition of a third language* (pp. 54–83). Clevedon, UK: Multilingual Matters.

Cummins, J. (2000b). *Language, power and pedagogy: Bilingual children in the crossfire.* Clevedon, UK: Multilingual Matters.

Cummins, J., & Swain, M. (1983). Analysis-by-rhetoric: Reading the text or the reader's own projections? A reply to Edelsky et al. *Applied Linguistics, 4*(1), 23–41.

Danzig, A. (1995). Applications and distortions of Basil Bernstein's code theory. In A. R. Sadovnik (Ed.), *Knowledge and pedagogy: The sociology of Basil Bernstein* (pp. 145–170). Norwood, NJ: Ablex Publishing Company.

Dittmar, N. (1976). *A critical survey of sociolinguistics: Theory and application.* P. Sand, P. A. M. Seuren, & K. Whiteley, Trans. New York: St. Martin's Press.

Edelsky, C., Hudelson, S., Flores, B., Barkin, F., Altweger, J., & Jilbert, K. (1983). Semilingualism and language deficit. *Applied Linguistics, 4*, 1–22.

Fillmore, C., D. Kempler, & Wang, S. Y. (1979). *Individual differences in language ability and language behavior.* New York: Academic Press.

Gee, J. P. (1999). *An introduction to discourse analysis: Theory and method.* New York: Routledge.

Gee, J. P. (2001). Progressivism, critique, and socially situated minds. In C. Dudley-Marling & C. Edelsky (Eds.), *The fate of progressive language policies and practices* (pp. 31–58). Urbana, IL: National Council of Teachers of English.

Genesee, F. (1984). On Cummins' theoretical framework. In C. Rivera (Ed.), *Language proficiency and academic achievement* (pp. 20–27). Clevedon, UK: Multilingual Matters.

Gleitman, L., & Landau, B. (1994). *The acquisition of the lexicon.* Cambridge: MIT Press.

Halliday, M. A. K. (1995). Language and the theory of codes. In A. R. Sadovnik (Ed.), *Knowledge and pedagogy: The sociology of Basil Bernstein* (pp. 127–144). Norwood, NJ: Ablex Publishing Company.

Hansegård, N. E. (1968). *Tvåspråkighet eller halvspråkighet?* Stockholm: Aldus series 253.

Heath, S. B. (1983). What no bedtime story means: Narrative skills at home and school. *Language and Society, 11*, 49–76.

Kasher, A. (1991). Pragmatics and Chomsky's research program. In A. Kasher (Ed.), *The Chomskyan turn* (pp. 122–149). Oxford, UK: Blackwell.

Kehler, A. (2002). *Coherence, reference, and the theory of grammar.* Stanford University, Palo Alto, CA: Center for the Study of Language and Information.

Kozol, J. (1991). *Savage inequalities.* New York: Crown Publishers, Inc.

Krashen, S. (1996). *Under attack: The case against bilingual education.* Culver City, CA: Language Education Associates.

Labov, W. (1970). The logic of non-standard English. In F. Williams (Ed.), *Language and poverty* (pp. 225–261). Chicago: Rand McNally.

Lightfoot, D. (1982). *The language lottery: Toward a biology of grammars.* Cambridge, MA: MIT Press.

MacSwan, J. & Mahoney, K. (2008). Academic bias in language testing: A construct validity critique of the IPT I Oral Grades K–6 Spanish (2nd ed.). *Journal of Educational Research and Policy Studies, 8*(2), 85–100.

MacSwan, J. & Rolstad, K. (2005). Modularity and the facilitation effect: Psychological mechanisms of transfer in bilingual students. *Hispanic Journal of the Behavioral Sciences, 27*(2), 224–243.

MacSwan, J. (2000). The threshold hypothesis, semilingualism, and other contributions to a deficit view of linguistic minorities. *Hispanic Journal of Behavioral Sciences, 20*(1), 3–45.

MacSwan, J. & Rolstad, K. (2003). Linguistic diversity, schooling, and social class: Rethinking our conception of language proficiency in language minority education. In C. B. Paulston & R. Tucker (Eds.), *Essential readings in sociolinguistics* (pp. 329–340). Oxford: Blackwell.

MacSwan, J., & Rolstad, K. (2006). How language tests mislead us about children's abilities: Implications for special education placements. *Teachers College Record, 108*(11), 2304–2328.

MacSwan, J., Rolstad, K., & Glass, G. V. (2002). Do some school-age children have no language? Some problems of construct validity in the Pre-LAS Español. *Bilingual Research Journal, 26*(2), 213–238.

Martin-Jones, M., & Romaine, S. (1986). Semilingualism: A half-baked theory of communicative competence. *Applied Linguistics, 7*(1), 26–38.

Milroy, J. & Milroy, L. (1999). *Authority in language: Investigating standard English.* New York: Routledge.

Newmeyer, F. J. (1986). *The politics of linguistics.* Chicago: The University of Chicago Press.

Newmeyer, F. J. (1988). *Linguistic theory in America* (2nd ed.). New York: Academic Press.

Nunberg, G. (1983, December). The decline of grammar. *The Atlantic Monthly.*

Paulston, C. B. (1975). Ethnic relations and bilingual education: Accounting for contradictory data. *Working Papers on Bilingualism, 6.* Ontario Institute for Studies in Education.

Paulston, C. B. (1983). *Swedish research and debate about bilingualism.* Stockholm: National Swedish Board of Education.

Petrovic, J. E. & Olmstead, S. (2001). Review of Jim Cummins, Language, power, and pedagogy: Bilingual children in the crossfire. *Bilingual Research Journal, 25,* 405–412.

Pinker, S. (1994). *The language instinct: How the mind creates language.* New York: W. Morrow.

Ramirez, D. Pasta, D., Yuen, S., Billings, D., & Ramey, D. (1991). *Final report. Longitudinal study of structured English immersion strategy, early-exit and late-exit transitional bilingual education programs for language-minority children,* Vols. 1 & 2. San Mateo, CA: Aguirre International.

Ritchie, W. C. & Bhatia, T. K. (1999). Child language acquisition: Introduction, foundations, and overview. In W. C. Ritchie & T. K. Bhatia (Eds.), *Handbook of child language acquisition* (pp. 1–46). San Diego: Academic Press.

Robins, R. H. (1967). *A short history of linguistics.* Bloomington: Indiana University Press.

Rolstad, K., Mahoney, K., & Glass, G. V. (2005). The big picture: A meta-analysis of program effectiveness research on English language learners. *Educational Policy, 19,* 572–594.

Rosenthal, A., Milne, A., Ellman, F., Ginsburg, A., & Baker, K. (1983). A comparison of the effects of language background and socioeconomic status on achievement among elementary-school students. In K. Baker & E. de Kanter (Eds.), *Bilingual education: A reappraisal of federal policy* (pp. 87–111). Lexington, MA: Lexington Books.

Sadovnik, A. R. (Ed.). (1995). *Knowledge and pedagogy: The sociology of Basil Bernstein.* Norwood, NJ: Ablex Publishing Company.

Schatzmann, L. & Strauss, A. (1955). Social class and modes of communication. *American Journal of Sociology, 60*(4), 329–338.

Skutnabb-Kangas, T. & Toukomaa, P. (1976). *Teaching migrant children's mother tongue and learning the language of the host country in the context of the socio-cultural situation of the migrant family.* Helsinki: The Finnish National Commission for UNESCO.

Skutnabb-Kangas, T. (1981). *Bilingualism or not? The education of minorities.* L. Malmberg & D. Crane, Trans. Clevedon, UK: Multilingual Matters, Inc.

Slobin, D. & Bowerman, M. (1985). *Crosslinguistic evidence for the language making capacity: What shapes children's grammar?* Hillsdale, NJ: Erlbaum.

Sperber, D. & Wilson, D. (1986). *Relevance: Communication and cognition.* Cambridge, UK: Cambridge University Press.

Tager-Flusberg, H. (1997). Putting words together: Morphology and syntax in the preschool years. In J. Berko-Gleason (Ed.), *The development of language* (pp. 159–209). Boston: Allyn and Bacon.

Thomas, W., & Collier, V. (1997). *School effectiveness for language minority students.* Washington, D.C.: National Clearinghouse for Bilingual Education.

Trudgill, P. (1974). *Sociolinguistics: An introduction to language and society.* London: Penguin Books.

Turner, C., Laria, A., Shapirio, E., & Perez, M. (1993). Poverty, resilience, and academic achievement among Latino college students and high school dropouts. In R. Rivera & S. Nieto (Eds.), *The education of Latino students in Massachusetts: Issues, research, and policy implications* (pp. 191–213). Boston: University of Massachusetts Press.

U.S. Commission on Civil Rights. (1975). *A better chance to learn: Bilingual-bicultural education.* Clearinghouse Publication 51.

Wiley, T. (1996). *Literacy and language diversity in the United States.* McHenrey, IL: Center for Applied Linguistics and Delta Systems, Co.

Willis, P. (1981). *Learning to labor: How working class kids get working class jobs.* New York: Columbia University Press.

CHAPTER 9

A POSTLIBERAL CRITIQUE OF LANGUAGE RIGHTS: TOWARD A POLITICS OF LANGUAGE FOR A LINGUISTICS OF CONTACT[1]

Christopher Stroud
*University of the Western Cape, South Africa,
and the Centre for Research on Bilingualism at
Stockholm University, Sweden*

An increasingly major preoccupation confronting postmodern/ late modern societies is how to accommodate the "non-mainstream speaker"—the transnational migrant, the indigenous minority, or the socioeconomically disadvantaged. In this context, it is fairly uncontested that some form of educational provision of nondominant languages is a necessary, though far from sufficient, condition for the nurturing of empowered and participatory citizens (Stroud, 2001). This is particularly

---

[1] This research was made possible by SAREC grant SWE/200549.

International Perspectives on Bilingual Education: Policy, Practice, and Controversy, pages 195–222
Copyright © 2010 by Information Age Publishing
All rights of reproduction in any form reserved.

the case for those who are most marginalized in society—mother-tongue speakers of nonofficial languages—as linguistic recognition of the least acknowledged is an important first step in also recognizing the official and informal structures of symbolic and material reproduction that continue to ensure the invisibility and silence of many minorities. A central argument in this chapter, however, is that much of the language (political) provision currently in place is counterproductive and, in point of fact, actually *reproductive* of the very forms of linguistic marginalization it is set to remedy. Not surprisingly, this also applies to the language-educational provisions that follow from such paradigms. The focus of this chapter is thus precisely on exploring the nature of the problems in contemporary language politics and in attempting to formulate new directions for a politics-of-language that addresses issues of social and economic justice for marginalized populations of minority- or nondominant-language speakers.

An important point of departure for this chapter is the assumption that any political philosophy of language is an articulation of a wider discourse of citizenship and governance. An example of this is how multilingualism is linked to citizenship and governance issues in a country such as Mozambique in both colonial and postcolonial times. Here, constructions of bilingualism have historically mediated tight linkages between the political economy of labor, governmentality, and Christianity. Language has been socially and politically construed in ways that serve to regiment and order peoples into administrative constituencies, in constructing moral images of speakers, and in the semiotic framing of discourses of tradition and modernity, agency, and citizenship (Gal & Irvine, 1995; Irvine & Gal, 2000). A notion such as codeswitching, for example, has been variously associated with moral attributes such as laziness and debauched and anti-social behavior, as well as resistance to state authority, whereas speaking a "pure" language was seen as an accomplishment of a loyal citizen. In particular, the colonial notion of *assimilado*, which comprised the colonial state's crowning attempt to form a colonial citizen from a colonial subject, rested heavily on the requirement of proficiency in Portuguese and on the exclusion of local languages.

In this chapter, I explore precisely how political discourses construct and performatively bring into existence a particular view of language. I focus specifically on a dominant political philosophy of language, namely, Linguistic Human Rights (LHR). LHR discourse is currently the most widespread discourse of linguistic emancipation and empowerment. LHR has its roots in a liberal notion of *citizenship* based on liberal *rights* theory—that is, a concern with state–civil society relations (principally the protection of the individual from the state [negative rights], but increasingly formulated in terms of state obligation to deliver [positive rights]), a distinction between the public (Habermasian) and the private spheres, juridically driven reform, and policymaking.[2] Rights in general have been touted as a way of managing diversity, and language rights in particular are seen as the solution to increased participation of language minorities in society, as a strategy for the preservation of languages, as a means to increase educational efficiency, and as a prerequisite for technological development more generally. Viewing political philosophies of language as a discursive construct that constitutes or legitimizes language as a particular type of object in a particular sociohistorical context (Heller, 2008, p. 52) allows us to ask specific questions around political philosophies of language. For example, rather than asking whether language is an appropriate type of object for a rights discourse—a common point of contention for many researchers—critics of LHR frameworks ask what *sort* of object/entity language is construed as in terms of rights discourses. Viewing language as a politically construed ontology (cf. Heller, 2008), it further makes sense to ask, (1) What institutional, symbolic, and linguistic resources does the notion of LHR produce? (2) What concrete political, administrative, and (linguistic) discursive practices are needed to promote LHR? (3) What tensions, contradictions, and competitions of position does the field of linguistic human rights favor?

Addressing such questions allows us to explore the ways in which LHR fashions minority language speakers as a particular type of (rights-bearing) political subject, and thus to critically discuss to what extent a minority language speaker, defined through rights discourse, is the best solution to contentious issues of equity and justice. I will suggest in fact that they are not, and that new discourses of citizenship in late modern transnational societies necessarily imply a new political philosophy of language. As the LHR paradigm underlies current educational provisions, critique of LHR naturally also has ramifications for educational language policy and curriculum development more specifically.

LANGUAGE RIGHTS: SHORT HISTORY AND PROBLEMS

What, then, are the origins of (language) rights discourses, and what are the dynamics behind their development? Bruthiaux (forthcoming) traces the origins of rights notions in the early writings of such thinkers as seventeenth-century John Milton and eighteenth-century John Wilkes, both of whom promoted freedom from the malign, repressive, and exploitative institutions of the state, churches, and courts of the time. Bruthiaux notes

---

[2] There is a misunderstanding that citizenship necessarily entails rights—there is an overlap in certain versions of citizenship, and although the arena of citizenship is where rights necessarily must manifest themselves, and where rights may be contested, and so forth, this is not a necessary outcome of the practice or deliberation of citizenship (e.g., deliberative democracy).

how "by [eighteenth] century's end and on both sides of the Atlantic, rights were understood as concerned with the preservation of liberty through legally enforceable statements of what the state should *not* do [emphasis in original]" (p. 2). Rights that protect the individual from unwelcome interference by the state, so-called negative rights, find reflex in the notion of language rights and can be contrasted with positive rights "or legally enforceable statements of what a proactive state should do" (Bruthiaux, forthcoming, p. 2; cf. Skuttnab-Kangas, 2000; Blommaert, 2005). Concern with language rights (in Europe) can be traced back to the growth of nation-states and the rise in the importance of language for national sentiment (Bruthiaux, forthcoming; Ruiz Veytez, 2001). Although religious rights were recognized as early as 1648 (Treaty of Westphalia), linguistic rights were only international acknowledged as late as the 1920s—mainly in the form of negative rights. However, as the modern nation-state has come to impact on ever more spheres of citizens' lives, the proactive support of language rights that was earlier the provenance of the church and social and cultural organizations has increasingly been serviced through public institutions and administrative structures. Especially since the 1960s, state-sponsored linguistic human rights remedies have become quite pervasive (cf. Kontra, Phillipson, Skutnabb-Kangas & Várády, 1999; May 2005). However, the notion of LHR has generated much conceptual contention and has proven to be highly problematic to implement. Authors such as Blommaert (2005), Stroud (2001), Stroud and Heugh (2004), and Wee (2005), among others, have suggested that the notion of rights is applicable to language only with difficulty, that rights discourses *de facto* create many of the problems they were originally set to resolve, that rights discourses assume a particular type of political agent, social order, and form of governmentality that is non-existent in many societies, that rights policies tend to ignore the many contingent materialities needed for their successful implementation, and that rights discourses construct unequal opportunities for individual and social agency. I review each of these considerations in turn.

On the Multiplicity of Rights

Rights are the outcome of contention and debate, and appeals to rights as a political tool are common in times of social transformation. The historical struggle for the rights of women and the poor for franchise, the contemporary proliferation of new rights for new minorities (e.g., the rights of sexual minorities to marriage, adoption, and military service) or rights recognizing the equality of traditional forms of marriage (e.g., polygamy in South Africa) are clear examples of this. In one sense, the very act of conceptualizing, claiming, and implementing rights of gender, sexuality, ethnicity, or intimacy is nothing less than the "discursive performance" of self/other definitions that are the stuff of contemporary politics of identity and constituency.

Given this context, it is not surprising that rights discourses present with a veritable flora of different rights notions: individual versus collective/cultural rights (see Kymlicka, 1995; MacMillan, 1986; Skuttnab-Kangas, 2000), instrumental and noninstrumental rights (Rubio-Marín, 2003), and solidarity rights (see Abi-Saab, 1980)—i.e., to what extent goods associated with rights are equitably and broadly distributed. Topics of contention, of course, are what type of rights language rights comprise—and what categories of speakers have the right to language rights (and under what conditions?).

Almost as pervasive are the discourses that underlie and justify language-rights appeals in the first place. Two general approaches to language rights (Bruthiaux, forthcoming) are formulated in terms of an ideological–moral discourse (see Skuttnab-Kangas, 2000) and a policy oriented/cost–benefit-inspired discourse (see Grin, 1996, 2005). Whereas Skuttnab-Kangas is a vocal promoter of the idea that rights should be accorded to languages on moral and ideological grounds, François Grin (2005) has instead argued that it should be part of a diversity management program that rests solidly on calculations of cost–benefit and tools-of-policy evaluation, where criteria such as the relative efficiency and cost-effectiveness of the different policy options vis-á-vis the allocation of resources, and in relation to the distribution of justice and fairness, should be accorded priority.

In general, the question of language as an object of rights appears not to be as straightforward as, for example, that of religion. An inescapable design feature of language is its unavoidability. Contrary to other (cultural) traits that a group may feel are in need of rights protection, such as dress, diet, or religion, "it is simply not possible to avoid privileging some language as a 'functional fact of human interaction'" (Wee, n.d.: 4). This means that speakers have no choice but to use a particular language in their interactions, and thus there is an important issue of agency and its lack in cases of language rights.

Problems Emanating from Rights Discourses

Many of the very problems that rights discourses are grappling with are, in one way or another, an effect of the rights paradigm itself. Linguistic human rights approaches tend to channel discourses on diversity into specific predetermined cultural and linguistic identities (Stroud, 2001; Stroud & Heugh, 2004; Wee, forthcoming), often undergirding ethnolinguistic stereotyping in the form of monolingual and uniform identities. Rights discourses encourage groups of speakers to work actively to differentiate themselves from others by claiming unique linkages of language and identity as a way of gaining political leverage in the competition for scarce resources (Stroud & Heugh, 2004; cf. Ford, 2005; Wee, forthcoming).

Although essentialism has been described as a potentially opportune political strategy (see May, 2005), there is the risk that group investment in politically successful identities may erase the distinction between strategic and nonstrategic essentialism, leading in some cases to unwillingness to give up particular identities or claims (Ford, 2005). This may further encourage a perspective on autonomy as nonnegotiable, rather than reciprocal negotiation (Wee, forthcoming, p. 7). The struggle for language rights may even predispose to ethnic conflict; Perry (2004) has estimated that 12 percent of rights claims are group rights that are ethnically potentially divisive.

LHR, as currently conceived, also privileges the official and group values and perceptions of what might constitute the language in question, and cannot entertain the legitimacy of alternative-language practices as part of the "language." In LHR discourses, languages are considered in terms of homogenous speech communities, and the fact that any speech community will comprise various groups (distinguished along parameters such as age, urbanity–rurality, modern–traditional, and socioeconomic status) is not easily dealt with. Although authors such as Skuttnab-Kangas (2000) do recognize the legitimacy of nonstandard varieties and the difficulty of distinguishing, say, speakers of lectal or perceived substandard varieties of "standard languages," such as Tsotsitaal, from "languages" such as Afrikaans, other authors such as Petrovic (2006) and Wee (2005) have pointed to a number of fundamental difficulties in attempting to extend a rights framework to such varieties.

How Rights Discourses are (Negatively) Adopted/ Appropriated in Different Sociopolitical Contexts

Citizenship and rights are not co-temporaneous or identical discourses. Whereas citizenship is contingent, historical, and political, rights are depoliticized, ahistorical, and universal (Yeatman, 2001). Thus the paradox of rights is that although they are universal, appeals to them are situated in local space and time and filtered through contingent local political, social, and economic structures by which the specifics of each nation-state polity constrain the choice of rights and to what extent that choice is actually provided for. Furthermore, language itself is "irreducibly dialectic in nature . . . an unstable mutual interaction of meaningful sign forms, contextualized to situations of interested human use and mediated by the fact of cultural ideology" (Silverstein, 1985, p. 220). Language practices, as well as thinking on language, are highly situated, historical, and contextualized phenomena.

An example from the South African context·illustrates one common way in which rights discourses are adapted to local, sociopolitical contexts. At the turn of democracy, South Africa put in place the Pan-South African Language Board (PANSALB), charged with the task of adjudicating and delivering decisions on matters of language-rights violations. However, the extent to which linguistic interests are actually represented and enacted in this liberal framework are minimal. According to Perry (2004), through a series of political machinations, PANSALB has become a "toothless watchdog" and has seen its status reduced to an advisory body only, with no legal means to enforce its decisions. This exemplifies the point made by Escoffier (1998, quoted in Stychin, 2001, p. 290) who claims that in general "Every institutionalized form of political rights (a passive achievement) also enables disciplinary and normalizing forms of domination (not necessarily good things)" (p. 226).

Often, in such cases, rights become a technique of social discipline that orders and regulates citizens into state-accepted social taxonomies[3] or that strategically disadvantages some groups over others.[4] In fact, Perry (2004) has suggested that the existence of a body or an institution such as PANSALB that is widely believed to be managing questions of language rights creates "an illusory sense of security" among stakeholders in civil society who might otherwise have taken a more active role in protecting language rights. Given that rights discourses are designed principally to enforce a legal limit on state power, it is somewhat paradoxical that it is the state itself that constrains the limits within which rights may apply.

The Contingent Materiality of Rights

Another problematic aspect of rights discourses has to do with their contingent materiality. Linguistic communities are typically bivalent collectivities (Fraser, 1995, p. 85) in that *both* recognition of a language and the economic viability of its community of speakers must be attended to in order to bring about productive use of a language. However, the liberal concept of citizenship does not take into account contingent political and socioeconomic constraints on the exercise of rights (see also McGroarty 2002, p. 25; Wiley, 2002), though recognition of minority languages and an accompanying legislative acknowledgement of linguistic diversity may be well catered for. On the other hand, as Bruthiaux (forthcoming) has noted, by talking openly and pragmatically about costs and benefits, *rights*

---

[3] This shortcoming is related in part to the fact that states have always been among the worst violators of (human) rights, and that all language minorities have a complex and ambivalent relationship to the classical-modern project of citizenship (to the state).

[4] It is also the case that many issues around language rights are covered in other legislation in South Africa—cf. the Committee on Religious, Cultural, and Language Rights.

discourses are easily transformed into *claims tout court* (needs and interests) and are therefore more appropriately processed in terms of how to more equitably distribute resources.[5]

Unequal Opportunities for Agency

A bearing assumption behind rights discourses is of the existence of a universal personhood to which rights will apply equally and justly without differentiation. However, in reality, different linguistic minorities have different histories and hold different positions in networks of political discourses. Universal definitions of social categories such as "language minority" may obscure these potential differences (Maher, 2002, p. 21). As Cowan, Dembour, and Wilson (2001) point out, the "[d]iscourse of rights is neither ethnically unambiguous nor neutral" (p. 11. cited in Wee, forthcoming, p. 4), and in practice, rights discourses carry widely divergent implications and produce very unequal subjects with different opportunities for agency. In the South African context, for example, the historically privileged Afrikaans-speaking group retain sufficient social and political capital to fully exercise their language rights—88 percent of all complaints of alleged rights violations reported to the Pan South African Language Board were submitted by speakers of Afrikaans, despite the fact that they comprise only 8 percent of the population (cf. the notion of "elite benefit" in this context) (De Varennes, 1996). It also throws into stark relief how a specific piece of legislation may have very heterogeneous effects depending on historical conditions of privilege that the rights legislation was actually brought in to redress.

To summarize the preceding sections, rights discourses have proved a powerful political tool in competition for scarce symbolic and material resources. Their situated and contended nature suggests that they are best seen as a spearhead of liberal–political struggle. The resources that LHR discourses produce are accessible mainly through state-sanctioned institutions that promote practices such as the description and normalization of (competing) hegemonic standard varieties of language connected to (strategically) essentialist identities. The area of contradiction and tension specific to the field of LHR revolves around authenticity of group membership and ownership of particular speech practices. This offers minorities a very limited political space and privileges a select set of semiotic practices for how marginalized speakers may express themselves and be heard—that is, *voice*. Not surprisingly, these aspects of rights discourses disadvantage

---

[5] Coulmas (1998) has noted how the requirement that poorer countries implement language rights perpetuates disparities in wealth between poor and wealthy states.

significant factions of speakers who subsequently lack agency and voice. We thus need to look anew at the rules for political engagement and the resources required for broader semiotic and democratic participation of marginalized sections of society, exploring alternatives to rights discourses that maximize the participation and voice of minimally privileged speakers. Importantly, the sociopolitically contingent particularities that plague the implementation of rights discourses detailed here are not easily rectified within the conventional political philosophy of liberal citizenship, as deep systemic and structural issues in late modern society are forcing a reconceptualization of citizenship in the direction of postliberal and postnational reconceptualizations. As we shall note, these inform different discursive constructions of late modern practices of multilingualism.

TRANSNATIONALISM, MULTIPLE CITIZENSHIPS AND NEW MULTILINGUAL DISPENSATIONS

The major theoretical problem adhering to LHR discourses emanates from the fact that they rest on a particular and limited view of citizenship, language, and governance that cannot adequately capture what it means to be a citizen in modern postcolonial and postnational or transnational and multiscaled state. Nor is LHR discourse able to conceptualize the new complexities that these states (and associated new citizenships) pose for language use or the potential they raise for language as a political instrument. In this section, I look briefly at two existing discourses of citizenship that are more appropriately attuned to questions of governance in late modernity, *cosmopolitan citizenship* and *deliberative democracy*, and ask in what way minority language speakers may be incorporated into institutions and practices of postliberal citizenship. By way of illustration, I will provide two short case studies that exemplify various aspects of the workings of multilingualism and voice in ways that highlight some of the issues that need to be addressed in terms of a new normative discourse of linguistic citizenship.

Cosmopolitan Citizenship: The Local in the Global

Citizenship has generally been closely identified with (historically gendered and racialized) practices exercised within a uniform and shared public space within the boundaries of a territorially defined nation-state. This has also been the case for language. However, in recent years, new political formations are appearing in contexts of massive demographic change (urbanization and new discourses of gender and social class) and technological innovation. These changes are fueled by vertical and horizontal processes of globalization and refigured through the particularities of the local urban context and local institutions.

Individuals now find themselves participating in a variety of sites in competition for resources distributed along multiple levels of scale, such as the nation, the supranation, the local, and the regional. Increasingly, private organizations, nongovernmental organizations (NGOs), and multinational corporations (multinationals) are providing the economic, symbolic, and material opportunities (e.g., medical care, security, transport, sewage disposals) that were traditionally either the provenance of the state or delegated to local governments. At the same time, many states have been reduced to mediating the local effects of global capitalism through structural adjustment exercises such as the International Monetary Fund (IMF) or the General Agreement on Tariffs and Trade (GATT)—many states in Africa are prime examples of this. In other words, the resources and agencies available to citizens now depends upon what organizations, channels, and institutions outside of the state proper they are able to access. The activity of politics is thus increasingly centered on a *politics-of-affinity* (Phelan, 1995), temporary coalitions of convenience and interest rather than a politics-of-identity.

The notion of cosmopolitan citizenship (Held, 2006) refers to the fact that although "the practice of democracy has conventionally been centered on the idea of locality and place (e.g., the nation-state) . . . future democracy will be centered exclusively on the international global domain" (Williams, 2008, p. 383). Democracy in Held's conception does not just pertain to government and formal politics, but also to "governance, the economy, and civil society" (Williams, 2008, p. 382). Importantly, Held (2006) sees democratic participation at the local level as an essential prerequisite of democratic structures at the transnational levels, with his remark that "the recovery of an intensive participatory and deliberative democracy at local levels as a complement to the deliberative assemblies of the wide-global order [portends] a political order of democratic associations, cities and nations as well as regions and global networks" (p. 309).

Calhoun (2001) also emphasizes the (continued) importance of the local in the re-imagining of social solidarity, stating:

> Local communities are often precisely the settings . . . in which social relationships establish bridges across race, religion, or other lines of categorical difference. The importance of the local resides in "public discourse" and the production and reproduction of "shared culture," which changes peoples' identities and understandings as "commonalities" with others are established, not found. (pp. 25–27)

What, then, would be the linguistic ramifications of cosmopolitan citizenship? What features or dimensions of language and multilingualism are highlighted in the pursuit of a cosmopolitan citizenship?

Transborder Languages and Development of Genres

Not surprisingly, these developments carry implications for sociolinguistic dynamics, specifically in terms of evolving practices and ideologies of multilingualism. Much of this social transformation involves encounters between speakers of different languages in multiple and various urban spaces (real and virtual) across which languages and their speakers travel. The Cameroonian linguist Chumbow (1999) has argued in the spirit of cosmopolitan citizenship that national borders ought to be reconceptualized as meeting places instead of the situation today in which "contacts at the borderline are more often contacts of conflict rather than for [sic] harmony" (Asiwaju, 1984 quoted in Chumbow, 1999, p. 56). He has pointed out that transborder languages have "lasting advantages for national development, peaceful co-existence and international cooperation" (p. 58). For example, millions of speakers, rather than being divided by their multilingualism in African languages, are actually linked into regional speech communities through linguistic continua (see also Prah, 1995). This demonstrates the point that "purely linguistic demarcation of language or dialects . . . does not translate into actual boundaries of communication" (Djité, 1993, p. 150). Speakers who for all intents and purposes speak different languages often do manage to communicate in practice (e.g., Xhosa speakers in the Southern part of South Africa can understand speakers of Zulu further north, and Swati and S. Ndebele are mutually comprehensible across the Mozambique, Zimbabwe, and Swaziland borders).

Over and above transborder languages, the exercise of cosmopolitan citizenship also underscores the importance of existing vibrant markets of multilingualism. This resonates with observations by Aronin and Singleton (2008), for example, who claim that contemporary multilingualism comprises a new "linguistic dispensation" (p. 1) in which "sets of languages[,] rather than single languages, now perform the essential functions of communication" (p. 2). Speech communities today increasingly need to be recognized as comprising translocal complex, multilayered, polycentric, and socioeconomically stratified semiotic spaces. So, rather than distinguish separate speech communities and distinct languages, it makes sense to speak of overlapping networks of activity, and of messages traveling across linked continua of forms.

These complex scaled aggregates of multilingual networks arise out of cross-border politics and trade and encourage an engagement of a broad coalition of actors, exploring commonalities *in* and *of* action. As new social movements create multiple, contested, and constantly changing social identities through collective experiences (Mouffe, 1992) the use of avenues of commonality predisposes to a politics of broad affiliation in which speakers may capitalize on fluid political identities in order to construct broad alliances with other constituencies not necessarily based in commonality of language (cf. Phelan, 1995; Stychin, 2001). This enhances respect for diversity and makes room for different forms of individuality—valuable assets for citizens in democratic societies (cf. Mouffe, 1992). The existence of these multilingual networks also helps local communities find ways of articulating common global and regional social interests and managing the situated impact of global events. They help expand the parameters of local democracy and promote new forms of minority-speaker participation across the arbitrary faultiness of historical borders, and in the interstices of state institutions.

Approaches to the politics of language and policy formulation have only recently attempted to come to terms with flux and contact of multilingual networks. Traditionally, work within the politics of multilingualism has been built around the idea of "linguistic distinctness," a perspective on language that "takes the world to be a neat patchwork of separate monolingual, geographical areas almost exclusively populated by monolingual speakers" (De Schutter, 2007, p. 3). This is tantamount to what Heller (2007) calls the "structural-functional view" of languages as bounded and delimitable systems that occupy equally bounded and delimitable spaces and functions. This paradigm treats language as an unproblematic and easily identifiable construct that serves as an intrinsic expression of a community or individual identity and that is "structured willy-nilly around the same received notions of language that have led to their oppression and/ or suppression" (Woolard, 1998, p. 7). Clearly, a narrow nation-state idea of a liberal conception of citizenship and language excludes the wider, more inclusive implications of emerging linked regional networks of participatory citizenship and language. In particular, there is little place for the linguistic versatility of multilingual portfolios for cosmopolitan citizenship.

Deliberative Democracy: Multiple Subjective Agencies

The importance of local relationships and everyday vernacular language for the wider political context cannot be overestimated. Giddens (1994) has said:

> Individuals who have a good understanding of their own emotional make-up, and who are able to communicate effectively with others on a personal basis, are likely to be well-prepared for wider tasks of citizenship. Communication skills developed within the arenas of personal life might well be generalizable across wider contexts. (p. 119)

Plummer (2001) has coined the term "intimate citizenship" to refer to the types of activities sustained in private, caring, contexts of solidarity that are crucial to further democratization and conceptualization of citizenship.

One body of thinking that has addressed the question of creating expanded participatory spaces for the expression of minority voices, and simultaneously attended to the issue of fluid and multiple political identities, broad alliances, and a flexible notion of public and private is that of deliberative democracy. The founding idea of deliberative democracy is that all citizens who may be directly subject to a particular decision, as well as their representatives, ought to be able to deliberate on problems in a rational and reflective way, with mutual respect for the values and interests of others, taking into account all perspectives in the search for framings and formulations of common concern on decisions that may hold more generally across various categories of citizen (Deveaux, 2005). Deliberation is especially useful with respect to minority groups undergoing social transformation, in which "a deliberative democratic approach to multicultural politics" inserts individuals centrally into "processes of cultural communication, contestation and resignification . . . within civil society" (Benhabib, 2002, p. 7). The inclusion of minority member voices not only provides essential data on local practices and perceptions but also contributes to democratic legitimacy (inclusiveness) and helps achieve a plausibility and acceptance among grassroots structures that is a necessary prerequisite for implementation (cf. Deveaux, 2005, p. 341). There is, then, an acknowledgement that communities are not homogeneous, and that public space is not uniform. Deliberative democracy also highlights the distinction between notions of *interest* versus *rights* versus *needs* as organizing tropes of citizenship activism, in which "[i]nterests are constructed in different sites and based in the subject positions of speakers" (Maher, 2002) and are able to accommodate different contradictory ideas of speakers.

However, much criticism has been leveled against deliberative democracy in some of its various interpretations. This criticism raises essential issues with respect to the political role of language and multilingualism. One such criticism has been that deliberative democracy may fall foul of a potential lack of democratic legitimacy in so far as only a few representatives and stakeholders will ever actively take part in any deliberations—something that is far from the "unconstrained deliberation of all about matters of common concern" (Benhabib, 2002, p. 7). Dryzeck (2000) proposes a notion of *discursive democracy* in order to deal with this problem, emphasizing "the contestation of discourses in the public sphere" . . . [where discourse is] "a shared way of comprehending the world embedded in language" (p. 10)—a bundle of assumptions, stances, and takes on an issue that many or few may identify with and see as a proxy for their own participation.

Another point of critique directed against the notion, and with interesting ramifications for language, warns of the potential antipluralist and elitist *modus operandi* of deliberative democratic practices. The claim here is that deliberative democracy assumes an ethnocentrically narrow, class and culture-determined concept of rational communication as a ground rule upon which all stakeholders must agree and around which they will want to reach consensus—some (abstract) notion of common-good. The "deficit" in this regard is not just a question of certain groups' being excluded because of lack of material resources or insufficient educational backgrounds, so simply increasing the social distribution of competencies relevant to deliberation more widely will not work (Sanders, 1997). Rather, it is a question of epistemological authority; a narrow focus on rationality, it is argued, excludes the feelings and complaints of disenfranchised groups and may constrain alternative rhetorical means through which a group may habitually choose to express its voice. This point also touches upon the idea of a uniform and shared public sphere that dominates and determines the form that political expression can take, what is considered legitimate language, and the import of epistemological authority. In later versions of deliberative democracy, an important recurrent theme has thus been the deconstruction or deemphasis of a sovereign and privileged Habermasian public sphere in favor of multiple, hierarchically layered, and contested public spheres. The idea of multiple spheres with more fluid boundaries is in line with the rejection of a single unitary subject or identity (Stychin, 2001, p. 294) and is a prerequisite for a more encompassing sense of citizenship. Fraser speaks of *subaltern counterpublics* in the sense of "the emergence of arenas in response to an exclusionary civil society" . . . [which] "provide important spaces both for withdrawal from official civil society and also for engagement with it to rectify exclusions" (Stychin, 2001, p. 288). Such a multiplicity of spheres allows "reconciliation . . . between normalization and transgression" (p. 288)—that is, the recognition of other orders of normativeness—and provides one way of managing the pull of social assimilation and separatism. This is an important point for those critics of deliberative democracy who would see consensus and agreement as hegemonic and centrifugal powers, whereas contest and negotiation allow for more dissent in individual voice to be heard. Thus different types of outcomes and different types of genres may comprise important components of deliberative processes in different fora. Deveaux (2005) speaks of bargaining rather than consensus, which better captures the idea of negotiation of interests. Mansbridge (1999) speaks of the importance of everyday language, whereas Sanders (1997) suggests that narrative and testimony specifically express an alternative type of "rationality" that is more accessible to many and that can thus comprise a more inclusive public discourse.[6] Perrin (2006) explicitly makes the point that thinking and talking are citizenship activities.

---

[6] One is reminded of the South African Truth and Reconciliation Committee proceedings here, as well as the local courts in Rwanda and processes of reintegration of child soldiers in Mozambique.

What perspective, then, does deliberative democracy encourage on language and multilingualism? An example of some aspects of language highlighted in practices of deliberative democracy can be found in the important role local multilingual practices play in the political and social lives of a local community. The transcript below is taken from a meeting of women traders in Maputo, Mozambique (cf. Stroud, 2004). More particularly, the example shows how the everyday multilingual practices of these women street traders transform debate and increase political participation more widely among speech community members—allowing for the consolidation of broader-based civic virtues and contesting public representations, identities, and states of affairs and providing a systematically structured means whereby the impact of global processes on local lives is mediated. The practices involve stretches of monolingual Ronga and Portuguese, interspersed with codeswitching between these two languages, as well as sequences that contain local forms of Mozambican Portuguese.[7]

AME: *Mas como nos prometeram "o futoro melhor" vamos la ver*	*But as they've promised us "a better future" let's wait and see*
ADA: *Nada*	*No way*
AME: *So que eu nao vejo nada*	*I don't see nothing/no way*
ADA: *Futoro pior*	*Worse future*
AME: *Futuro pior sim*	*Yes, worse future*
ESP: E que kuzindzela nakoni ka kazata	To hope for anything is difficult
AME: *Muito mesmo*	Very much so
ADA: Na vatama vaku nyimani hikusa a hlomulu wa bindza	They will say you just must cope because life is difficult/suffering is hard
AME: *Tens razao tens razao e verdade*	*You're right, you're so right*
ESP: Mm	Hm
AME: *Niguem aguenta com o sofrimento*	*Nobody can cope with suffering*
ADA: *Futuro pior*	*Worse future*
AME: *E verdade*	*It's true*
ADA: *So que se a gente tivesse votado dlkama era muito bom*	*So, if people were to vote for Dlkama it would be very good*
AME: *tambem digo pa! Tambem digo juro*	*I say the same! Say just the same*

The short stretch of codeswitched discourse among the women took place at a time when the first multiparty and democratic elections were

---

[7] In the following text, plain text is used for segments of Ronga and italics for Portuguese.

underway in Mozambique after years of civil war. The dialogue takes the form of an extended and co-constructed complaint, much of which expresses a suspicion of the governing party, Frente de Libertação de Moçambique (Mozambican Liberation Front [FRELIMO]) and of politicians more generally. In large parts of their discourse, they are actively resisting authority and expressing contrary opinions through recontextualizing and reversing conventional meanings and by expropriating the dominant, authorized discourse in acts of subversive resignification (Butler, 1990, p. 123). The resignification has to do with the meaning accorded to the governing FRELIMO party's first election slogan, *o futuro melhor* (the better future). Throughout the FRELIMO campaign, there was a noticeable tension between the meanings ascribed to this slogan on behalf of FRELIMO and the meanings associated with it in popular parlance. Whereas FRELIMO did its utmost to firm up the linkage between the slogan and the party—for example, by means of street processions chanting the slogan, T-shirts with the words written underneath the smiling face of then President Chissano, TV advertisements, and the like—these women deconstructed this metonymy. Just by uttering the election slogan, a whole set of public discourses was brought into play, as well as reactions to these discourses, inspiring participants to a brisk exchange of contentions. All participants concur in an expression of disbelief in, and distrust of, the promises of politicians, and the very stuff of the interaction was a pained discussion of the veracity of the claim to a better future; all agree that the election will probably not change their situation all that much—despite the promises of politicians, the future remains as bleak as ever. The short-term outcome of the interaction is to offset the local realities of a pained group of *comerciantes* against the sleek fictions manufactured in political slogans.

The point to observe here is that these political and personal stances were accomplished through local forms of language that created intimacy and solidarity among speakers. The women used the elaborate resources of informal and hybrid varieties of Portuguese, as well as the local language Ronga and codeswitching between the two. Such linguistic strategies have the advantage that they admit speakers of various degrees of proficiency into the community, as well as incorporating multilinguals speaking syncretic varieties of a language, comprising loans, transfers, and codeswitches. These speakers' demands for political voice and justice are thus linked to a particular sociocultural and linguistic representation. The processes illustrated here not only create novel political and ethical positions, but the local, informal social, and interdependent nature of civil and political participation in which the women are engaging also challenges the idea of the abstract and independent citizen laid down in a limiting notion of citizenship as this is exercised through narrow, public/formal relationships. In this example, conventional discursive formations and modalities of power are subverted in the multilingual speech practices of these women, proving the "political" to be "all power structured relations from the interpersonal to the international" (McEwan, 2005: 189 quoted in Kerfoot, forthcoming).[8]

The mode of enunciation used by the women reconfigures the meaning of speaking in these particular languages, and the use of local varieties in intimate contexts of this type challenges the emphasis of LHR discourse on formally sanctioned and publically recognized linguistic practices. LHR discourses necessarily assume that language is "an identifiable and relatively stable property of a group or community" in order that it may be "institutionally accommodated in such a manner as to respect the norms of liberalism" (Wee, n.d., p. 3). One consequence of an *autonomous* view of language, and an *essentialist* view of identity in relation to language, is that it implies a particular sociolinguistic ordering, regularization, and hierarchization of language ecologies that may not be readily acceptable (or accessible) to indigenous communities (Stroud, 2001; Stroud & Heugh, 2004). In other words, rights discourses constitute new hierarchies of difference and disadvantage (e.g., between varieties within a speech community) rather than consensus and accommodation.

Rights discourse also ignores the important role played by linguistic hybridity. As we have noted, within the LHR paradigm, a linguistics-of-standardization, officialization, and intellectualization reconstructs minority languages in the image of official standard languages so as to embody the social ideologies, class differences, and standard/nonstandard distinctions common to prestigious languages and at the same time levels multilayered and complex blended identities of minority speakers almost to political insignificance. Thus, ignoring hybridity "obscures the multiplicity of our cultural inheritances and the complex ways in which they shape our contexts of choice" (Carens, 2000, quoted in Wee, n.d., 8). This is well illustrated with the vendor example. Here, it is precisely the deployment of hybrid, stereotyped, fractured, and marginal forms of discourse that allow these women to move with ease across different spaces of the political in their complaint, providing them the opportunity to bridge private life and social and political institutions.

In this section, I have discussed how different types of citizenship find expression through language, the political potential of multilingualism, and how this potential is not acknowledged in LHR discourses. We have noted how a rights perspective on language may actually contribute to the creation, marginalization, and disempowerment of minority language groupings that the paradigm purportedly wishes to redress. The final part

---

[8]This can be contrasted with an *affirmative* politics (Fraser, 1995), which approaches problems of equity through recognizing extant cultural and social identities and basing claims of equity or redistribution on these claims, thereby leaving "intact most of the underlying political-economic system (p. 85).

of the chapter deals with a discussion of the notion of linguistic citizenship as an alternative to linguistic human rights, and how linguistic citizenship can be seen as an extension of, and a semiotically informed complement to, postliberal and postnational citizenships.

LINGUISTIC CITIZENSHIP

We have seen how late modern democratic structures and processes need to address tensions between *identity and identification*, recognize a *plurality of public voices and positions* and *new public spheres outside of the state proper*, and deal with the blurring of the borders between *public and private*. New discourses of citizenship need to contend with the fact that people are linked in many different ways and that their interests and subject positions vary greatly and may not coincide with groupings such as ethnicity, race, gender, or sexuality, or even large homogeneous categories such as social class that liberal–citizenship politics tend to assume. The role of the state in mediating and melding global institutions to the local means that citizens now need to engage as interested parties in subnational, supranational, and other such organizations and institutions. This also carries many implications for language and its political formulations. Not surprisingly, the complexity of the nexus of multilingualism and citizenship is not accommodated in LHR discourses. Rights-based remedies underemphasize the real political–linguistic issues in late modern, postliberal societies.

In order to reposition language into discourses of postliberal citizenship more widely and to capture a better understanding of language as a (material sociopolitical) resource in complex late modern contexts of multilingualism, an alternative approach to a politics of language is required.[9] I have called such an approach *linguistic citizenship*. Linguistic citizenship refers predominantly to a view on language and politics that recognizes the manifold challenges posed by late modern contexts of migration and multilingualism for democracy and voice and that takes as a central point of departure the desirability of constructing agency and maintaining voice across media, modalities, and context. It is a new construct that combines the principles of cosmopolitan citizenship and deliberative democracy but that also attends particularly to the role of language and multilingualism as a political resource in complex, transnational, scaled societies. Language, from the perspective of linguistic citizenship, is both the means and the target for democratic effort, and multilingualism is both a facilitative and

---

[9] Other interesting recent attempts to rethink the politics of language rights are, for example, the collection of papers in Kymlicka and Patten (2003).

constraining factor in the exercise of democratic citizenship and voice. In particular, it takes linguistic diversity and difference as a prime means (rather than a problem) for the material realization of democracy. It recognizes the manifold sites and the many linguistic practices through which citizenship is managed, attempting to account for the way both local and transnational solidarities are built across categorical identities through interpersonal negotiation in multiscaled spaces (fluid political identities, broad alliances, and so forth). We have seen how approaches to local languages defined in pastoralist and invariably static terms as authentic expressions of primeval identities (such is the case with LHR discourses) cannot address the issues of mobility, linguistic transportation, and scales of relevance arising from the pressures of transnational developments. Linguistic citizenship thus contributes toward the political theorization of a linguistics-of-contact rather than a linguistics-of-community (Pratt, 1998).

Such a project must necessarily involve an alternative take on ownership of, and agency over, multilingual resources and their meanings. Speakers themselves must also make some stake in the norms of communication (institutional and otherwise), as well as language logistics and the transport and delivery of meanings across multiscaled participatory spaces. Linguistic citizenship focuses attention on how speakers themselves may exercise control over their language, deciding what languages are and what they may mean, and how language issues can be discursively tied to a wider range of social issues (Stroud, 2001). Central to the exploration of linguistic citizenship, therefore, is an approach to language in terms of a sociolinguistics of multilingual mobility rather than linguistic localization, in which issues of how multiple encodings of a discourse are transfigured across signage, contexts, and languages are in focus—that is, a focus on the "inevitably transformative dynamics of socially situated meaning-making processes" (Iedema, 2001, p. 30) that Iedema (2001, 2003) has termed *resemiotization*. Resemiotization is about how meaning shifts from context to context, from practice to practice, or from one stage of a practice to the next (2003, p. 41). The notion of resemiotization is of crucial interest, for insight into how the material manifestation of language (as well as *choice* of language) reflects "the social dynamics that shape our meanings as they emerge" (Iedema, 2003, p. 40) and "serves to realize the social, cultural and historical structures, investments and circumstances of our time" (p. 50) out of which meanings are generated.

A notion of linguistic citizenship is thus attuned to the implications of multitude of identities, subject positions, and positions of interest that suggest reframing semiotic practices of citizenship away from a totalizing sense of language and toward such notions as *fracturedness, hybridity, partiality,* and *perspective.* Rather than the idea of language, central to linguistic citizenship are the notions of genre and multilingual repertoires. These notions provide for (new) positions of subjectivity and ways of talking about and managing social transformation in late modernity. Genres organize multi-lingual resources into "complexes of communicative-formal features that make a particular communicative event recognizable as an instance as a type" (Blommaert, 2008; cf. Briggs & Bauman, 1992), recognizable by community members as conventional performances of subjectivities and activities. Importantly, new genres comprise the textual practices for "cultural innovation and change" and offer up new epistemological or cultural forms for the formation and expression of particular types of identity, and so so on (Blommaert, 2008, p. 47). Briggs and Bauman (1992) have noted how genres comprise powerfully political and ideological formations.

One offshoot of such a perspective on language and citizenship is a different take on the complexity in the (re)production and consolidation of notions of minority language speaker—specifically, in how language minority intersects with other social categories and identities. It encourages reflection on what a notion of minority language speaker would actually comprise if conceptualized in non-essentialist terms and taking into consideration the multiple identities and social locations of speakers (Wee, in preparation). As with other politically mobilizing identities, it merits asking the question of how the notion of minority speaker can be more realistically understood as a contested concept while nevertheless serving as a centripetal notion for sustained political engagement around language (cf. articles in Gouws, 2005).

Some Implications of an Alternative Perspective for the Provision of Education in Marginalized Languages

To close this chapter, I will briefly draw out the implications of the notion of linguistic citizenship in a concrete example of educational language planning and classroom practice. LHR-inspired educational implementations are designed around a multicultural model of affirmative policy that recognizes extant groupings and diverse positions of linguistic interest in society as status quo. This is manifest in educational language planning in a concern with the spatial and temporal distribution of languages across academic content and years (e.g., in such notions as additive and transitional bilingual programs). The underlying linguistic rationale for this is the structural–functional view of language and the mosaic metaphor of multilingualism. Distinct and standard normative varieties are taught, notions of correctness are upheld, and different languages compete for space in the official arena of schooling. Certain genres of language—so-called cognitive academic language use and normative language—are privileged and pedagogically enforced, and the epistemological authority of speakers is only recognized when voiced in these educationally legitimate genres.

Educational language planning based in ideas of linguistic citizenship, on the other hand, would highlight the transport and movement (transposition or translation) of meanings and speaker voice across genres, modalities, and repertoires rather than the temporal and spatial *localization* of language(s)—a *practices* rather than a program/structure view. Furthermore, it would give priority to a reflective, critically metalinguistic take on language in keeping with the need for a critical look at the role that language can play in a transformative politics of social and linguistic identity. Rather than a focus on *language* per se, linguistic citizenship would take the notion of *voice* as a pedagogical point of departure that informs a mode of working with genres and registers with respect to how meanings are transported across a range of media and modalities in ongoing constructions of subjectivity. This stance reflects different takes on identity versus identification and toward related notions of linguistic ownership, authenticity, and expertise—that is, nativeness. The permeable and shifting nature of boundaries between languages and the dissolution of the notion of community in favor of a "linguistics of contact" offer a different perspective on the distinction between (systemic linguistic) concepts such as L1 and L2 and suggest cultivating pedagogical strategies for "crossing" between language and social constructs (cf. Stroud & Wee, 2007), thereby also recognizing the semiotics of a plurality of public voices and positions. The classroom organized according to principles of linguistic citizenship, in other words, is reconstituted as an arena for the negotiation of difference and commonality rather than the assumption or imposition of commonality (in language, speech norms, or social identity) (cf. Stroud, 2001). Canagarajah (in Makoni & Pennycook, 2007, pp. 237–238) expresses similar thoughts thus:

> [R]ather than focusing on rules and conventions, we have to focus on strategies of communication. This shift will enable our students to be prepared for engagement in communities of practice and collaboratively achieve communication through the use of pragmatic strategies. Our pedagogical objective is not to develop mastery of a "target language" (that cliché in our field), but to develop a repertoire of codes among our students . . . through all this we are helping students shuttle *between* communities, and not to think of only joining *a* community.

An example of how a pedagogical application of linguistic citizenship that clearly illustrates how features such as resemiotization and use of hybridity in the service of voice may pan out in practice is provided by Kerfoot (forthcoming). Hers is a study of an Adult Basic Education (ABET) program before and in the immediate aftermath of South Africa's transition to democracy, where the challenges facing citizens in attaining basic rights

> involve[d] the development of the capabilities for participatory development and governance: the kind of skills required under the new dispensation [we] re substantially different from those needed for pre-1994 mobilization and resistance. Effective participation require[d] facilitation, advocacy and management abilities: the mundane but critical practices of engaging accountable authorities. (Marais, 2001, p. 284)

The program was designed to train ABET facilitators from historically disadvantaged communities. Participation was multiracial and multilingual, with seven language groups from predominantly rural areas taking part and with all participants reasonably proficient in both English and Afrikaans. Kerfoot found that the practices that allowed participants to exit the course with a newfound agency and exercise of voice in rights-building initiatives across a range of contexts involved the shifting use of different languages, language varieties, registers, and modes of representation to engage community members. These "recoding moves" encouraged the legitimate recontextualization of a message in different registers (high versus low Afrikaans for older speakers; Orange River Afrikaans variety for younger speakers), which served "to promote intergroup dialogue and to reshape existing distinctions between formal and informal speech along with the power relations bound up in them" (Kerfoot, forthcoming, p. 25).

In a similar manner, the development and deployment of multisemiotic means of representing problems and issues in space (e.g., the use of newsprint and thick koki pen, as well as mindmaps and bullets to afford more spatial representations of ideas), alternating with mixed and temporal logics of representation (Kress, 2003), erased hierarchy and "constructed participants as equals capable of collectively addressing social issues" (Kerfoot, forthcoming). The use of spatial logics in writing changed both the "force" and the "feel" of the text (Kress, 2003, p. 16), crystalizing key moments of synthesis while representing in material form the restructured roles and relationships of the facilitator and the other participants. At the same time, it provided a durable, accessible, legitimate record of discussions and decisions. Kerfoot concludes that the recoding and resemiotizations in the transport of meanings and understandings allow voices previously silenced to be heard in ways not possible through "normative" literacy practices, not least in the way in which these practices permitted new "social arrangements and knowledge structures, altering the channels along which ideas flowed" (Kerfoot, forthcoming, p. 25).

CONCLUSION

I have discussed in depth the efficacy of much contemporary thought on language as a political construct in discourses of rights and suggest the need for a new (normative) discourse on language and multilingualism. A critical examination of LHR discourses with respect to the notion of language and multilingualism they construct showed that LHR is not adequate for understanding the semiotic practice of citizenship in contemporary late modern society. I put forward that the notion of citizenship and language delimited in liberal models of citizenship is not strategically viable, because LHR discourse offers only a restricted set of strategies for managing linguistic diversity that often also disregard or obscure essential features and practices of (multilingual) language use in everyday contexts. I have thus argued that the social realities (for minority speakers) are mediated through more diverse and complex configurations of citizenship—namely, postliberal or postnational citizenship, which I discuss in terms of deliberative democracy and cosmopolitan citizenship—than it is possible to capture in a liberal rights formulation. And I have presented these postliberal positions as being more sensitive to and cognizant of transnational migrants and multiple types of linguistic minority and as carrying specific implications for a politics and understanding of language.

At base, the main tension/problem simply resides in the (inherent) tendency of rights discourses to treat language as an apolitical, universal, abstract, and asocial object—of necessity, rights abstract away from concrete historical and sociopolitical contexts and are universal, depoliticized statements—and according to Yeatman (2001) determines a specific type of individual. The notion of language in LHR is thus one appropriate to a generalized public sphere, constructed around processes such as standardization, purified notions of language, and dislocation from patterns and practices of language as it occurs in quotidian contexts.

However, language is richly political, sociopolitically/economically contingent, and historiographically particular and is part of the citizenship domain *par excellens*. Rights discourses are always *situated* rights, localized in practice and inserted into the quotidian *Realpolitik* of nation-state management. Furthermore, competition over the symbolic resources of language is always part and parcel of competition over access to and distribution of more material and social goods. My argument here is that language falls firmly within citizenship discourses, and that it is the very medium whereby citizenship is enacted and performed. Contemporary notions of cosmopolitan citizenship and deliberative democracy require a very different stance on, and construct of, language and multilingualism. In fact, in order to reap the fruits of cosmopolitan citizenship and realize the goals of deliberative democracy, attention needs to be directed to the organization of multilingualism in a sociolinguistics of mobility and process rather than community and structure, and to notions such as resemiotization and the transport of messages across (multilingual) spaces of varying scalarity. This can be captured with the notion of *linguistic citizenship*, a conception of linguistic diversity as politics and potential rather than as a political problem.

REFERENCES

Abi-Saab, G. (1980). The legal formulation of a right to development. In J. Dupuy (Ed.), *The right to development at the international level* (pp. 159–175). The Hague: Sijthoff and Nordhoff.

Aronin, L. & Singleton, D. (2008). Multilingualism as a new linguistic world order. *International Journal of Multilingualism, 5*(1), 1–16.

Asiwaju, A. I. (Ed.). (1984). *Partitioned Africans.* Lagos, Nigeria: Lagos University Press.

Benhabib, S. (2002). *The claims of culture: Equality and diversity in the global era.* Princeton, NJ: Princeton University Press.

Blommaert, J. (2005). Situating language rights: English and Swahili in Tanzania revisited. *Journal of Sociolinguistics, 9*(3), 390–417.

Blommaert, J. (2008). *Grassroots literacy: Writing, identity and voice in Central Africa.* London & New York: Routledge.

Briggs, C. & Bauman, R. (1992). Genre, intertextuality and social power. *Journal of Linguistic Anthropology, 2*(2), 131–172.

Bruthiaux, P. (forthcoming). *Language rights in historical and contemporary perspective.* Manuscript in preparation.

Butler, J. (1990). *Gender trouble: Feminism and the subversion of identity.* New York & London: Routledge.

Calhoun, C. (2001, May). *The necessity and limits of Cosmopolitanism: Local democracy in a global context.* Paper presented at the meeting of UNESCO on Identity and Difference in the Global Era, Rio de Janeiro, Brazil.

Canagarajah, S. (2006). After disinvention: Possibilities for communication, community and competence. In S. Makoni & A. Pennycook (Eds.), *Disinventing and Reconstituting Languages* (pp. 233–239). Clevedon, UK: Multilingual Matters.

Carens, J. H. (2000). *Culture, citizenship, and community: A contextual exploration of justice and evenhandedness.* Oxford: Oxford University Press.

Chumbow, B. (1999). Transborder languages of Africa. *Social Dynamics, 25*(1), 51–69.

Coulmas, F. (1998). Language rights: Interests of state, language groups and individual. In Benson, et al. *Language Sciences, 29*(1), 53–72. Oxford: Blackwell.

Cowan, J. K., Dembour, M., & Wilson, R. A. (2001). Introduction. In J. K. Cowan, M. Dembour, & R. A. Wilson (Eds.), *Culture and rights: An anthropological perspective* (pp. 1–26). Cambridge, UK: Cambridge University Press.

De Schutter, H. (2007). Language policy and political philosophy: On the emerging linguistic justice debate. *Language Problems and Language Planning, 31*(1), 1–23.

De Varennes, F. (1996). *Language minorities and human rights.* The Hague: Kluwer Law International.

Deveaux, M. (2005). A deliberative approach to conflicts of culture. In A. Eissenberg & J. Spinner-Halev (Eds.), *Minorities within minorities: Equality, rights and diversity* (pp. 340–362). Cambridge, UK: Cambridge University Press.

Djité, P. (1993). Language and development in Africa. *International Journal of the Sociology of Language, 100/101*, 149–166.

Dryzek, J. S. (2000). Discursive democracy vs. liberal constitutionalism. In M. Saward (Ed.), *Democratic Innovation* (pp. 78–89). London: Routledge.

Escoffier, J. (1998). *American homo: Community and perversity.* Berkeley: University of California Press.

Ford. R. T. (2005). *Racial culture: A critique.* Princeton, NJ: Princeton University Press.

Fraser, N. (1995). From redistribution to recognition? Dilemmas of justice in a post-socialist age. *New Left Review, 212*(July/August), 68–91.

Gal, S., & Irvine, J. (1995). The boundaries of languages and disciplines: How ideologies construct difference. *Social Research, 62*(4), 967–1001.

Giddens, A. (1994). *Beyond left and right: The future of radical politics.* Palo Alto, CA: Stanford University Press.

Gouws, A. (Ed.). (2005). *(Un-)thinking citizenship: Feminist debates in contemporary South Africa.* Cape Town: UCT Press/Ashgate Publishing.

Grin, F. (1996). Economic approaches to language and language planning: An introduction. *International Journal of the Sociology of Language, 121*, 1–15.

Grin, F. (2005). Linguistic human rights as a source of policy guidelines: A critical assessment. *Journal of Sociolinguistics, 9*(3), 448–460.

Held, D. (2006). *Models of democracy* (3rd ed.). Cambridge, UK: Polity Press.

Heller, M. (Ed.). (2007). *Bilingualism: A social approach.* New York & London: Palgrave Macmillan.

Heller, M. (2008). Bourdieu and "literacy education". In J. Albright and A. Luke (eds.), *Pierre Bourdieu and Literacy Education* (pp. 50–67). New York & London: Routledge.

Iedema, R. (2001). Resemiotization. *Semiotica, 137*(1), 23–39.

Iedema, R. (2003). Multimodality and resemiotization: Extending the analysis of discourse as multi-semiotic practice. *Visual Communication, 2*, 29–57.

Irvine, J. & Gal, S. (2000). Language ideology and linguistic differentiation. In P. Kroskrity (Ed.), *Regimes of Language* (pp. 35–83). Santa Fe: SAR Press.

Kerfoot, C. (forthcoming). Making and shaping participatory spaces: *The multilingual citizen: Towards a politics of language for agency and change.* Resemiotization and citizenship agency. In L. Lim, C. Stroud and L. Wee, manuscript in preparation. Manchester: St Jerome Publishing.

Kontra, M., Phillipson, R., Skutnabb-Kangas, T, & Varády, T. (Eds.). (1999). *Language: A right and a resource, approaching linguistic human rights.* Budapest: Central European University Press.

Kymlicka, W. (1995). *Multicultural citizenship: A liberal theory of minority rights.* Oxford: Oxford University Press.

Kymlicka, W. & Patten, A. (Eds.). (2003). *Language rights and political theory.* Oxford: Oxford University Press.

Kress, G. (2003). *Literacy in the new media age.* London: Routledge.

MacMillan, C. M. (1986, June). *The character of language rights: Individual, group or collective rights?* Paper presented at the meeting of the Canadian Political Science Association, Winnepeg, Canada.

Maher, K. (2002). Who has the right to rights? Citizenship's exclusions in an age of migration. In A. Brysk (Ed.), *Globalization and human rights* (pp. 19–43). Berkeley: University of California Press.

Makoni, S. & Pennycook, A. (2007). Disinventing and reconstituting languages. In S. Makoni & A. Pennycook (Eds.), *Disinventing and reconstituting languages* (pp. 1–41). Clevedon, UK: Multilingual Matters.

Mansbridge, J. (1999). Everyday talk in the deliberative system. In S. Macedo (Ed.), *Deliberative politics: Essays on democracy and disagreement* (pp. 211–238). Oxford: Oxford University Press.

Marais, H. (2001). *South Africa limits to change: The political economy of transition.* Cape Town: UCT Press & London: Zed Books.

May, S. (2005). Language rights: Moving the debate forward. *Journal of Sociolinguistics, 9*(3), 319–347.

McEwan, C. (2005). Gendered citizenship in South Africa: Rights and beyond. In A. Gouws (Ed.), *(Un-)thinking citizenship: Feminist debates in contemporary South Africa* (pp. 177–198). Cape Town: UCT Press/Ashgate Publishing.

McGroarty, M. (2002). Evolving influences on educational language policies. In J. Tollefson (Ed.), *Language policies in education: Critical issues* (pp. 17–36). Mahwah, NJ: Lawrence Erlbaum Associates.

Mouffe, C. (1992). Feminism, citizenship and radical democratic politics. In J. Butler & J. Scott (Eds.), *Feminists theorize the political* (pp. 369–384). New York: Routledge.

Perrin, A. (2006). *Citizen speak: The democratic imagination in American life.* Chicago: University of Chicago Press.

Perry, T. (2004). Language rights and ethnic politics: A critique of the Pan South African Language Board [electronic version]. *PRAESA Occasional Papers, 12.* Retrieved from http://web.uct.ac.za/depts/praesa/Occasional%20 Paper%2012 %20text%20layout.pdf.

Petrovic, J. (2006, November). *Linguistic human rights and the (post)liberal conundra of dialect and language.* Paper presented at the meeting of the American Educational Studies Association, Spokane, Washington.

Phelan, S. (1995). The space of justice: Lesbians and democratic politics. In L. Nicholson and S. Seidman (Eds.), *Social postmodernism* (pp. 332–356). Cambridge, UK: Cambridge University Press.

Plummer, K. (2001). The square of intimate citizenship: Some preliminary proposals. *Citizenship Studies, 5*(3), 237–251.

Prah, K. (1995). *African languages for the mass education of Africans.* Bonn, Germany: German Foundation for International Development.

Pratt, M. L. (1998). *Imperial eyes: Travel writing and transculturation.* London and New York: Routledge.

Rubio-Marín, R. (2003). Language rights: Exploring the competing rationales. In W. Kymlicka & A. Patten (Eds.), *Language rights and political theory* (pp. 52–79). Oxford: Oxford University Press.

Ruiz Veytez, E. J. (2001). The protection of linguistic minorities: A historical approach. *International Journal of Multicultural Studies, 3,* 5–14.

Sanders, L. M. (1997). Against deliberation. *Political Theory, 25*(3), 347–376.

Silverstein, M. (1985). Language and the culture of gender. At the intersection of structure, usage and ideology. In E. Mertz & R. Parmentier (Eds.), *Semiotic mediation: Sociological and psychological perspectives* (pp. 219–229). Orlando: Academic Press.

Skutnabb-Kangas, T. (2000). *Linguistic genocide in education—Or worldwide diversity and human rights?* Mahwah, NJ: Lawrence Erlbaum.

Stroud, C. (2001). African mother tongue programs and the politics of language: Linguistic citizenship versus linguistic human rights. *Journal of Multilingual and Multicultural Development, 22*(4), 339–355.

Stroud, C. (2004). The performativity of codeswitching: Women street vendors in Mozambique. *International Journal of Bilingualism, 8*(2), 145–166.

Stroud, C. & Heugh, K. (2004). Linguistic human rights and linguistic citizenship. In D. Patrick & J. Freeland (Eds.), *Language rights and language survival: A sociolinguistic exploration* (pp. 191–218). Manchester: St Jerome.

Stroud, C. & Wee, L. (2007). Identity, second language literacy and remedial crossing: Exploring liminalities in social positioning in the classroom. *TESOL Quarterly, 41*(1), 33–54.

Stychin, C. (2001). Sexual citizenship in the European Union. *Citizenship Studies, 5*(3), 285–301.

Wee, L. (2005). Intra-language discrimination and Linguistic Human Rights: The case of Singlish. *Applied Linguistics, 26*(1), 48–69.

Wee, L. (n.d.). Language and liberalism: Implications for language rights. Manuscript in preparation.

Wee, L. (forthcoming). Essentialism and language rights. In L. Lim, C. Stroud and L. Wee (Eds.). Language and liberalism: Manuscript in Preparation. Manchester: St Jeromes Publishing.

Wiley, T. (2002). Accessing language rights in education: A brief history of the U.S. context. In J. Tollefson (Ed.), *Language policies in education: Critical issues* (pp. 39–64). Mahwah, NJ: Lawrence Erlbaum Associates.

Williams, C. (2008). *Linguistic minorities in democratic context.* London: Palgrave Macmillan.

Woolard, K. (1998). Language ideology as a field of inquiry. In B. Schieffelin, K. Woolard, & P. Kroskrity (Eds.), *Language ideologies: Practice and theory* (pp. 3–47). Oxford: Oxford University Press.

Yeatman, A. (2001). Who is the subject of human rights? In D. Meredyth & J. Minson (Eds.), *Citizenship and cultural policy* (pp. 104–119). London: Sage Publications.

LaVergne, TN USA
10 December 2009
166591LV00002B/14/P